Vienna

Mark Honan

Vienna

2nd edition

Published by
Lonely Planet Publications
Head Office: PO Box 617, Hawthorn, Vic 3122, Australia
Branches: 155 Filbert St, Suite 251, Oakland, CA 94607, USA
                       10a Spring Place, London NW5 3BH, UK
                       71 bis rue du Cardinal Lemoine, 75005 Paris, France

Printed by
SNP Printing Pte Ltd, Singapore

Photographs by
Austrian National Tourist Office (ANTO)   Glenn Beanland   Jon Davison
Mark Honan   Richard Nebesky   Tamsin Wilson

Front cover: An angel in the Stephansdom, Vienna (Jon Davison)

First Published
March 1995

This Edition
June 1998

National Library of Australia Cataloguing in Publication Data

Honan, Mark
Vienna

Includes Index.
ISBN 0 86442 557 0.

1. Vienna (Austria) – Guidebooks. I. Title.

914.36130453

text & maps © Lonely Planet 1998
photos © photographers as indicated 1998

Mark Honan

After a university degree in philosophy opened up a glittering career as an office clerk, Mark decided that there was more to life than form-filling and data-entry. He set off on a two year trip around the world, armed with a backpack and a vague intent to sell travel stories and pictures upon his return to England. Astonishingly, this barely formed plan succeeded and Mark became the travel correspondent to a London-based magazine. He toured Europe in a campervan, mailing back articles to the magazine and gathering the experience that would later enable him to contribute to Lonely Planet's series of Europe guidebooks. He has since written Lonely Planet guidebooks to *Vienna*, *Austria* and *Switzerland*, as well as updating the *Solomon Islands* and contributing to an edition of *Central America* and *Mexico*. He is currently updating *Austria*. Although more than happy not to be a clerk anymore, he finds, curiously, that life as a travel writer still entails a good deal of form-filling and data-entry.

From the Author

Thanks to everyone who responded to my numerous and diverse inquiries: Johannes Hartl and Dr Weiss from the Wien Bundespolizeidirektion were particularly helpful, as were Mrs Winter from the Vienna Tourist Board, and Marion and Ingrid from ANTO in London. Special thanks to Irmgard Lauria for finding me a settled base in Vienna during my research, and to Franz Schubert for his local insights. The Bratislava section was updated with the help of Lonely Planet's *Czech & Slovak Republics*.

From the Publisher

This book was coordinated at Lonely Planet's Melbourne office by the dynamic duo: Louise Klep (mapping and design) and Darren Elder (editorial). Lou Callan and Jane Fitzpatrick assisted with proofing. Jenny Jones and Tass Wilson also assisted with mapping. Illustrations were drawn by Jane Hart and Tass Wilson, and the cover was designed by Margie Jung. Quentin Frayne edited the language section.

Thanks

Many thanks to the travellers who used the last edition and wrote to us with helpful hints, interesting anecdotes and other useful advice: Thomas Coohill, Lawrence Gowen, Peter Keenan, Lloyd McCune, Milton Peek, Thomas Roush, Christine & Craig Seppi, Johanna Strand and Frank Vergona.

Warning & Request

Things change – prices go up, schedules change, good places go bad and bad places go bankrupt. So, if you find things better or worse, recently opened or long since closed, please tell us and help make the next edition even more accurate and useful.

We value all of the feedback we receive from travellers. Julie Young coordinates a small team who read and acknowledge every letter and email, and ensure that every morsel of information finds its way to the appropriate authors, editors and publishers.

Everyone who writes to us will find their name in the next edition of the appropriate guide and will also receive a free subscription to our quarterly newsletter, *Planet Talk*. The very best contributions will be rewarded with a free Lonely Planet guide.

Excerpts from your correspondence may appear in new editions of this guide; in our newsletter, *Planet Talk*; or in updates on our Web site – so please let us know if you don't want your letter published or your name acknowledged.

Contents

Introduction

'The streets of Vienna are paved with culture, those of other cities with asphalt.' So remarked the Austrian writer Karl Kraus (1874-1936). Perhaps that's an exaggeration, but you can see his point. Vienna (Wien) conjures countless images: elaborate imperial palaces, coffee houses crammed with rich cakes and Baroque mirrors, angelic choirboys, Art Nouveau masterpieces, and white stallions strutting in measured sequence in the Spanish Riding School.

Then there's Mozart, Beethoven, Haydn, Schubert, Strauss, Brahms, Mahler, Schönberg and many others. Vienna's musical heritage has an almost physical presence, and adds at least as much to a view of the city as its many visible traits. The mighty Danube River may slice through 2840km of Europe, from the Black Forest to the Black Sea, but it owes its fame largely to Vienna; thanks to the Strauss waltz, it will be forever pictured 'blue' in numerous hearts and minds.

Today's city is the glorious legacy of an all-conquering Habsburg dynasty that controlled much of Europe for over 600 years. There was a time, after the humiliating occupation by the victorious Allies of WWII, when Vienna had an aura of being unable to live up to its own reputation. The hugely impressive building façades seemed just that – façades with no function. Vienna was seen as a haunt for genteel old ladies, whiling away their autumn years sipping coffee in a *Konditorei*.

But now the city has recovered its old panache and verve, and from the rubble of WWII the Viennese have built an enviable economic clout. Its architectural gems never stopped shining, its musical prowess never ceased impressing, yet added to the tradition and culture is a new vitality. Modern high-rise developments along the Danube are a manifestation of the city's forward-looking approach. The old ladies may still be in Vienna, endlessly sipping their coffee, but it has become a city in which young people can feel at home again. Visitors of any age can find plenty to enjoy in Vienna.

Facts about Vienna

HISTORY

Evidence of Palaeolithic inhabitation of the Danube Valley is to be found in the 25,000-year-old statuette, the *Venus of Willendorf*. When the Romans arrived on the scene there were already Celtic settlements in the Danube Valley, the result of migrations east from Gaul some 500 years earlier. The Romans established Carnuntum (now Petronell) as a provincial capital of Pannonia in the year 9 AD. Around the same time a military camp, Vindobona, was built about 40km to the west. This effectively marked the northern border of the Roman Empire and served to discourage advances by Germanic tribes north of the Danube. The camp was right in the middle of Vienna's Innere Stadt (the 1st district in the centre of town), located within a square bordered by Graben, Tiefer Graben, Ruprechtskirche and Rotenturmstrasse. A civil town sprang up outside the camp, which flourished in the 3rd and 4th centuries. At this time a visiting Roman emperor, Probus, introduced vineyards to the hills of the Wienerwald (Vienna Woods).

In the 5th century the Roman Empire collapsed and the Romans were beaten back by invading tribes. The importance of the Danube Valley as an east-west crossing meant that there were successive waves of tribes and armies trying to wrest control of the region. Before and after the Romans withdrew came the Teutons, Slavs, Huns, Goths, Franks, Bavarians, Avars and Magyars. In the 7th century the Bavarians controlled territory between the Eastern Alps and the Wienerwald, with the Slavs attempting to encroach on the region from the south-east.

Charlemagne, the king of the Franks, brushed aside all those in his path and in 803 established a territory in the Danube Valley west of Vienna, known as the Ostmark (eastern march). The Ostmark was overrun by Magyars upon his death in 814, but was re-established by Otto I, the Great, in 955. Otto was subsequently crowned the Holy Roman emperor of the German princes by Pope John XII. In 996 the Ostmark was first referred to as Ostarrichi, a clear forerunner of the modern German *Österreich* (Austria), meaning eastern empire. The first documentation of a settlement on the site of the old Vindobona military camp appears with a reference to 'Wenia' in the annals of the archbishopric of Salzburg in 881.

The Babenbergs

Leopold von Babenberg, a descendant of a noble Bavarian family, became the margrave (German noble above count) of the Ostmark in 976. The Babenbergs proceeded to gradually extend their sphere of influence: in the 11th century most of modern day Lower Austria (including Vienna) was in their hands; a century later (1192) Styria and much of Upper Austria was safely garnered. This was a period of trade and prosperity for the region. In 1156 the Holy Roman emperor, Friedrich Barbarossa, elevated the territory to that of a duchy. The same year, the Babenbergs, under Duke Heinrich II, established their permanent residence in Vienna.

Vienna, already an important staging point for armies on their way to and from the Crusades, was first documented as a city *(civitas)* in 1137. The city continued to flourish, welcoming artisans, merchants and minstrels. Stephansdom (St Stephen's Cathedral) was consecrated (then a Romanesque church) in 1147 and a city wall was built. A city charter was granted to Vienna by the duke in 1221.

In 1246 Duke Friedrich II died in a battle with the Hungarians over the mutual border. He left no heirs, which allowed the Bohemian king, Ottokar II, to move in and take control. Ottokar held sway over a huge area (all the way from the Sudeten to the Adriatic Sea) and refused to swear allegiance to the new Holy Roman emperor, Rudolf of Habsburg. His pride was costly – Ottokar died in a battle against his powerful adversary at Marchfeld in 1278. Rudolf granted his two sons the fiefdoms of Austria and Styria in 1282. Thus began the rule of one of the most powerful dynasties in history. The Habsburgs were to retain the reigns of power right up to the 20th century.

The Habsburg Dynasty

The Habsburgs gradually extended their dominion: Carinthia (Kärnten) and Carniola were annexed in 1335, followed by Tirol in 1363. Rudolf IV (who ruled from 1358 to 1365) went as far as forging some documents (the *Privilegium maius*) to elevate his status to that of an archduke. He also laid the foundation stone of Stephansdom and founded the University of Vienna. These acts helped to placate the wealthy Viennese families, who had their privileges reduced in the previous century.

In 1453 Friedrich III managed to genuinely acquire the status that was faked by Rudolf IV and was elected Holy Roman emperor. Furthermore, he persuaded the pope to raise Vienna to a bishopric in 1469. Friedrich's ambition knew few bounds – his motto was *Austria Est Imperator Orbi Universo* (A E I O U), which expressed the view that the whole world was Austria's empire. To try to prove this he waged war against King Matthias Corvinus of Hungary, who managed to occupy Vienna from 1485 to 1490. Friedrich's tomb rests inside the Stephansdom.

Friedrich instigated the famous and extremely successful Habsburg policy of acquiring new territories through politically motivated marriages – Burgundy, the Netherlands, Spain (and its overseas lands) were all gained in this manner. Meantime a genetic side effect emerged, albeit discreetly played down in official portraits: the hooked Habsburg nose, thick lips and distended lower jaw became a family trait.

The Habsburg empire was soon too vast to be ruled by one person, and in 1521 the Austrian territories were passed on to Ferdinand by his elder brother Charles. Ferdinand later inherited Hungary and Bohemia through his own marriage. Insurrection in Vienna prompted Ferdinand to decree a new city charter under which self-rule was abolished, and Vienna came directly under the control of the sovereign.

The Turkish Threat

Ferdinand became preoccupied with protecting his territories from the incursions of the Turks, who were rampant under the leadership of Suleiman the Magnificent. The Turks overran the Balkans and killed Lewis II in their conquest of Hungary. In 1529 they commenced a siege against Vienna. It lasted for 18 days and was curtailed partly by the early onset of winter. The inner city had not been breached, though the outer districts lay in ruins. Although they withdrew, the Turks remained a powerful force, and it was this ongoing threat that prompted Ferdinand to move his court to Vienna in 1533, the first Habsburg to permanently reside in the city. This move increased the city's prestige.

In 1556 Charles abdicated as emperor and his brother, now Ferdinand I, was crowned in his place. Charles' remaining territory was inherited by his own son, Philip, thereby finalising the split in the Habsburg line. In 1571 the emperor granted religious freedom, upon which the vast majority of Austrians turned to Protestantism. In 1576 the new emperor, Rudolf II, embraced the Counter-Reformation and much of the country reverted to Catholicism – not always without coercion. The problem of religious intolerance was the cause of the Thirty Years' War, which started in 1618 and had a devastating effect on the whole of central Europe. In 1645 a Protestant Swedish army marched within sight of Vienna but did not attack. The Peace of Westphalia treaty ended the conflict in 1648 and caused Austria to lose territory to France.

For much of the rest of the century, Austria was preoccupied with halting the advance of the Turks into Europe. In the meantime, in 1679, Vienna suffered a severe epidemic of the bubonic plague and 75,000 to 150,000 Viennese died. The city had barely recovered when the Turks struck again, with a siege in

The Turks & Vienna

The Ottoman Empire viewed Vienna as 'the city of the golden apple', and it wasn't the *Apfelstrudel* they were after in their two great sieges. The first, in 1529, was undertaken by Suleiman the Magnificent, but the 18 day endeavour was not sufficient to break the resolve of the city. The Turkish sultan subsequently died at the siege of Szigetvár, yet his death was kept secret for several days in an attempt to preserve the morale of the army. The subterfuge worked for a while. Messengers were led into the presence of the embalmed body, which was placed in a seated position on the throne, and they then unknowingly relayed their news to the corpse. The lack of the slightest acknowledgment of the sultan towards his minions was interpreted as regal impassiveness.

At the head of the Turkish siege of 1683 was the general Kara Mustapha. Amid the 25,000 tents of the Ottoman army that surrounded Vienna he installed his 1500 concubines. These were guarded by 700 black eunuchs. Their luxurious quarters contained gushing fountains and regal baths, all set up in haste but with great opulence.

Again, it was all to no avail – perhaps the concubines proved too much of a distraction. Whatever the reason, Mustapha failed to put garrisons on the Kahlenberg and was surprised by a quick attack from Charles of Lorraine heading a German army and supported by a Polish army led by King Sobieski. Mustapha was pursued from the battlefield and defeated once again, at Gran. At Belgrade he was met by the emissary of the sultan. The price of failure was death, and Mustapha meekly accepted his fate. When the Austrian imperial army conquered Belgrade in 1718 the grand vizier's head was dug up and brought back to Vienna in triumph, where it is preserved in the Historisches Museum der Stadt Wien (but is no longer exhibited). ■

1683. The Viennese were close to capitulation when they were rescued by a Christian force of German and Polish soldiers. Combined forces subsequently swept the Turks to the south-eastern edge of Europe. The removal of the Turkish threat saw a frenzy of Baroque building in Vienna – Johann Bernhard Fischer von Erlach and Johann Lukas von Hildebrandt began to change the face of the city. Under the musical emperor, Leopold I, Vienna also became a magnet for musicians and composers.

The Years of Reform

The death of Charles II, the last of the Spanish line of the Habsburgs, saw Austria get involved in the War of the Spanish Succession (1701-14). At its conclusion Charles VI, the Austrian emperor, was left with only subsidiary Spanish possessions (such as the Low Countries and Italy). Charles then turned to the problem of ensuring his daughter, Maria Theresa, would succeed him as he had no male heirs. To this end he drew up the *Pragmatic Sanction*, co-signed by the main European powers. Maria Theresa duly ascended to the Habsburg throne in 1740. However, to ensure she stayed there it was

first necessary to win the War of the Austrian Succession (1740-48). The Seven Years' War (1756-63) was also fought to retain Habsburg lands (though Prussia won Silesia in this conflict).

Maria Theresa's rule lasted 40 years, and is generally acknowledged as a golden era in which Austria developed as a modern state. Centralised control was established along with a civil service. The army and economy were reformed and a public education system was introduced. Vienna's reputation as a centre for music grew apace. Her son, Joseph II, who ruled from 1780 to 1790 (though was also jointly in charge from 1765), was even more of a zealous reformer. He issued an edict of tolerance for all faiths, secularised religious properties, and abolished serfdom. Yet Joseph moved too fast for the staid Viennese and was ultimately forced to rescind some of his measures.

The Crumbling Empire

The rise of Napoleon proved to be a major threat to the Habsburg empire. He inflicted defeats on Austria in 1803, 1805 and 1809, and in the latter two years also occupied Vienna. Franz II, who had taken up the Austrian crown in 1804, was forced by Napoleon in 1806 to give up the German crown and the title of Holy Roman Emperor. The cost of the war caused state bankruptcy and a currency collapse in 1811, from which the Viennese economy took years to recover.

European conflict dragged on until the Congress of Vienna, in which Austria and its capital regained some measure of pride. The proceedings were dominated by the Austrian foreign minister, Klemens von Metternich. Austria was left with control of the German Confederation until forced to relinquish it in the Austro-Prussian War in 1866.

On the home front, all was not well in post-Congress Vienna. The arts and culture as pursued by the middle class flourished (the so-called Biedermeier period), but the general populace had a harder time. Metternich had established a police state and removed civil rights. Coupled with poor wages and housing, this led to revolution in March 1848. The war minister was hanged from a lamppost, Metternich was ousted and Emperor Ferdinand I abdicated. The subsequent liberal interlude was brief, and the army helped re-impose an absolute monarchy. The new emperor, Franz Josef I, was just 18 years old.

Technical advances helped to improve the economic situation and in 1857 Franz Josef ordered the commencement of the massive Ringstrasse developments around the Innere Stadt. The city council *(Gemeinderat)* was re-established in 1861 but only 1% of Viennese – all privileged landowners – were eligible to vote.

Franz Josef became head of the dual Austro-Hungarian monarchy, created in 1867 by the *Ausgleich* (compromise), which was Austria's response to defeat by Prussia the previous year. A common defence, foreign and economic policy ensued but unity was not complete, as two separate parliaments remained. Another period of prosperity began, which particularly benefited Vienna. The city hosted the World Fair in 1873. Its infrastructure was improved (trams electrified, electricity stations and gasworks built) and fledgling health and social policies were instigated. Universal suffrage was introduced in Austro-Hungarian lands in 1906.

Peace in Europe had been maintained by a complex series of alliances (Austria-Hungary was linked to the German empire and Italy under the Triple Alliance). The situation changed in 1914 when the emperor's nephew was assassinated in Sarajevo on 28 June. A month later Austria-Hungary declared war on Serbia and WWI began.

The Republic

In 1916 Franz Josef died and his successor, Charles I, abdicated at the conclusion of the war in 1918. The Republic of Austria was created on 12 November 1918. Under the peace treaty signed by the powers on 10 September 1919, the new republic's planned union with Germany was prohibited, and it was forced to recognise the independent states of Czechoslovakia, Poland, Hungary and Yugoslavia. Previously those countries, along with Romania and Bulgaria, had been largely under the control of the Habsburgs. The loss of so much land caused severe economic difficulties – the new states declined to supply vital raw materials to their old ruler and Vienna's population was soon on the verge of famine. But by the mid-1920s the federal government had succeeded in stabilising the currency and establishing new trading relations.

In 1919 the franchise was extended to all Viennese adults, who could then vote for the city government by secret ballot. The socialists (Social Democrats) gained an absolute majority and retained it in all free elections up until 1996. They embarked on an impressive series of social policies and municipal programmes, particularly covering communal housing and health. The Karl-Marx-Hof is the best example of the municipal buildings created in this so-called 'Red Vienna' period. It originally contained 1325 apartments and was designed by Karl Ehn. It stretches for 1km along Heiligenstädter Strasse, north of Franz Josefs Bahnhof.

The rest of the country, however, was firmly under the sway of the conservative federal government, causing great tensions between city and state. On 15 July 1927, in a very dubious judgement, right-wing extremists were acquitted of an assassination charge. Demonstrators gathered outside the Palace of Justice in Vienna (the seat of the Supreme Court) and set fire to the building. The police responded by opening fire on the crowd, killing 86 people (including five of their own number). The rift between Vienna's Social Democrats and the federal government grew.

The Rise of Fascism

Political and social tensions, coupled with a worldwide economic crisis, gave federal chancellor Engelbert Dolfuss an opportunity in 1933 to establish an authoritarian regime. In February 1934 civil war erupted, with the right wing proving victorious. Vienna's city council was dissolved and all progressive policies instantly stopped. In July the National Socialists (Nazis) assassinated Dolfuss. His successor, Schuschnigg, was unable to stand up to increasing threats from Germany. In 1938 he capitulated and included National Socialists in his government.

On 11 March 1938 German troops marched into Austria and encountered little resistance. Hitler, who had departed Vienna decades before as a failed and disgruntled artist, returned to the city in triumph, and held a huge rally at Heldenplatz. Austria was incorporated into the German Reich under the *Anschluss* on 13 March. A national referendum in April actually supported the Anschluss.

The arrival of the Nazis was to have a devastating affect on Vienna's Jews in particular, though many non-Jewish liberals and intellectuals also fled the city. After May 1938, Germany's Nuremberg racial laws were also applicable in Austria. Jews were stripped of many of their civil rights; they were excluded from some professions and universities and were required to wear the yellow Star of David. Vienna's Jewish community was rocked by racial violence on the night of 9 November 1938, when their shops were looted and all but one of their temples burnt down. (For more on this, see the Jewish Museum in the Things to See & Do chapter.) Many Jews managed to flee the country, but about 60,000 Austrian Jews were sent to the concentration camps. All but 2000 perished.

Austria was part of Germany's war machine during WWII from 1939 to 1945. Allied bombing was particularly heavy in Vienna in the last two years of the war and most major public buildings were damaged or destroyed, plus about 86,000 homes. The city was liberated on 11 April by Russian troops advancing from Hungary.

Post-WWII

Austria was declared independent again on 27 April 1945 and a provisional federal government established under Karl Renner. The country was restored to its 1937 frontiers and was occupied by the victorious Allies – the USA, the Soviet Union, Britain and France. The whole country was thus divided into four zones, one for each occupying power. Vienna, within the Soviet zone, was itself divided into four zones. Fortunately there was free movement between each zone, and Vienna escaped the east-west division suffered by Berlin. Control of the central zone alternated between the four powers on a monthly basis.

Delays caused by frosting relations between the superpowers ensured that the Allied occupation dragged on for 10 years. It was a tough time for the Viennese – the rebuilding of national monuments was slow and expensive and the black market dominated the flow of goods. On 15 May 1955 the Austrian State Treaty was ratified, with Austria proclaiming its permanent neutrality. The Allied forces withdrew, and in December 1955 Austria joined the United Nations. As the capital of a neutral country on the edge of the Warsaw Pact, Vienna attracted spies and diplomats in the Cold War years. Kennedy and Khrushchev met here in 1961, and Carter and Brezhnev in 1979. Various international organisations located themselves in the city.

Austria's international image suffered following the election in 1986 of President Kurt Waldheim who, it was revealed, served in a German *Wehrmacht* unit implicated in WWII war crimes. In 1992 he was succeeded by Thomas Klestil, like Waldheim a candidate of the right-wing Austrian People's Party (ÖVP). (A belated recognition of Austria's less than spotless WWII record came with Chancellor Franz Vranitzky's admission in 1993 that Austrians were 'willing servants of Nazism'.) In the federal government, the Social Democrats (SPÖ) have enjoyed sole or coalition power (with the ÖVP) since the 1970s.

In the post-war years Austria has worked hard to overcome economic difficulties. It established a free trade treaty with the European Union (EU, then known as the EEC) in 1972, and application for full membership eventually followed. Austrians endorsed their country's entry into the EU in the referendum on 12 June 1994; a resounding 66.4% were in favour, though since then the people have been rather more ambivalent about the advantages of EU membership. Austria officially joined the EU on 1 January 1995, and commenced its first six month stint in the EU presidency in July 1998.

GEOGRAPHY
Vienna (elevation 156m) occupies an area of over 400 sq km in the Danube Valley, the most fertile land for cultivation in Austria. Vines and fruits are grown along the river, with vineyards extending as far as the suburbs of Vienna. More than 700 hectares are under cultivation in the Vienna region, and nearly 90% of the wine produced is white. The largest wine-growing area is Stammersdorf in the north.

The Danube formerly flowed through northern Vienna in a series of offshoots and backwaters, all of which were susceptible to flooding. The flow was regulated from 1870 to 1875 by the digging of a straight channel, which forms the present course of the river. This was supplemented 100 years later by the building of the New Danube channel, a further provision against flooding. The long, thin island that was created between the two

channels is now a recreation area. The Old Danube was formerly the main course of the river; it is now an enclosed, curving stretch of water, and the site of beaches and boating activities.

CLIMATE
Austria comes within the central European climatic zone, though the eastern part of the country (where Vienna is situated) has what is called a Continental Pannonian climate, characterised by a mean temperature in July above 19°C and annual rainfall usually under 800mm.

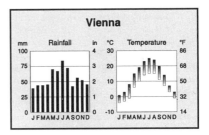

Maximum temperatures in Vienna are: January 11°C, April 15°C, July 25°C and October 14°C. Minimum temperatures are lower by about 10°C (summer) to 4°C (winter). The difference in temperature between day and night and summer and winter are greater than in the west of the country. July and August can be very hot, and a hotel with air-conditioning would be an asset at this time. Winter is surprisingly cold, especially in January, and you would need to bring plenty of warm clothing. Damp maritime winds sometimes sweep in from the west. Average rainfall is 710mm per year, with most falling between May and August.

ECOLOGY & ENVIRONMENT
Austrians are well informed about environmental issues and the country has signed up to various international agreements intended to reduce pollution and preserve natural resources. Austria actually exceeds EU

environmental dictates in many regards. Measures to preserve the environment range from banning leaded petrol to setting up an 'Eco Fund' to promote natural forms of energy (wind and solar power etc).

Recycling is well established in Vienna. Residents diligently divide tin cans, paper and plastic from the rest of their refuse for recycling purposes. This isn't only dictated by conscience, they are compelled to do so by law. In addition, 'hazardous' materials such as aerosols must be put aside to be collected twice a year by the municipal authorities. Recycling bins are a common sight in Vienna's streets.

Glass containers (especially beer bottles) often have a return value, and some supermarkets have an automatic bottle-returning area *(Flaschen Rücknahme)*. It's all very efficient. You put your bottle into the recess and the machine works out what type it is and the appropriate return value. Once you've deposited all your bottles you press the button and the machine gives you a credit note against the rest of your shopping.

Vienna's widespread use of environmentally friendly trams has helped to keep the city's air of a reasonable quality, and the Wienerwald (Vienna Woods) also helps by acting as an efficient 'air filter'. Data on air quality is shown on display panels in various public locations.

At the vanguard of environmental building projects in Vienna is the artist Friedensreich Hundertwasser (see the Peace Empire and a Hundred Waters boxed text in the Things to See & Do chapter), who gave a distinctive face-lift to the façade of the Spittelau incinerator. This plant reprocesses waste matter, burning 250,000 tonnes of waste annually to supply heating for 40,000 homes in Vienna. It has one of the lowest emission levels of any incinerator worldwide.

FLORA & FAUNA

Protected green zones comprising woods, meadows and parks occupy 52% of land in the city of Vienna. Trees include beech, oak, pine and spruce in the Wienerwald, and the famous horse chestnut trees that line avenues in the Prater and elsewhere. Vienna's public parks and gardens are attended to by 1500 gardeners who coax some two million blossoms into life every year.

The Danube River contains 60 fish species native to Austria, including perch, salmon, eels and catfish. The Danube between Vienna and the Slovakian border is a protected area, the Donau-Auen National Park. Close to Vienna, on the shores of the Neusiedler See, is a protected bird sanctuary (see the Excursions chapter), where there are many rare species. Herons, kingfishers, bitterns, warblers and many others can be seen, and storks nest on the rooftops of nearby towns.

Lainzer Tiergarten is home to wild sheep and boars, and all species of deer that are native to central Europe. On the domestic front, there are over 46,000 dogs living in the city. The Viennese love their dogs and are unwilling to curtail their canines' habits of excreting in the street. Former mayor Helmut Zilk tried to address this problem by flying in consultants from Paris to demonstrate fancy faeces hoovering machines. Unfortunately, dog owners were unimpressed and have declined to touch their doggies' do-dos with barge poles or anything else. Numerous pigeons provide further waste disposal problems.

GOVERNMENT & POLITICS

As well as being Austria's capital, Vienna is (and has been since 1922) one of nine federal provinces *(Bundesländer)*. Every federal province has its own head of government *(Landeshauptmann)* and provincial assembly *(Landtag)*. Each provincial assembly has a fair degree of autonomy in deciding local issues and also elects representatives to the Federal Council *(Bundesrat)*, the upper house of the national legislative body. The lower house, the National Council *(Nationalrat)*, is elected every four years by all adults over the age of 18 (though they must have reached 18 in the calendar year preceding the election).

In Vienna, the provincial assembly is elected every five years. The last election in

October 1996 ushered in the first post-war coalition. The Social Democrats (SPÖ), formerly with an absolute majority, won 43 seats out of 100. The right-wing opposition comprised the Freedom Party (FPÖ) with 29 seats and the Austrian People's Party (ÖVP) with 15; the Green Party won six seats. The FPÖ has seen a huge surge in popularity since 1986 under the leadership of Jörg Haider, who has expressed admiration for several of Adolf Hitler's policies.

Vienna's provincial assembly also functions as the city council *(Gemeinderat)*. Likewise, the offices of provincial governor and mayor are united in the same person. The city hall *(Rathaus)* is the seat of these offices.

ECONOMY

Vienna is a base for precision engineering, metal products and the manufacture of electrical and electronic goods. Banking and insurance are also important, as is the city's strong trading links with eastern Europe. The port of Vienna is the largest facility for container transloading in inland Europe, and has increased in importance with the opening of the Main canal connecting the Rhine and the Danube.

Tourism is one of Vienna's biggest earners, and guest workers from eastern Europe and elsewhere are the backbone of this industry. Vienna, like the rest of the country, is increasingly gearing itself towards big-spending tourists, with a rise in the number of four and five-star hotels and a fall in those with one or two stars. About 25% of visitors hail from Germany. The easier accessibility of nearby Prague and Budapest, although providing competition to Vienna, has actually helped pull more visitors into the region.

The city coalition government is very gradually loosening the old socialist administration's centralised grip on the Viennese economy, yet it still has fingers in various commercial pies, such as holdings in many restaurants and cinemas. Roughly 25% of all city housing is owned by the municipal authority.

Austrians enjoy good welfare services, free education and health care, and a benign pensions and housing policy. Vienna's unemployment rate is similar to the national figure, hovering around 7%. The inflation rate is usually under 2%.

POPULATION & PEOPLE

Vienna has a population of 1,640,000, approximately one-fifth of the population of Austria as a whole. Population density in the city is 410 people per sq km. Native Austrians are mostly of Germanic origin, though Vienna itself has more ethnic diversity. Industrial expansion in the late 19th century brought European migrants into the capital, particularly from the Czech-speaking parts of the then empire.

In May 1993 around 600,000 foreigners were living legally in the country. About 65,000 of these were war refugees from the former Yugoslavia. Other foreigners mostly hailed from Turkey, Poland, Germany, the Czech Republic and Slovakia. Vienna itself experienced an immigration increase of 91,043 over emigration between 1990 and 1992. In September 1992 a survey established that the public perception of what posed the greatest current threat to the country was being 'overrun by waves of refugees' (voiced by an incredible 38% of respondents). Given such sentiments, it's not surprising that the federal government has tightened up immigration controls considerably – since then, immigration into Vienna has approximately matched emigration.

National service is compulsory for Austrian males (six months plus two months at a later time), though they may opt out of the military in favour of civil-service duties. Women are not conscripted; currently, they cannot even volunteer to join the armed services, though this is likely to change soon.

ARTS
Music

Above all other artistic pursuits, Vienna is known for music. Composers throughout Europe were drawn to Austria and especially Vienna in the 18th and 19th centuries by the willingness of the Habsburgs to patronise this medium. In fact many of the royal family were themselves gifted musicians – Leopold I was a composer, Charles VI (violin), Maria Theresa (double bass) and Joseph II (harpsichord and cello) all played instruments. The various forms of classical music – symphony, concerto, sonata, opera and operetta – were explored and developed by the most eminent exponents of the day.

As early as the 12th century Vienna was known for its troubadours (called *Minnesänger*) and strolling musicians. In 1498 Maximilian I relocated the court orchestra from Innsbruck to Vienna. Opera originated in Italy around 1600 yet it was in Vienna that it attained its apotheosis. The genre was reformed by Christoph Willibald von Gluck (1714-87) who married the music to a more dramatic format (such as with his works *Orpheus & Eurydice* and *Alceste*).

Classicism Opera was taken to further heights by Wolfgang Amadeus Mozart, who succeeded Gluck as court composer (albeit at less than half of the former's salary!) in 1787. Mozart achieved a fusion of Germanic and Italianate styles (the librettos were first in Italian and later, innovatively, in German). Pundits consider Mozart's greatest Italian operas to be *The Marriage of Figaro* (1786), *Don Giovanni* (1787) and *Così fan Tutte* (1790); the libretto in each case was by Lorenzo da Ponte. Mozart's *The Magic Flute* (1791) was a direct precursor of the German opera of the 19th century.

Mozart's mentor was Joseph Haydn, the other dominant musical figure of the 18th century. Haydn has been credited with ushering in the classicism era in Viennese music. He also worked with both Mozart and Beethoven and influencing both of their work. In the course of his life he wrote the two great oratorios, *The Creation* (1798) and *The Seasons* (1801), as well as concertos, symphonies, operas, Masses and sonatas.

The Viennese Classical School

Vienna is the city of music. Its reputation grew out of the classical era of the late 1700s and early 1800s. At that time the Habsburgs were at the height of their power, and their love of music helped elevate it to one of the favourite pastimes of the aristocracy. The three greatest classical composers, Mozart, Haydn and Beethoven, were all drawn to Vienna, and their innovative and inspirational work saw the beginning of a golden era. Today, Vienna's music lives on in the Burgtheater, Staatsoper, and the other concert halls and parks. Music is difficult to avoid (not that you'd want to) as you wander the streets, passing by buskers playing the classics and people dressed as Mozart peddling tickets to concerts.

Wolfgang Amadeus Mozart

Mozart (1756-91) was only 35 when he died yet he had the time and ability to compose some 626 pieces, including 24 operas, 49 symphonies, over 40 concertos, 26 string quartets, seven string quintets, and numerous sonatas for piano or violin. Praise for his music came from many quarters – Haydn believed him to be the 'greatest composer' of whom he knew in name or person; Schubert effused on the 'magic of Mozart's music that lights the darkness of our lives'.

Mozart was born in Salzburg, and his career started young. His musician father, Leopold, taught him how to play the harpsichord at age three. Two years later Leopold gave him a small violin, but without giving any musical instruction. A few days afterwards young Mozart asked a quartet of musicians if he could join in their playing. The musicians laughingly agreed, but were amazed when the prodigy proceeded to play his part perfectly. One went as far as to call it witchcraft. Mozart senior was quick to exploit his son's astounding talent. Along with Wolfgang's sister, Maria Anna (four years older, and also exceptionally gifted), they toured Europe giving recitals and receiving plaudits wherever they went.

At age six Wolfgang performed in front of Empress Maria Theresa at Schönbrunn – enthusiastically jumping up into her lap when she marvelled at his performance. At age eight he had already toured London, Paris, Rome, Geneva, Frankfurt and the Hague. Four of his sonatas were published before he turned nine, and he could demonstrate the ability to write down complex pieces after just one hearing. In 1770, still only 14 years old, Mozart was appointed director of the archbishop of Salzburg's orchestra. The work did not challenge his talents and after petitioning the archbishop to be released he departed for Paris in 1777.

In 1781 Mozart was summoned to Vienna by the archbishop to help with the celebrations of the accession of Joseph II. Although he left the archbishop's employ soon after he remained in Vienna and it was here that Mozart was to have his most productive years – his music encompassing light-hearted, joyous themes, dramatic emotions and melancholic gloom.

Although always productive musically, Mozart was a compulsive gambler, and lost large sums at billiards, ninepins and cards. He was also something of a ladies' man – at age 24 he proclaimed, 'If I had married everyone I jested with, I would have well over 200 wives'. On 4 August 1782 he married Constanze Weber in the Stephansdom (he had earlier fallen in love with her sister Aloysia, but she was now married to another) and she bore him six children, but only two (Carl and Franz, who also became a composer and pianist) survived to be adults.

Mozart was dispatched to the earth on a rain-filled December day after a meagerly attended, frugal funeral ceremony. His body was wrapped in a sack and doused with lime (an imperial decree to prevent epidemics) before being buried in a ditch in the Cemetery of St Mark's.

The film *Amadeus* (1985), by Milos Forman and Peter Shaffer, portrayed Mozart as infuriating, enthusiastic, volatile, emotionally immature and effortlessly gifted, an interpretation perhaps not very far removed from the truth (though Mozart once announced that nobody had worked harder than himself at studying musical composition).

Joseph Haydn

Although not as famous (or flamboyant) as Mozart or Beethoven, Joseph Haydn is generally considered one of the three greatest classical composers. He was prolific and his life's work includes 108 symphonies, 68 string quartets, 47 piano sonatas, and about 20 operas.

Haydn (1732-1809) had an extraordinary upbringing. Born in Rohrau, Lower Austria, to humble parents, he left home (virtually never to return) at the age of six, when his musical talent was recognised and he moved to Hainburg to live with a cousin, who was choirmaster. At eight he was invited to be chorister at the Stephansdom in Vienna, where he stayed for nine years. When his voice broke, at 17, he was unceremoniously expelled from both the cathedral choir and choir school and left to his own devices – a fate his brother, Michael, also endured.

Uneducated in musical theory, Haydn studied musical works intensely, most notably those of Bach, so he could compose his own music. A chance encounter brought him to the attention of Italian composer Niccoló Porpora, who guided and corrected Haydn with his compositions.

After a decade of being a freelance musician, Haydn was engaged as musical director for the Bohemian count Ferdinand Maximilian von Morzin. But the count suffered financial difficulties and the orchestra, Haydn included, was dismissed.

The Esterházys, one of the Austrian Empire's richest and most influential families, then invited him to enter their services as assistant musical director. And although the head of the Esterházy family was to change several times, Haydn remained in the family's services until his death 38 years later. Prince Miklós, the second head of the family during Haydn's time, supported Haydn in all his endeavours and was a passionate performer on the baryton (an obsolete cello-like instrument).

It was during this period that Haydn developed a close friendship with Mozart. The two were inspired by each other's work, Haydn teaching Mozart how to write quartets. Mozart then dedicated a set of six to his 'beloved friend'.

After Prince Miklós' death in 1790, most of the court musicians were dismissed by Prince Antai, who did not share his father's love of music. Haydn retained his salary but no duties were required of him. With little to do he was persuaded to visit England to write and perform six symphonies. Fêted by the aristocracy and royals (King George III invited him to remain) and generally regarded as a genius, Haydn remained in England for 18 months, and returned for a shorter period in 1794. He wrote 12 symphonies (including the Symphony No 102 in B-flat Major – one of his greatest works) during his two trips to England, and the place and people had a very powerful effect on him.

Back in Vienna, Haydn was inspired, writing several very significant pieces including the oratorios *The Creation* (inspired by Handel's oratorios, which he heard in London) and *The Seasons*, and six masses for his new patron, Miklós II, which are among the 18th century's greatest.

Haydn's private life was not as successful as his professional life. In 1760 he married Maria Anna Keller, something he described as the biggest mistake of his life. Maria had no love of music – her dislike apparently extended to lining pastry pans with Haydn's manuscripts – and the couple quarrelled frequently. However, Haydn found love with his long-term mistress, Italian soprano Luigia Polzelli.

Just before Haydn died, Vienna was besieged by Napoleon's forces and the elderly composer refused to move to the safety of the inner city. As a mark of respect Napoleon had a guard of honour placed outside his house. Two days before he died Haydn was moved by a visit by a French officer who sang an aria from *The Creation*.

Ludwig van Beethoven

Beethoven (1770-1827), like many other composers of the era, was born into music. His grandfather was Kapellmeister of the choir of the archbishop-elector of Cologne and his father, Johann, was also a singer in the choir. However, unlike Mozart, he was no child prodigy. In spite of his father's urgings, it was not until his teens that Beethoven began to show his genius.

After four years with the Bonn opera, the archbishop-elector, Maximilian Francis, was persuaded to send Beethoven to Vienna to study with Mozart in 1787; however, his visit was cut short after his mother died two months later. Mozart was very impressed with the young Beethoven, especially his ability to improvise, and predicted he would make a great name for himself.

Beethoven's reputation began to grow in Bonn and he gained many supporters, even being employed as a teacher by several influential families. The money from teaching helped support his family, after his father had squandered much of the family fortune on alcohol. Fate had it that Haydn visited Bonn at this time and, after being shown some of Beethoven's manuscripts, agreed to take him as a student.

Beethoven came to Vienna for the second time in late 1792. He was 21 years of age and already a superb piano virtuoso, but he still had much to learn as a composer. Ultimately Haydn wasn't to be his only teacher. Soon after arriving Beethoven began taking lessons in secret from Johann Georg Albrechtsberger, Stephansdom's organist, who was very learned in musical technique. Later he also studied vocal composition with Antonio Salieri, the imperial Kapellmeister.

Money again became an issue for Beethoven after Haydn left for his second trip to England, but patrons such as Prince Lichnowsky (who also supported Mozart) supported him and any thoughts he had of returning to Bonn were abandoned (partly because the city had fallen to the French). Later, when he threatened to leave Vienna after a quarrel with some musicians, several nobles (including the prince) offered him an annuity of 4000 florins. To receive this grand sum all Beethoven had to do was remain in Vienna and write music, which he did until his death.

Beethoven's career had three distinct periods. The first, which largely comprised chamber music, was from his adolescence to his 32nd year. In the second period, when he began to improvise, Beethoven's hearing began to fail him – he briefly contemplated suicide (what worse fate than deafness could there be for a musician?) but he abandoned such thoughts because he felt he had too much to contribute to his art. As total deafness approached, Beethoven withdrew from the public performances that helped make him so popular. He produced fewer pieces (one of which was the Symphony No 9 in D Minor, one of his greatest and most influential works), but many consider his final 10 years his best period.

Beethoven never married, but appears (from letters) to have contemplated it at least three times. He died from cirrhosis of the liver aged 57, and more than 20,000 people attended his funeral. ■

Ludwig van Beethoven hailed from Bonn and came to Vienna to study, first with Mozart and later under Haydn. He stayed in the city up to the time of his death, living at as many as 80 different addresses. He was greatly inspired by the Viennese countryside (eg in the *Pastoral Symphony* of 1808). Among his piano sonatas, overtures and concertos are the opera *Fidelio* and the *Ninth Symphony* (concluding with the majestic *Ode to Joy*). Beethoven began to lose his hearing at age 30, understandably a cause of deep depression to him, and was profoundly deaf while still composing some of his major works.

Franz Schubert (1797-1828), a native Viennese, was responsible for giving the ancient *Lieder* (German-language songs) tradition a new lease of life, creating a craze of what became known as 'Schubertiade' musical evenings.

The Waltz The waltz originated in Vienna at the beginning of the 19th century and went down a storm at the Congress of Vienna. The early masters of this genre were Johann Strauss the Elder (1804-49), who was also the composer of the *Radetzky March*, and Joseph Lanner (1801-43).

But the man who really made this métier his own was Johann Strauss the Younger (1825-99), composer of 400 waltzes. Young Strauss became a musician against the wishes of Strauss senior (who had experienced years of struggle), and set up a rival orchestra to his father's. He composed Vienna's unofficial anthem, the *Blue Danube* (1867), and *Tales from the Vienna Woods*. This joyful if lightweight style became so popular that more 'serious' composers began to feel somewhat disenfranchised. The operetta form became equally fashionable. The younger Johann Strauss proved also to be a master of this style, especially with his eternally popular *Die Fledermaus* (1874) and *The Gipsy Baron* (1885). Franz Lehár (1870-1948) was another notable operetta composer.

Other 19th Century Styles In the late 19th century Vienna was still attracting musicians

and composers from elsewhere in Europe. Anton Bruckner (1824-96) arrived from Upper Austria and settled in Vienna with his appointment as organist to the court in 1868. He is known for dramatically intense symphonies and church music. Johannes Brahms (1833-97) and Gustav Mahler (1860-1911) were both German. Richard Strauss (1864-1949) was also German, and though he spent time in Vienna he tended to favour Salzburg. Brahms enjoyed Vienna's village atmosphere and said it had a positive effect on his work, which was of the classical-romantic tradition. Mahler is known mainly for his nine symphonies, and was director of the Vienna Court Opera from 1897 to 1907. Hugo Wolf (1860-1903) rivalled Schubert in his facility at Lieder composition, though he later went insane.

The New School Vienna's musical eminence continued in the 20th century with the innovative work of Arnold Schönberg (1874-1951), who founded what has been dubbed the 'New School' of Vienna. Schönberg developed theories on twelve-tone composition, yet some of his earlier work (eg *Pieces for the Piano op. 11* composed in 1909) went completely beyond the bounds of tonality. Schönberg was also a competent artist. The most influential of his pupils were Alban Berg and Anton Webern, who both explored the twelve-tone technique.

Music Today The *Heurigen* (wine taverns) in Vienna have a musical tradition all their own, with the songs often expressing very maudlin themes. It's known as *Schrammelmusik*, and is usually played by musicians wielding a combination of violin, accordion, guitar and clarinet. In the field of rock and pop Vienna has made little impact (unless you count the briefly emergent Falco), though the city does have several jazz clubs, and was home to Joe Zawinul of Weather Report.

Today, Austrian orchestras such as the Vienna Philharmonic have a worldwide reputation. Vienna's music institutions like the Vienna Boys' Choir, the Staatsoper (State

Opera), the Musikverein and the Konzerthaus are unrivalled, as are its music festivals. A visit to some sort of musical event is an essential part of any trip to Vienna.

Sculpture & Design
The Verdun Altar in Klosterneuburg abbey dates from the Romanesque period. Fine examples of Baroque sculpture are the Donner Fountain by George Raphael Donner in Neuer Markt, and Balthasar Permoser's statue of Prince Eugene in the Lower Belvedere. Baroque even extended to funeral caskets, as created by Balthasar Moll for Maria Theresa and Francis I. Neo-classical sculpture is typified in the equestrian statue of Emperor Joseph II in Josefsplatz by the Hofburg.

The Biedermeier period was strongly represented in furniture, examples of which can be seen in the Museum für angewandte Kunst (Museum of Applied Art). After Biedermeier, the technique of bending wood in furniture became popular, particularly in the backs of chairs. The bentwood chair became known as the Viennese chair.

In 1903 the Wiener Werkstätte (Vienna Workshops) were founded. They created a range of quality, if expensive, household products, as well as garments and jewellery. Aesthetic considerations were given precedence over practicality, resulting in some highly distinctive styles, such as Josef Hoffmann's silver tea service (displayed in the Museum für angewandte Kunst). Another key figure involved in the Wiener Werkstätte was Kolo Moser.

Architecture
Excavations of Roman ruins can be seen within Vienna's 1st district at Michaelerplatz, Am Hof 9 and Hoher Markt. Romanesque architecture barely survives in modern Vienna, though some churches (eg Stephansdom and Michaelerkirche) are built around earlier Romanesque churches.

The Gothic style didn't really take hold in Austria until the accession of the Habsburgs. The most impressive Gothic structure in Austria is Vienna's Stephansdom. It displays a typical characteristic of the Gothic style in Austria with its three naves of equal height, a feature also to be found in the Minorite churches.

While Renaissance architecture had little penetration in Vienna, Baroque proved to be a high point for Austria in terms of both architecture and painting. Building fervour was fuelled by the removal of the Turkish threat in 1683. Learning from the Italian model, Johann Bernhard Fischer von Erlach (1656-1723) developed a national style called Austrian Baroque. This mirrored the exuberant ornamentation of Italian Baroque but gave it a specifically Austrian treatment. Dynamic combinations of colour are coupled with irregular or undulating outlines. Examples of Fischer von Erlach's work in Vienna include the Nationalbibliothek and Karlskirche. Another prominent Baroque architect was Johann Lukas von Hildebrandt (1668-1745), responsible for the palaces of Belvedere and Schwarzenberg, and the Peterskirche.

Rococo, the extreme version of Baroque, was a great favourite with Maria Theresa. She chose this fussy style for most of the rooms of Schloss Schönbrunn when she commissioned Nicolas Pacassi to renovate it in 1744. Austrian rococo is sometimes referred to as late-Baroque Theresian style.

Rococo was succeeded by neo-classicism, a less showy style of which Vienna's Technical University is an example. The period between the Congress of Vienna (1814-15) and the revolutions of 1848 was called the Vormärz (pre-March), or Biedermeier when applied to art.

In the second half of the 19th century, historicism took hold; this is seen principally in the Ringstrasse developments instigated by Emperor Franz Josef I. A great diversity of retrograde styles can be seen here, such as French Gothic (Votivkirche), Flemish Gothic (Rathaus), Grecian (Parlament), French Renaissance (Staatsoper) and Florentine Renaissance (Museum für angewandte Kunst).

The backlash came at the end of the 19th century with the emergence of Art Nouveau (Jugendstil), an art and architecture style that

Architectural Styles

Romanesque This style dates from the 10th to 13th centuries. Romanesque churches are characterised by thick walls, closely spaced columns and heavy, rounded arches. Little of this style remains in Vienna today.

Gothic The Gothic style was popular from the 13th to 16th centuries. This new aesthetic was made possible by engineering advances, permitting thinner walls and (in churches) taller, more delicate columns and great expanses of stained glass. Distinctive features included pointed arches and ribbed ceiling vaults, external 'flying buttresses' to support the thinner walls, and elaborate carved doorway columns. Stephansdom is the best example.

RICHARD NEBESKY
Stephansdom

Renaissance The 16th century saw a new enthusiasm for classical forms and an obsession with grace and symmetry. In Austria, Italian architects were imported to create Renaissance buildings, and they usually incorporated Italian and local features.

Baroque This resplendent, triumphal style is closely associated with the rebuilding (and re-imposition of Catholicism) in the region after the Thirty Years' War. Emotional sculpture and painting, marble columns, and rich, gilded finishing create the extravagant and awe-inspiring interiors. One of Vienna's best Baroque structures is Schloss Belvedere.

Rococo This is essentially late, over-the-top Baroque. Florid in the extreme, elaborate and 'lightweight', it was popular with architects in the late 18th century. The interior of Schloss Schönbrunn displays this style.

MARK HONAN
Schloss Belevedere

Historicism The revival of old styles of architecture became popular after the 1848 revolutions. Neo-classical, neo-Renaissance and neo-Gothic styles all came to the fore and are evident in most of the building on Vienna's Ringstrasse. The neo-classicism style used grand colonnades and pediments, and often huge, simple, symmetrical buildings.

Modern At the turn of the century the sensuous and decorative style called Art Nouveau ('new art'; called *Sezessionstil* in Austria) took hold, its main practitioners in Vienna being the Secession architects. The more sinuous and decorative features of this style became subservient to functional considerations, both in design and building materials. ∎

MARK HONAN
Art Nouveau bank, Fleischmarkt

spread through much of Europe. In Vienna the movement flowered with the founding of the Secession movement in 1897. Otto Wagner – designer of the Postsparkasse (Post Office Savings Bank) and the Kirche am Steinhof – was one of the leading architects in the field. (For more information on the Secessionists see Karlsplatz in the Things to See & Do chapter.) It was Wagner who led the movement towards a more modern, functional style as the 20th century unfolded. Alfred Loos (1870-1933) was perhaps an even more important figure in the move towards a new functionalism. He was a bitter critic of the Ringstrasse buildings, yet he was also quickly disillusioned with the ornamentation in Secessionist buildings.

The dominance of the Social Democrats in the city government of the new Republic gave rise to a number of municipal building projects, not least the massive Karl-Marx-Hof apartment complex. Post-war architecture was mostly utilitarian. More recently some strange multicoloured, haphazard-looking structures have been erected in Vienna, the work of the maverick artist and architect, Friedensreich Hundertwasser. Austria's premier post-modern architect is Hans Hollein.

Literature

The outstanding Viennese work of the Middle Ages was the *Nibelungenlied* (The Song of the Nibelungs), written around 1200 by an unknown hand. This epic poem told a tale of passion, faithfulness and revenge in the Burgundian Court at Worms. Its themes were adapted by Richard Wagner in his *The Ring of the Nibelungen* operatic series.

The first great figure in the modern era was the playwright Franz Grillparzer (1791-1872), who anticipated Freudian themes in his plays which are still performed at the Burgtheater. Other influential playwrights who still regularly get an airing are Johann Nestroy, known for his satirical farces, and Ferdinand Raimaund *(The Misanthrope)*.

Adalbert Stifter (1805-68) is credited as being the seminal influence in the development of an Austrian prose style. Austria's

literary tradition really took off around the turn of the century, around the same time as the Vienna Secessionists and Sigmund Freud were creating their own waves. Influential writers who emerged at this time included Arthur Schnitzler, Hugo von Hofmannsthal, Karl Kraus and the poet Georg Trakl. Kraus' apocalyptic drama *Die letzten Tage der Menschheit* (The Last Days of Mankind) employed a combination of reports, interviews and press extracts to tell its tale – a very innovative style for its time. Kraus had previously founded *Die Fackel* (The Torch), a critical literary periodical. Peter Altenberg was a poet who depicted the bohemian lifestyle of Vienna, and he currently resides in the Café Central in the form of a plaster dummy.

Robert Musil was one of the most important 20th century writers, but he only achieved international recognition after his

---

Viennese Actionism

Viennese Actionism spanned from 1957 to 1968 and was one of the most extreme of all modern art movements. It was linked to the Vienna Group and had its roots in abstract expressionism. Actionism sought access to the unconscious through the frenzy of an extreme and very direct art: the actionists quickly moved from pouring paint over the canvas and slashing it with knives, to using bodies (live people, dead animals) as 'brushes', and using blood, excrement, eggs, mud, and whatever came to hand as 'paint'. The traditional canvas was soon dispensed with altogether. The artist's body instead became the canvas, the site of art became a deliberated event (the scripted action, staged both privately and publicly) and even merged with reality.

It was a short step from self-painting to inflicting wounds upon the body, and engaging in physical and psychological endurance tests. For 10 years the actionists scandalised the press and public, incited violence and panic – and got plenty of publicity. Often poetic, humorous and aggressive, the actions became increasingly politicised, addressing the sexual and social repression that pervaded the Austrian state. *Art in Revolution* (1968), the last action to be realised in Vienna, resulted in six months' hard labour all round. ∎

death. He was born in Klagenfurt in 1880 and died in poverty in Geneva in 1942, with his major literary achievement, *Der Mann ohne Eigenschaften* (The Man without Qualities), still unfinished. Fortunately, enough of this work was completed for it to fill three volumes (English translation available) and reveal a fascinating portrait of the collapsing Austro-Hungarian monarchy. Another major figure in the 20th century was Heimito von Doderer (1896-1966). He grew up in Vienna and first achieved recognition with his novel *The Strudlhof Staircase*. His magnum opus was *Die Dämonen* (The Demons), an epic fictional depiction of the end of the monarchy and the first years of the Austrian Republic, with specific reference to Vienna. It looks at all strata of society and is published in English in three volumes.

The Wiener Gruppe (Vienna Group) was formed in the 1950s by HC Artmann. Its members incorporated surrealism and Dadaism in their sound compositions, textual montages, and actionist happenings. (See the Viennese Actionism boxed text earlier.) Public outrage and police intervention were a regular accompaniment to their meetings. The group's activities came to an end in 1964 when Konrad Bayer, its most influential member, committed suicide.

Thomas Bernhard (1931-89) was born in Holland but grew up and lived in Austria. He was obsessed with negative themes such as disintegration and death, but in later works like *Cutting Timber* he turned to controversial attacks against social conventions and institutions. His novels are seamless (no chapters or paragraphs, few full stops) and seemingly repetitive, but surprisingly readable once you get into them. He also wrote plays and short stories. Bernhard was influenced by Ludwig Wittgenstein's writings, and even wrote an autobiographical novel about his friendship with the philosopher's nephew. Both *Cutting Timber* and *Wittgenstein's Nephew* are published in English translations by Vintage.

The best known living writer is Peter Handke (born 1942). His output encompasses innovative and introspective prose works and stylistic plays. Contemporary female writers include the provocative novelist Elfriede Jelinek, who dispenses with direct speech and indulges in strange flights of fancy, but is worth persevering with. Translations of her novels *The Piano Teacher*, *Lust* and *Women as Lovers* have been published in paperback by Serpent's Tail. Another prominent contemporary author is Friederike Mayröcker, once described as 'the avant-garde's bird of paradise' by a critic.

Film

Austrian endeavours in the film industry go mostly unnoticed outside the German-speaking world. There are a few exceptions. The film director Fritz Lang was responsible for the innovative science fiction silent film *Metropolis* (1926), and *M* (1931) starring Peter Lorre. Well-known actors are Klaus Maria Brandauer who starred in *Mephisto* (1980) and other films; and of course there's former Mr Universe Arnold Schwarzenegger, whose build fills the screen in such action epics as *The Terminator* series, *Total Recall* (1990), *True Lies* (1994), and he played Mr Freeze in *Batman & Robin* (1997).

Theatre

Vienna's tradition in the theatre was bolstered by the quality of operas and operettas produced in the golden age of music. In addition, Greek dramas, avant-garde, mime, comedy, farce and other genres are regularly performed. Vienna is home to the four federal theatres, the Staatsoper, Volksoper, Akademietheater and Burgtheater. The Burgtheater is the premier performance venue in the German-speaking world. Municipal theatres include the Theater an der Wien, the Raimundtheater and the Etablissement Ronacher. Private theatres are the Volkstheater, Theater in der Josefstadt, Kammerspiele, Wiener Kammeroper, Theater der Jugend, Künstlerhaus, Konzerthaus and Schauspielhaus. The Theater in der Josefstadt is known for the modern style of acting evolved by Max Reinhardt.

Painting

Examples of Gothic church art in Austria are best seen in the Middle Ages collection in the Orangery in the Unteres Belvedere. Early Renaissance art is represented in Austria by the Danube School, which combined landscapes and religious motifs; exponents included Rueland Frueauf the Younger, Wolf Huber, Max Reichlich and Lukas Cranach.

Baroque artists responsible for many church frescoes were Johann Michael Rottmayr and Daniel Gran. A prominent canvas painter was Franz Anton Maulbertsch, who combined mastery of colour and light with intensity of expression. The leading Biedermeier painters were Georg Ferdinand Waldmüller and Friedrich Gauermann, who captured the age in portraits, landscapes and period scenes. Some of Waldmüller's evocative if idealised peasant scenes can be seen in the Historisches Museum der Stadt Wien and the Oberes Belvedere. Rudolf von Alt was an exponent of watercolour.

Prominent painters of the historicism period were Hans Makart and August von Pettenkofen. Anton Romako's work anticipated the age of expressionism.

The leading painter of the Art Nouveau age, and one of the founders of the Viennese Secession movement, was Gustav Klimt (1862-1918). Trained in the traditional mould, he soon developed a colourful and distinctive style, full of sensuous female figures, flowing patterns and symbolism.

Egon Schiele and Oskar Kokoschka were important exponents of Viennese expressionism. The work of these 19th and 20th century Austrian painters are best viewed in the Oberes Belvedere.

SCIENCE & PHILOSOPHY

The Vienna Circle was a group of philosophers centred on Vienna University in the 1920s and 30s. The term logical positivism was created to describe their views. They owed an initial debt to the work of the Austrian philosopher and scientist Ernst Mach (whose name lives on as a measure of the speed of a body in relation to the speed of sound). The group formulated the verifiability principle, which sought to find meaning in phenomena by the method of its verification. Mathematical propositions and statements of pure logic are true and meaningful in virtue of the fact that they are tautological and self-evident ('2 + 2 = 4' can be regarded as a statement of identity, and will always be true). Metaphysical questions, like 'is there a God?', are meaningless because they cannot be verified. However, science illuminates the world and confers meaning on it by the fact that its questions are answerable and empirically verifiable. Thus, for the Vienna Circle, the test of verifiability determined whether something had meaning. The Vienna Circle emigrated with the arrival of the Nazis in 1938. The movement remained influential, though it lost some of its appeal when philosophers couldn't agree whether the verifiability principle itself was tautological or subject to empirical verification.

Sir Karl Popper (1902-94) was loosely connected with the Vienna Circle, but mainly in a critical capacity. He was born in Vienna and lived and worked there until he also emigrated rather than face the Nazis. He had an impact on the way the nature of scientific inquiry was understood, with his views that the hallmark of science is falsifiability rather than verifiability. He pointed out that general scientific laws could never be logically proved to always apply, they could only be disproved if and when contrary data became manifest. (This would make them meaningless according to the verifiability principle of the logical positivists.) Scientific laws are therefore accepted until they are seen to require revision (as in the way that Newtonian physics was refined by Einstein), thus leading to the advancement of scientific endeavour. Popper was also known for his work in the field of social and political philosophy.

Ludwig Wittgenstein (1889-1951) made a significant impact with his philosophical writings, not least on the Vienna Circle. He was born in Vienna and died in Cambridge, England, where he spent the latter part of his

Sigmund Freud

Sigmund Freud was born in Freiberg, Moravia, on 6 May, 1856. Three years later his father, a Jewish wool merchant, relocated the family to the Leopoldstadt quarter in Vienna. Freud was educated in Vienna and graduated as a Doctor of Medicine in 1881 (his degree took three years longer to complete than was usual, as he spent much of his time engaged in neurological research that wasn't part of the curriculum). In 1886 he set up his first office as a neurologist at 01, Rathausstrasse 7, and later that year married Martha Bernays, who went on to bear him six children. In 1891 he moved his practice to 09, Berggasse 19. He first came up with the term 'psychoanalysis' in 1896.

Although many academics and physicians were hostile towards his published works, Freud was able to gather round him a core of pupils and followers, who would meet in his waiting room on Wednesday evenings. Among their number was the Swiss psychologist Carl Jung, who later severed his links with the group (in 1914) because of personal differences with Freud. In 1923 Freud was diagnosed as having cancer of the palate, an affliction that caused him great pain and forced him to undergo surgery over 30 times. The illness prompted him to mostly withdraw from public life; his daughter, Anna (a child psychiatrist), often appeared in his stead at meetings and conventions.

The arrival of the Nazis in 1938 instigated a mass evacuation by many of Vienna's Jews. Freud was allowed to emigrate to London on 4 June, accompanied by Anna. The rest of his children also managed to escape, but other family members weren't so fortunate – four of his elderly sisters were detained in the city, and finally killed in a concentration camp in 1941. Freud breathed his last in London on 23 September, 1939. ■

---

career as a research fellow at the university. Much of his output was concerned with the scope and limitations of language. His *Tractatus* was an adamant treatise ordered as a series of logical statements. By analysing language using language he ended up in the paradoxical situation of having to say what he admitted could only be shown. Nevertheless, Wittgenstein was so convinced that this work had achieved all that it was possible for such a text to do, that it effectively heralded an end to philosophical inquiry. He therefore retired from the scene and retreated to the obscurity of a teaching post in rural Austria.

He returned to Cambridge in 1929 and proceeded to all but contradict the thrust of his earlier work. His new theories were less rigid and attempted to illuminate the inventiveness of language. Wittgenstein has been hailed as one of the most influential 20th century philosophers, yet in his personal life he cut a rather lonely figure. One of his great fears was that his writings would be destroyed by fire (only the *Tractatus* was published in his lifetime), and he obsessively stored these in a fireproof safe.

Sigmund Freud (1856-1939), the founder of psychoanalysis, had a love-hate relationship with Vienna, the city where he lived and worked for most of his life. He too fled from the Nazis in 1938. Freud believed that the repression of infantile sexuality was the cause of neurosis in adult life. Central to his treatments was getting the patient to recognise unconscious conflicts. Early on he employed hypnosis to uncover these conflicts, which he later abandoned in favour of free association and the study of symbolism in dreams. *The Interpretation of Dreams* (1900) was his first major work.

In *Beyond the Pleasure Principle* (1920) Freud contended that the two dominant principles of the mind were the pleasure-pain complex and the repression-compulsion complex, the latter being the instinctive drive of an organism to return to its previous state.

His last psychoanalytical work was *The Ego and the Id* (1923), a new theory in which the tensions between the id (basic urges), the ego (the conscious personality) and the superego (idealised ingrained precepts) were explored. Inferiority complexes and guilt feelings were the frequent result of such tensions. Although Freud's views have always been attacked, his legacy to the 20th century remains enormous. A mental landscape of Oedipus complexes, phallic objects and Freudian slips are only a few of the manifestations. Generations of patients supine on couches is another.

SOCIETY & CONDUCT

It is customary to greet people you come across with the salute *Grüss Gott* and to say *Auf Wiedersehen* when departing. This applies to shop assistants, café servers and the like. Not greeting someone will be taken as a personal affront. When being introduced to someone it is usual to shake hands.

Some older Viennese still cling to the language and etiquette of the old empire, known as *Kaiserdeutsch* or *Schönbrunndeutsch*. This can be seen as pompous or charming depending upon your point of view. It may manifest itself at introductions, with men addressing women as *Gnädige Frau* (gracious lady) and formally adding *Küss die Hand* (I kiss your hand), perhaps backing this up by actually performing the act or clicking the heels. People often address each other using full formal titles.

The Viennese tend to dress up when going to the opera or theatre, so the wearing of jeans and trainers by foreigners at such events is tolerated but rather frowned upon. You will find conservative behaviour exhibited in various other ways too, such as in the rigid respect for the 'don't walk' red figure on traffic lights; even if there's no traffic anywhere in sight, people will obediently wait for the lights to change (in theory you could be fined around AS100 if the police spot you jaywalking).

At a meal, Austrians dining together normally raise their glasses and say *Prost* before taking their first sip of wine; look people in the eye while you're doing it – some may consider you insincere otherwise. Similarly, there will be a signal before you should start to eat, such as the exchange of a *Guten Appetite*.

RELIGION

Religion plays an important part in the lives of many Austrians. If you venture out into the countryside you'll see small roadside shrines decorated with fresh flowers. Freedom of religion is guaranteed under the constitution. Even the religious rights of children are protected: up to age 10 a child's religious affiliation is in the hands of its parents, yet from age 10 to 12 the child must be consulted about its preferred religion, and from age 12 to 14 a change of religion cannot be imposed upon any child. Upon reaching 14 children have full independence to choose their own faith.

The 1991 census revealed that in Vienna there were 890,000 Roman Catholics, 80,000 Protestants and 160,000 following other religions; 400,000 people were non-religious or undeclared.

The tourist office has the *Grüss Gott* brochure listing religious services for various denominations, and the *Vienna Reporter* newspaper lists services in English. A Roman Catholic service is held in English at the Votive Church (Votivkirche) on Sunday at 11 am.

LANGUAGE

The Viennese speak German, with an accent similar to that found in Bavaria. Though the grammar is the same as standard German, there are also many words and expressions that are used only by the Viennese. Many Viennese speak some English, and young people are usually quite fluent. Tourist office and train information staff almost invariably speak English; hotel receptionists and restaurant servers usually do too, especially in higher class places. Nevertheless, some knowledge of German would be an asset and any attempt to use it, no matter how clumsy, will be appreciated. One characteristic of German is that all nouns are written with a capital letter.

Pronunciation

Unlike English or French, German has no real silent letters: you pronounce the **k** at the start of the word *Knie*, 'knee', the **p** at the start of *Psychologie*, 'psychology', and the **e** at the end of *ich habe*, 'I have'.

Vowels As in English, vowels can be pronounced long (eg as in 'pope'), or short (eg as in 'pop'). As a rule, German vowels are long before single consonants and short before double consonants: the **o** is long in the word *Dom*, 'cathedral', but short in the word *doch*, 'after all'.

a	short, like the 'u' in 'cut', or long, as in 'father'
au	as in 'vow'
ä	short, as in 'act', or long, as in 'hair'
äu	as the 'oi' in 'boy'
e	short, as in 'bet', or long, as in 'day'
ei	like the 'i' in 'pile'
eu	as the 'oi' in 'boy'
i	short, as in 'sit', or long, as in 'see'
ie	as in 'see'
o	short, as in 'not', or long, as in 'note'
ö	like the 'er' in 'fern'
u	like the 'u' in 'pull'
ü	similar to the 'u' in 'pull' but with stretched lips

Consonants Most German consonants sound similar to their English counterparts. One important difference is that **b**, **d** and **g** sound like 'p', 't' and 'k', respectively, at the end of a word.

b	normally like the English 'b', but as 'p' when at the end of a word
ch	like the 'ch' in Scottish *loch*
d	normally like the English 'd', but like 't' when at the end of a word
g	normally like the English 'g', but at the end of a word, either as 'k', or as the 'ch' in 'loch' if preceded by **i**
j	like the 'y' in 'yet'
qu	like 'k' plus 'v'
r	can be trilled or guttural, depending on the region

s	normally like the 's' in 'sun', but like the 'z' in 'zoo' when followed by a vowel
sch	like the 'sh' in 'ship'
sp, st	the **s** sounds like the 'sh' in 'ship' when at the start of a word
tion	the **t** sounds like the 'ts' in 'hits'
ß	like the 's' in 'sun' (written as 'ss' in this book)
v	as the 'f' in 'fan'
w	as the 'v' in 'van'
z	as the 'ts' in 'hits'

Greetings & Civilities

Good day.	*Guten Tag.*
Hello.	*Grüss Gott.*
Goodbye.	*Auf Wiedersehen.*
Bye.	*Tschüss.*
Yes.	*Ja.*
No.	*Nein.*
Please.	*Bitte.*
Thank you.	*Danke.*
That's fine, you're welcome.	*Bitte sehr.*
Sorry. (excuse me, forgive me)	*Entschuldigung.*

Some Viennese Words

See the Places to Eat chapter for more vocabulary on Viennese food and drink. Most of the following Viennese dialect and slang words would not be understood by High German speakers. On the other hand, the 'normal' German equivalent would be understood by the Viennese.

Beisl	small tavern for food and drink
Bim	tram
Blunzn	black pudding
Faschiertes	minced meat
Gerstl	money
Gefüllte Paprika	stuffed green pepper
Guglhupf	Viennese cake
Haberer	friend
Hasse	sausage
I'hob an dulliö.	I'm drunk.
Obers	cream
Maroni	(roasted) chestnut
Maut	tip (to waiter etc)

Moos	money
Müch	milk
Paradeiser	tomatoes
Scherzl	crust of bread
Stamperl	glass (for Schnapps)
Stiftl	glass (for wine)
Verdrahn	to sell
Wimmerer	sunburn
Weimberl	raisin

Some Useful Phrases

Do you speak English?	*Sprechen Sie Englisch?*
Does anyone here speak English?	*Spricht hier jemand Englisch?*
I (don't) understand.	*Ich verstehe (nicht).*
Just a minute.	*Ein Moment.*
Please write that down.	*Können Sie es bitte aufschreiben.*
How much is it?	*Wieviel kostet es?*

Useful Signs

Camping Ground	*Campingplatz*
Entrance	*Eingang*
Exit	*Ausgang*
Full, No Vacancies	*Voll, Besetzt*
Guesthouse	*Pension, Gästehaus*
Hote	*Hotel*
Information	*Auskunft*
Open/Closed	*Offen (or Geöffnet)/ Geschlossen*
Police	*Polizei*
Police Station	*Polizeiwache*
Train Station	*Bahnhof (Bf)*
Rooms Available	*Zimmer Frei*
Toilets	*Toiletten (WC)*
Youth Hostel	*Jugendherberge*

Getting Around

What time does ... leave?	*Wann fährt ... ab?*
What time does ... arrive?	*Wann kommt ... an?*
What time is the next boat?	*Wann fährt das nächste Boot?*
next	*nächste*
first	*erste*
last	*letzte*
the boat	*das Boot*

the bus (city)	*der Bus*
the bus (intercity)	*der (Überland) Bus*
the tram	*die Strassenbahn*
the train	*der Zug*
I'd like ...	*Ich möchte ...*
a one-way ticket	*eine Einzelkarte*
a return ticket	*eine Rückfahrkarte*
1st class	*erste Klasse*
2nd class	*zweite Klasse*
Where is the bus stop?	*Wo ist die Bushaltestelle?*
Where is the tram stop?	*Wo ist die Strassen- bahnhaltestelle?*
Can you show me (on the map)?	*Können Sie mir (auf der Karte) zeigen?*
far/near	*weit/nahe*
Go straight ahead.	*Gehen Sie geradeaus.*
Turn left.	*Biegen Sie links ab.*
Turn right.	*Biegen Sie rechts ab.*

Around Town

I'm looking for ...	*Ich suche ...*
a bank	*eine Bank*
the city centre	*die Innenstadt*
the ... embassy	*die ... Botschaft*
my hotel	*mein Hotel*
the market	*den Markt*
the police	*die Polizei*
the post office	*das Postamt*
a public toilet	*eine öffentliche Toilette*
the telephone centre	*die Telefonzentrale*
the tourist office	*das Verkehrsamt*
beach	*Strand*
bridge	*Brücke*
castle	*Schloss, Burg*
cathedral	*Dom*
church	*Kirche*
hospital	*Krankenhaus*
island	*Insel*
lake	*See*
main square	*Hauptplatz*
market	*Markt*
monastery, convent	*Kloster*
mosque	*Moschee*

FACTS ABOUT VIENNA

mountain	*Berg*
old city	*Altstadt*
palace	*Palast*
ruins	*Ruinen*
sea	*Meer*
square	*Platz*
tower	*Turm*

Accommodation

Where is a cheap hotel?	*Wo ist ein billiges Hotel?*
What is the address?	*Was ist die Adresse?*
Could you write the address, please?	*Könnten Sie bitte die Adresse aufschreiben?*
Do you have any rooms available?	*Haben Sie noch freie Zimmer?*
I'd like ...	*Ich möchte ...*
a single room	*ein Einzelzimmer*
a double room	*ein Doppelzimmer*
a room with a bath	*ein Zimmer mit Bad*
to share a dorm	*einen Schlafsaal teilen*
a bed	*ein Bett*
How much is it per night/per person?	*Wieviel kostet es pro Nacht/pro Person?*
Can I see it?	*Kann ich es sehen?*
Where is the bath/shower?	*Wo ist das Bad/die Dusche?*

Food

bakery	*Bäckerei*
grocery	*Lebensmittelgeschäft*
delicatessen	*Delikatessengeschäft*
restaurant	*Restaurant, Gaststätte*
breakfast	*Frühstück*
lunch	*Mittagessen*
dinner	*Abendessen*
I'd like the set lunch, please.	*Ich hätte gern das Tagesmenü, bitte.*
Is service included in the bill?	*Ist die Bedienung inbegriffen?*
I'm a vegetarian.	*Ich bin Vegetarier* (m)/ *Vegetarierin* (f).

Time & Dates

today	*heute*
tomorrow	*morgen*
in the morning	*morgens*
in the afternoon	*nachmittags*
in the evening	*abends*
Monday	*Montag*
Tuesday	*Dienstag*
Wednesday	*Mittwoch*
Thursday	*Donnerstag*
Friday	*Freitag*
Saturday	*Samstag, Sonnabend*
Sunday	*Sonntag*
January	*Januar*
February	*Februar*
March	*März*
April	*April*
May	*Mai*
June	*Juni*
July	*Juli*
August	*August*
September	*September*
October	*Oktober*
November	*November*
December	*Dezember*

Numbers

0	*null*
1	*eins*
2	*zwei* (*zwo* on phone or public anouncements)
3	*drei*
4	*vier*
5	*fünf*
6	*sechs*
7	*sieben*
8	*acht*
9	*neun*
10	*zehn*
11	*elf*
12	*zwölf*
13	*dreizehn*
14	*vierzehn*
15	*fünfzehn*
16	*sechzehn*
17	*siebzehn*
18	*achtzehn*
19	*neunzehn*

FACTS ABOUT VIENNA

20	*zwanzig*
21	*einundzwanzig*
22	*zweiundzwanzig*
30	*dreissig*
40	*vierzig*
50	*fünfzig*
60	*sechzig*
70	*siebzig*
80	*achtzig*
90	*neunzig*
100	*hundert*
1000	*tausend*
one million	*eine Million*

Health

I'm ...	*Ich bin ...*
diabetic	*Diabetikerin* (f)/
	Diabetiker (m)
epileptic	*Epileptikerin* (f)/
	Epileptiker (m)
asthmatic	*Asthmatikerin* (f)/
	Asthmatiker (m)

| I'm allergic to anti-biotics/penicillin. | *Ich bin gegen Anti-biotika/Penizillin allergisch.* |

antiseptic	*Antiseptikum*
aspirin	*Aspirin*
condoms	*Kondome*
constipation	*Verstopfung*
contraceptive	*Verhütungsmittel*
diarrhoea	*Durchfall*
medicine	*Medizin*
nausea	*Übelkeit*
sunblock cream	*Sunblockcreme*
tampons	*Tampons*

Emergencies

Help!	*Hilfe!*
Call a doctor!	*Holen Sie einen Arzt!*
Call the police!	*Rufen Sie die Polizei!*
Go away!	*Gehen Sie weg!*

Facts for the Visitor

WHEN TO GO

Visitors descend on Vienna year-round. When to go depends on what you want to do or see. In July and August, for example, you won't be able to see the Lipizzaner stallions or the Vienna Boys' Choir, but you will be able to enjoy the Vienna Summer of Music. See the Public Holidays & Special Events section later in this chapter for seasonal events to aim for.

It's not only singers and horses that disappear in July and August – many Viennese also go on holiday at this time. These months can be oppressively hot, yet summer remains the most popular time for tourists to visit. June is dire for budget accommodation, but from July to September things are much easier with the opening of student residences. In winter you'll find things less crowded and the hotel prices lower (except over Christmas and Easter), though it can get too cold for comfort around the New Year. Weatherwise, spring and autumn are probably the most comfortable seasons for sightseeing. September is a busy month for tourism.

WHAT TO BRING

Anything you don't bring you can easily buy in Vienna. Objects you might want include a torch (needed for the Third Man Tour), padlocks, some string (clothesline) and a light raincoat. A few hostels charge extra for sheets so you may want to bring your own. If you take a water bottle to fill up you won't have to keep buying expensive drinks when sightseeing.

ORIENTATION

Vienna stands imperiously in the Danube Valley, with the rolling hills of the Wienerwald (Vienna Woods) undulating beyond the suburbs in the north and west. The Danube River divides the city into two unequal halves. The old city centre and nearly all the tourist sights are south of the river. The Danube Canal (Donaukanal) branches off from the main river and winds a sinewy course south, forming one of the borders of the historic centre, the 1st district (known as the *Innere Stadt*). The rest of the old centre is encircled by the Ringstrasse, or Ring, a series of broad roads sporting sturdy public buildings and sites of touristic interest. Beyond the Ring is a larger traffic artery, the Gürtel (literally meaning 'belt'), which is fed by the flow of vehicles from the outlying motorways.

Stephansdom (St Stephen's Cathedral), with its distinctive slender spire, is in the heart of the Innere Stadt and is the city's principal landmark. The majority of hotels, pensions, restaurants and bars are in the Innere Stadt, and west of the centre between the Gürtel and the Ringstrasse. Farther west is an important tourist sight, Schloss Schönbrunn.

On the north bank of the Danube is the long, thin Danube Island (Donauinsel), with the New Danube (Neue Donau) running along its northern shore. A loop of water beyond this is the Old Danube (Alte Donau), the remnant of the original course of the river. It encloses a flattened half-circle of land, with the Donaupark at its heart and beaches and water-sport centres along its shores. North and east of the Old Danube are relatively poor, residential districts, of no real interest to tourists.

Addresses

Vienna is divided into 23 districts *(Bezirke)*, fanning out from the 1st district, the Innere Stadt. Take care when reading addresses. The number of a building within a street *follows* the street name. Any number *before* the street name denotes the district. This system has been used throughout this book. If you know the postcode of somewhere you can always work out approximately where it is, as the middle two digits of the four-number code correspond to the district, eg a postcode of 1010 means the place is in district one, and 1230 refers to district 23. Generally speaking, the higher the district number the further it is from the centre. Another thing to note is that the same street number may cover several adjoining premises, so if you find that what is supposed to be a pizza restaurant at Wienstrasse 4 is really a rubber fetish shop, check a few doors either side before you resign yourself to a radical change of diet.

MAPS

For most purposes, the free map of Vienna provided by the tourist office will be sufficient. It shows bus, tram and U-Bahn routes and major city-wide sights on a general map and a central blow-up. (Some of its key items aren't explained – for that you'll have to buy *Vienna From A to Z*; see the introduction to the Things to See & Do chapter). For a street index, you'll need to buy a map. The most authoritative series of maps on Vienna and Austria are produced by Freytag & Berndt. It has maps to different scales; at 1:20,000 you can get either a fold-up map or a more extensive, book-style *Städteatlas*.

TOURIST OFFICES
Local Tourist Offices

The main tourist office (Map 8; ☎ 513 88 92, 513 40 15) is at 01, Kärntner Strasse 38. It is small and hectic but there is extensive free literature on hand. The city map is excellent, as is the *Young Vienna Scene* booklet, which contains lots of useful information despite the chummy style. The bi-annual *Vienna Scene* addresses all ages. There are also free

lists of museums, events, hotels and restaurants. The office is open daily from 9 am to 7 pm, and also offers a room-finding service that is subject to a AS40 commission per reservation.

Advance requests for brochures, telephone inquiries and anything out of the ordinary are better dealt with at the head office of the Vienna Tourist Board (Map 5; ☎ 211 14; fax 216 84 92) at Obere Augartenstrasse 40, A-1025, Wien. However, the office is not very conveniently situated and doesn't really expect tourists to show up on its doorstep. Opening hours are Monday to Friday from 8 am to 4 pm.

The Niederösterreich Touristik-Information (Map 8; ☎ 513 80 22; fax -30; email noe.tourist-info@ping.at), 01, Walfischgasse 6, is a section of a travel agent, giving information on Lower Austria. This province includes the Wachau (the wine-growing area between Krems and Melk) and the Wienerwald (Vienna Woods). However, for detailed information you'll need to contact the region's local tourist offices. It's open Monday to Friday from 8 am to 6 pm.

The Österreich Werbung, or Austria Information Office (Map 7; ☎ 588 66; fax -20; email oeinfo@oewien.via.at), 04, Margaretenstrasse 1, is open Monday to Friday from 10 am to 5 pm (6 pm on Thursday), and has information on the whole country.

Information and room reservations (AS40 commission) are also available in various offices specially situated at entry points to the city:

Airport – Arrivals hall, open daily from 8.30 am to 9 pm
Train stations – Westbahnhof (Map 4), open daily from 7 am to 10 pm, and Südbahnhof (Map 7), open daily from 6.30 am to 10 pm (9 pm from 1 November to 30 April)
From the west by road – A1 autobahn exit Wien-Auhof (Map 2), open daily from 8 am to 10 pm (Easter to October), from 9 am to 7 pm (November) and from 10 am to 6 pm (December to pre-Easter)
From the south by road – A2 exit Zentrum (Map 2), Triester Strasse, open daily from 9 am to 7 pm (Easter to June, and October) and 8 am to 10 pm (July to September)

Top Left: Metal sculptures, Volksprater
Top Right: Street musicians
Bottom Left: Vienna Boys' Choir
Bottom Right: Touts dress in period costume to sell tickets to classical concerts

MARK HONAN

MARK HONAN

GLENN BEANLAND

JON DAVISON

Top Left: Interior of the Kunsthistorisches Museum
Top Right: St Michael's Gate, Hofburg
Middle Right: Detail of a door to the Kunsthistorisches Museum
Bottom: Sunset on the Alte Burg, Hofburg

From the north by road – At the Floridsdorfer Brücke (Map 5; bridge) on Danube Island (Donauinsel), open from 9 am to 7 pm (May to September)

Tourist Offices Abroad

The Austrian National Tourist Office (ANTO) has branches in about 20 countries. Elsewhere, its functions may be taken care of by the Austrian Trade Commission, or the commercial counsellor at the Austrian Embassy. Make contact by telephone or letter in the first instance – some offices are not geared to receive personal callers. ANTO offices abroad all have email, they include:

Australia
  (☎ 02-9299 3621; fax 9299 3808; email oewsysd@world.net) 1st floor, 36 Carrington St, Sydney, NSW 2000
Canada
  (☎ 416-967 3381; fax 967 4101) 2 Bloor St East, Suite 3330, Toronto, Ont M4W 1A8
Czech Republic
  Österreich Werbung (☎ 2-26 85 18; fax 26 67 16; email oewprag@traveller.cz), Krakovská 7, CR-12543 Prague 1
Germany
  Österreich Information (☎ 089-66 67 10; fax 66 67 12 01; email oewmuc@mail.isar.net), Postfach 1231, D 82019, Taufkirchen, Munich
Hungary
  Osztrák Nemzeti Idegenforgalmi Képviselet (☎ 1-351 11 91; fax 351 11 95; email oewbud@hungary.net), Rippl Rónai utca 4, H 1068, Budapest
Italy
  Austria Turismo (☎ 02-467 51 91; fax 43 99 01 76; email oewmil@oewmil.inet.it), Casella Postale No 1255, I 20121, Milan; also in Rome
South Africa
  (☎ 11-442 7235; fax 788 2367) Cradock Heights, 2nd floor, 21 Cradock Ave, Rosebank, 2196 Johannesburg
Switzerland
  Österreich Werbung (☎ 01-451 15 51; fax 451 11 80; email oewzrh@access.ch), Zweierstrasse 146, Postfach, CH 8036, Zürich
UK
  (☎ 0171-629 0461; fax 499 6038; oewlon@easynet.co.uk) PO Box 2363, London W1A 2QB
USA
  (☎ 212-944 6880; fax 730 4568; email antonyc@ix.netcom.com) PO Box 1142, New York, NY 10108-1142
  (☎ 310-477 3332; fax 477 5141) PO Box 491938, Los Angeles, CA 90049

There are also tourist offices in Amsterdam, Brussels, Paris, Madrid, Copenhagen, Stockholm and Tokyo. New Zealanders can get information from the Austrian consulate in Wellington (see the Austrian Embassies section).

Other Information Offices

The city information office in the Rathaus (Map 8; City Hall) is open Monday to Friday from 8 am to 6 pm. Somebody will also answer phone inquiries (☎ 525 50) on Saturday and Sunday from 8 am to 4 pm, as well as during office hours. It provides information on social, cultural and practical matters, geared as much to residents as to tourists.

Jugend Info (Map 8; Youth Info; ☎ 17 79; email jugendinfo.vie@blackbox.ping.at), 01, Dr Karl Renner Ring, in the below-ground Bellaria Passage, sells tickets for a variety of events at reduced rates for those aged between 14 and 26. There's plenty of information on rock concerts and other events around town and it's open from Monday to Saturday from noon to 7 pm.

DOCUMENTS
Visas

Visas are not required for EU, Scandinavian, US, Canadian, Australian or New Zealand citizens. Most visitors may stay a maximum of three months (six months for Japanese). If you need to stay longer you should simply leave the country and re-enter. British and other EU nationals, plus the Swiss, may stay as long as they like, though if they are taking up residency they should register with the local police within five days of arrival. Any other nationals seeking residency should apply in advance in their home country.

South African and some Arab and Third World nationals (eg Kenyans, Nigerians, Egyptians, Saudi Arabians) require a visa. The visa will have a validity of up to three months; the procedure varies depending upon the nationality – some nationals may be required to show a return ticket. Visa extensions are not possible: you will need to leave and reapply.

There are no border controls between EU

nations signed up to the Schengen Agreement, namely Austria, Belgium, France, Germany, Italy, Luxembourg, the Netherlands and Spain. Once you've entered one of these countries, you don't need a passport to move between them. Similarly, a visa valid for any of them ought to be valid for them all, but double check with the relevant embassy.

Photocopies

It's a good idea to photocopy all important document details, leaving one copy with someone at home and keeping the other with you, separate from the originals.

Other Documents & Cards

Don't forget to arrange travel insurance before you leave home – good-value annual policies are available nowadays. An International Student Identity Card (ISIC) can get the holder decent discounts on admission prices, but in Austria these discounts usually only apply to those under 25 or 27. Hostelling International (HI) membership is required to stay in youth hostels; it would be cheaper to join in your home country, rather than paying for the guest stamp in Austria. See the Getting There & Away chapter for useful travel passes and documentation required for car drivers.

EMBASSIES
Austrian Embassies Abroad

Austrian embassies abroad include:

Australia
(☎ 02-6295 1533; fax 6239 6751) 12 Talbot St, Forrest, ACT 2603
Canada
(☎ 613-789 1444) 445 Wilbrod St, Ottawa, Ont K1N 6M7
Ireland
(☎ 01-269 4577; fax 283 0860) 15 Ailesbury Court Apartments, 93 Ailesbury Rd, Dublin 4
New Zealand
Austrian Consulate (☎ 04-801 9709; fax 385 4642), 22-4 Garrett St, Wellington – does not issue visas or passports; contact the Australian office for these services

UK
(☎ 0171-235 3731; fax 235 8025) 18 Belgrave Mews West, London SW1 8HU
USA
(☎ 202-895 6700; fax 895 6750) 3524 International Court NW, Washington, DC 20008

Foreign Embassies in Vienna

For a complete listing, look in the telephone book under *Botschaften* (embassies) or *Konsulate* (consulates). Of the embassies mentioned below, consulate details are the same unless indicated. Double-check visa requirements if you plan to make excursions to neighbouring Hungary, the Czech Republic or Slovakia: Australians and New Zealanders require a visa for each country (British and Americans don't) and should be able to acquire one in Vienna the same day.

Australia
(Map 8; ☎ 512 85 80) 04, Mattiellistrasse 2-4
Canada
(Map 8; ☎ 531 38-3000) 01, Laurenzerberg 2
Czech Republic
(☎ 894 31 11) 14, Penzingerstrasse 11-13
France
Embassy: (☎ 505 47 47-0) 04, Technikerstrasse 2
Consulate: (☎ 535 62 09) 01, Wipplinger Strasse 24-26
Germany
(☎ 711 54-0) 03, Metternichgasse 3
Hungary
(Map 8; ☎ 533 26 31) 01, Bankgasse 4-6
Ireland
(☎ 715 42 46-0) 03, Landstrasser Hauptstrasse 2, Hilton Center
Italy
Embassy: (☎ 712 51 21-0) 03, Rennweg 27
Consulate: (☎ 713 56 71) 03, Ungarngasse 43
Japan
(☎ 501 71-0) Büro, 04, Argentinierstrasse 21
New Zealand
The New Zealand Embassy (☎ 0228-22 80 70) in Bonn, Germany, has responsibility for Austria; in Vienna there's only an honorary consul (☎ 318 85 05)
Slovakia
(☎ 318 90 55) 19, Armbrustergasse 24
Slovenia
(☎ 586 13 04-0) 01, Nibelungengasse 13
South Africa
(☎ 320 64 93) 19, Sandgasse 33
Switzerland
(☎ 795 05-0) 03, Prinz Eugen Strasse 7

UK
  Embassy: (Map 7; ☎ 716 13-0) 03, Jaurèsgasse 12
  Consulate: (☎ 714 61 17) 03, Jaurèsgasse 10
USA
  Embassy: (Map 4; ☎ 313 39) 09, Boltzmann-gasse 16
  Consulate: (Map 8; ☎ 313 39) 01, Gartenbau-promenade 2

CUSTOMS

For duty-free purchases, anybody aged 17 or over may bring into Austria 200 cigarettes or 50 cigars or 250 grams of tobacco, plus 2L of wine and 1L of spirits. Note that duty-free shopping within the EU is planned to be abolished in July 1999. If you buy duty-paid alcohol and tobacco in high street shops in other EU countries there is theoretically no restriction, but to ensure these goods remain for personal use, guideline limits are 800 cigarettes (or 200 cigars, 1kg tobacco), 10L of spirits, 90L of wine and 110L of beer. No duty is payable on items brought in for personal or professional use, nor on gifts or souvenirs up to a value of AS1000.

MONEY
Currency

The Austrian Schilling (AS, or *ÖS* in German) is divided into 100 Groschen. Banknotes come in denominations of AS20, AS50, AS100, AS500, AS1000 and AS5000. There are coins to the value of 500, 100, 50, 25, 10, five and one Schillings, and for 50, 10, five and two Groschen. There is no limit on the value of Schillings that can be imported or exported.

Austria, subject to meeting entry criteria, will be part of the EU single currency on 1 January 1999, at which point the exchange rate of the Schilling will be irrevocably fixed for non-cash transactions such as cheques, credit cards and electronic transfers. By 1 January 2002, Euro notes and coins will be circulated and bank accounts will be converted to Euros. The Schilling will cease to be legal tender on 1 July 2002.

Travellers Cheques & ATMs

American Express and Thomas Cook are the best known Travellers cheques. An alter-

Who's on the Money?

The people chosen to be honoured on banknotes are sometimes quite revealing about a society. Yet something that is so familiar is often barely looked at; many Austrians couldn't tell which famous people appear on the currency.

Occupying a modest place on the AS20 note is Moritz Michael Daffinger (1790-1849), a Biedermeier artist and designer in the applied arts field; his image is backed with the Albertina graphic arts collection, which houses some of his work. Sigmund Freud (1856-1939), psychoanalyst supreme, stares pensively out from the AS50 note; on the reverse is the Josephinium, the Museum of Medical History. The AS100 note is the domain of the statesman and academic Eugen Böhm-Bawerk (1851-1914), who was president of the Academy of Sciences from 1911 to 1914, which appears on the back. Occupying pride of place on the AS5000 note (rather ironically, for a man who died a pauper) is Wolfgang Amadeus Mozart (1756-91); on the reverse is the State Opera Building, which stages many Mozart operas.

Until recently, the Art Nouveau architect Otto Wagner (1841-1918) appeared on the AS500 note, and Nobel Prize-winning physicist Erwin Schrödinger (1887-1961) resided on the AS1000 note. Both these were replaced in 1997 by a AS500 note bearing Rosa Mayreder, artist and women's rights activist, and a AS100 note portraying Karl Landsteiner, Nobel Prize-winner in Medicine.

Commentators had questioned the need to issue new notes just a few years before the Schilling was due to be scrapped in favour of the Euro, but at least the new issue means there's a female figure to be found in the nation's pockets. ■

native (or additional) way to manage your money is to rely on getting cash advances with a Visa card, EuroCard or MasterCard; ATM Bankomat machines for this are numerous, including at all the main train stations, the airport and 200 branches of Bank Austria. They are accessible 24 hours a day. You can usually take up to AS2500 (AS5000 for a EuroCard) at each transaction, and there's no commission to pay at the Austrian end. If you feed enough money into your credit card account at the beginning of your trip, you can avoid most of the charges made by the credit card company for such advances.

Credit Cards
Visa, EuroCard (Access, MasterCard) are accepted a little more widely than American Express and Diners Club, although a surprising number of shops and restaurants refuse to accept any credit cards at all. Plush shops and restaurants will accept cards, though, and the same applies for hotels. Train tickets can be bought by credit card in main stations.

International Transfers
To get money sent to Austria, a direct transfer of funds through a bank is quick and (hopefully) easy, but an international money order is cheaper. There's no charge at the Austrian end to receive an American Express Moneygram.

Currency Exchange
The following are approximate exchange rates to purchase Austrian Schillings when this book went to press:

Australia	A$1	=	AS8.80
Canada	C$1	=	AS8.79
Czech Republic	1K	=	AS0.35
Germany	DM1	=	AS7.04
Hungary	Ft1	=	AS0.06
Japan	¥1	=	AS0.101
New Zealand	NZ$1	=	AS7.70
Switzerland	Sfr1	=	AS8.72
UK	UK£1	=	AS21.05
USA	US$1	=	AS12.85

Changing Money
Exchange rates can vary a little between banks. It pays to shop around, not only for exchange rates but also for commission charges. Changing cash attracts a negligible commission but the exchange rate is usually between 1 and 4% lower than for cheques.

The American Express office (Map 8; ☎ 515 40; fax -777), 01, Kärntner Strasse 21-23, is open Monday to Friday from 9 am to 5.30 pm, and Saturday from 9.30 am to noon. It has a travel section and financial services, and will hold mail (not parcels) free of charge for up to four weeks for customers who have American Express cheques or cards. For cashing its own cheques there is

no commission to pay. For cashing the cheques of other institutions, commission is AS25 to AS40. The commission for cash is AS10 or more. Although the exchange rates aren't great, American Express usually works out the best place to change travellers cheques.

For changing cash, go to the post office as no commission is charged; its commission for Travellers cheques is AS60. Train stations charge a AS64 minimum for cheques, and about AS20 for cash. Bank Austria charges from AS95 for cheques and AS30 for cash. Avoid buying and changing a lot of low-value cheques as many places charge commission per cheque. Look especially carefully at the commission rates offered by exchange booths *(Wechselstuben)* – we've seen rates of 5% plus AS15 per cheque! Moneychangers at the airport charge at least AS110 commission though the exchange rates are standard.

Banks are open Monday to Friday from 8 or 9 am to 3 pm, with late opening on Thursday until 5.30 pm; smaller branches close from 12.30 to 1.30 pm. Train stations have extended hours for exchange at ticket counters or at exchange offices. Exchange offices are open daily from 7 am to 10 pm in Westbahnhof, and from 6.30 am to 10 pm (9 pm from 1 November to 31 March) in Südbahnhof. Branch post offices can exchange money up to 5 pm on weekdays, and on Saturday morning. Some post offices have longer hours for exchange.

Costs
Vienna is averagely expensive for a western capital. A survey by the Union Bank of Switzerland in 1997 placed Vienna as the 19th most expensive city in the world, excluding rent (London was 9th, New York was 14th, Sydney was 20th).

Budget travellers can get by on about AS450 per day if they camp or stay in hostels, stick to student cafés, cheap lunch specials or self-catering, and only have the occasional drink. Staying in a cheap pension and dispensing with self-catering will require about AS800 a day – add AS150 to be sure of a room with private shower/WC. To stay in a mid-price hotel, have a moderate lunch, a decent dinner, some money to spend on evening entertainment and not be too concerned about how expensive a cup of coffee is, a daily allowance of about AS1500 would be needed. These estimates don't include extras like souvenirs, postage or tours, and only allow a moderate sum for sightseeing admission prices, so you could end up spending significantly more per day than this.

Tipping & Bargaining

Hotel and restaurant bills include a service charge, but hotel porters and cleaning staff usually expect something for their services. It is also customary to tip in restaurants and cafés unless you're dissatisfied with something. Round up small bills and add an extra 5 to 10% to larger ones: except in plush places, simply say the total amount you want the server to take when you hand over the money. Taxi fares do not include an element for tips and the driver will expect around 10% extra. Tour guides, cloakroom attendants and hairdressers are also usually tipped.

Bargain hard in flea markets. Otherwise, prices are fixed, but it can't hurt to ask for 'a discount for cash' if you're making several purchases. In theory, hotel prices are not negotiable; in practice, you can often haggle for a better rate in the low season or if you're staying more than a few days.

Discounts are possible for students and seniors: see Documents and Senior Citizens in this chapter. The Vienna Card (see the Things to See & Do chapter) also gives useful discounts.

Taxes & Refunds

Value-added tax (*Mehrwertsteuer* or MWST) is set at 20% for most goods. Prices are always displayed inclusive of all taxes, even (usually) service charges in hotels and restaurants.

All non-EU tourists are entitled to a refund of the MWST on purchases over AS1000. To claim the tax, a U34 form or tax-free cheque and envelope must be completed by the shop at the time of purchase (show your passport), and then get it stamped by border officials when you leave the EU. (If you're leaving Austria for another EU country, you can't get this customs stamp in Austria, you have to get it from customs staff where you finally quit the EU.) Vienna airport has a counter for payment of instant refunds, as do those at Salzburg, Innsbruck, Linz and Graz. Counters are also at Westbahnhof and Südbahnhof, and at major border crossings. The refund is best claimed upon departing the EU, as otherwise you'll have to track down an international refund office or claim by post.

Before making a purchase, ensure the shop has the required paperwork; some places display a 'Tax Free for Tourists' sticker. Also confirm the value of the refund; it's usually advertised as 13%, which is the refund of the 20% standard rate of VAT after various commissions have been taken. But some items are subject to a lower rate of VAT: for paintings and sculpture it's only 10%.

DOING BUSINESS

Vienna is a major conference location, hosting 268 international conferences in 1996. Not surprisingly, the city can provide plenty of facilities and services for the business visitor. To start a business in Austria, there are a lot of bureaucratic hoops to leap through, and you would need to be a citizen of the EU or the USA. The first useful port of call would probably be the trade office at the Austrian embassy in your home country.

Business Locales

Donaupark in the 22nd district has the Vienna International Center (UNO City), where international organisations are based, including the UN (the third most important base after New York and Geneva) and the International Atomic Energy Agency (rather ironic, considering that Austrians rejected nuclear power in a 1978 referendum). The park also has the Austria Center Vienna (Map 5; ☎ 23 69; fax -303), Austria's largest convention hall, with 14 conference rooms and 170 offices and meeting rooms. UNO City has extraterritorial status – it is leased to the UN for a rent of AS1 per annum. Take your passport when visiting. (Guided tours of the Austria Center are conducted regularly.)

The Hofburg (☎ 587 36 66; fax 535 64 26), in the Innere Stadt, also hosts conferences, banquets and exhibitions. Over a third of international conferences are held in Vienna's hotels. The Vienna Tourist Board head office (see the Tourist Offices section) has congress information. Smaller trade fairs may be held in UNO City, though the main centre for trade fairs is the Messegelände in the Prater.

Business Park Wien Süd is being built near the Shopping City Süd, by the A21 motorway. When it's finished in 1999 it'll be the biggest business park in Austria, and will include offices plus production, manufacturing and storage buildings.

Business Services

The following organisations could help you set up and run a business in Vienna. For public Internet facilities, see Internet Access & Email in this chapter.

Wirtschaftskammer Österreich (☎ 501 05), 04, Hauptstrasse 63 – Austrian Chamber of Commerce

Wiener Wirtschaftsförderungsfonds (WWFF; ☎ 4000-867 90; fax -7073; email vienna@wwff .gv.at), 08, Ebensdorferstrasse 2 – Vienna Business Promotion Fund, a non-profit organisation selling Vienna as a business location to potential investors

Dun & Bradstreet Information Services (☎ 588 61-0; fax 586 33 59), 01, Opernring 3-5 – marketing information and credit reports

Regus Business Centre (☎ /fax 599 24-0), 06, Mariahilfer Strasse 123 – office rental from a few hours upwards; secretarial services, telephone service, catering and conference facilities

Berlitz Sprachschule (☎ 512 82 86; fax -4), 01, Graben 13 – translation and interpreting services

GRT-Price Waterhouse (☎ 501 88-0; fax -4), 04, Prinz Eugene Strasse 72 – public accountants and tax advisers

Kreditschutzverband von 1870 (KSV; ☎ 534 84), 01, Zelinkagasse 10 – Austrian association for the protection of creditors; legal advice, business information data bases

POST & COMMUNICATIONS
Post

The main post office (Map 8) is at 01, Fleischmarkt 19. It's open 24 hours a day for collecting and sending mail, changing money and using the telephone. Only a few services (like paying bills) are not round the clock. There are also post offices open daily at Südbahnhof and Franz Josefs Bahnhof (both 24 hour), and at Westbahnhof (closes from 1 to 4 am). Post offices usually have photocopiers but they're expensive (AS3 a sheet) – instead, try the universities, or the Rank Xerox shop at the southern end of Kärntner Strasse (AS1.20 a sheet self-service).

Branch post offices are open Monday to Friday from 8 am to noon and 2 to 6 pm, and Saturday from 8 to 10 am (noon for district head offices). They generally have a counter for changing money, but this closes at 5 pm on weekdays.

Sending Mail Postcards and letters within Austria cost AS6.50 and AS7 respectively. Letters (up to 20g) cost AS6.50/7 non-priority/priority to Europe and AS7.50/13 elsewhere. Stamps are available in tobacconist *(Tabak)* shops as well as post offices. The normal weight limit for letter post *(Briefsendung)* is 2kg, which would cost AS125/260 to Europe and AS135/450 to elsewhere. Printed matter (books, brochures, etc) can be sent at a reduced rate, and up to a 5kg limit. Airmail takes about four days to the UK, seven days to the USA and about 10 days to Australasia. By surface mail *(Erdwegpakete)* you can send packages up to 20kg.

Receiving Mail Poste restante is *Postlagernde Briefe* in German. Mail can be sent care of any post office and is held for a month; a passport must be shown to collect. Ask people who are sending you letters to write your surname in capitals and underline it. The full address for the main post office is: Hauptpostlagernde, Fleischmarkt 19, A 1010, Vienna. American Express (see Money earlier in this chapter) will also hold mail for four weeks for customers who have its card or cheques.

Note that like other Continentals, the Viennese 'cross' the number seven with a horizontal line and begin the number one with a rising diagonal stroke connecting to the top of the vertical downstroke, which looks rather like a lopsided, uncrossed seven. The net result of this is that unless you (or whoever writes to you) gets into the habit of crossing sevens when addressing envelopes, letters to No 77 will probably be delivered to confused residents of No 11, and eventually returned to sender or despatched with due diligence to the recycling bin.

Telephone

The telephone code for Vienna is 0222 for calls made inside Austria. If you're ringing from outside the country you must dial 1 instead.

Telephone calls within Austria are 33% cheaper on weekends and between 6 pm and 8 am on weekdays – phones are still expensive though, despite only needing AS1 to get connected. On long-distance calls, inserting at least AS9 is recommended; Schillings tick away at the local rate while you're waiting for the dialled party to pick up the receiver, and once you get through, each Schilling only lasts about 10 seconds.

Post offices invariably have telephones. Be wary of using telephones in hotels, as they are more expensive (perhaps twice the price of the normal AS1 per unit – AS3.50 per unit in five-star hotels). You can save money and avoid messing around with change by buying a phone card (Telefon-Wertkarte). For AS48 you get AS50 worth of calls, and for AS95 and AS190 you get AS100 and AS200 worth of calls respectively.

In Vienna telephone numbers don't always have the same number of digits: the reason for this is that some telephones numbers have an individual line, others a party line, and sometimes numbers are listed with an extension that you can dial direct (without a pause after the main number). This is relevant for reading phone

Telephone Number Warning
The Viennese telephone system is being upgraded. Most numbers have now been changed, though there are a few numbers (eg in the 19th district) awaiting the extra digit. If the number has recently been replaced, you will get a recorded message telling you to dial ☎ 1619, ☎ 1611, or to check the phone book. ■

numbers listed in the telephone book: if, for example, you see the number '123 45 67-0', the '0' signifies the number has extensions. Whether you dial the '0' at the end or not, you will (with a few exceptions) get through to that subscriber's main telephone reception. If you know a specific extension of somebody you want to speak to, dial that instead of the '0' and you'll get straight through to that person.

Fax numbers are often a telephone extension of the main number, and it's fairly common to see them listed only by their extension, perhaps following the letters 'DW' (the German abbreviation indicating 'extension'). In this book, any telephone extensions are separated from the main number by a hyphen, and fax extensions are shown only by a hyphen and the extension number (ie you'd have to dial the main number first to reach it).

If you get the rising three-bleep anthem it means you've dialled an invalid number. Check the phone book or call ☎ 1611 for directory assistance. Patience is called for as it's nearly always engaged (indicated by fast beeps). If you get the recorded message, hang on as you're now in the queue and will speak to a human being eventually. If the frustration of constant failure gives you sleepless nights, try calling in the early hours when you'll have more success.

International Calls For the directory of international telephone numbers, dial ☎ 1612 for Germany, ☎ 1613 for the rest of Europe, and ☎ 1614 for outside Europe. To direct-dial abroad, first call the overseas access code (00), then the appropriate country code, then the relevant area code (minus the initial '0' if there is one), and finally the subscriber number. For calling to Austria from abroad, the country code is 43.

Per minute at normal/cheap rate, telephone calls from Austria cost about AS10/7.50 to the UK, AS15/10 to the USA, and AS22/17 to Australia, New Zealand or South Africa. If direct-dialling is not possible, call ☎ 09 for the international operator; as with the information lines, you may have to wait a while to be connected.

To reverse the charge (ie call collect), you also need to dial ☎ 09; this is only possible to some countries (eg USA, Canada and Ireland). To other countries you have to dial an international access number and still pay AS1 per minute, even though it's a reverse-charge call. You may prefer to do this anyway, as the operator will speak the language of that country. Some of the numbers are:

Australia:	☎ 022 903 061
Canada:	☎ 022 903 013
New Zealand:	☎ 022 903 064
UK:	
BT	☎ 022 903 044
Mercury	☎ 022 903 441
USA:	
AT&T	☎ 022 903 011
Sprint:	☎ 022 903 014

Fax & Telegraph

Luxury hotels will offer fax services but it would be cheaper to go to the post office. To send a fax from the post office costs AS12 for 10 pages plus the cost of the telephone time; receiving faxes costs just the AS12. Some hotels *may* let you receive the odd fax free of charge.

Telegrams can also be sent from the main post offices but they're very expensive, eg to Europe it's AS7.30 per word plus AS50, and even each word of the address is charged!

Nobody sends telexes nowadays; the only place it can be done is at the Telegraphen-zentralstation (☎ 534 160) at 01, Börseplatz, but even then you would need an Austrian telephone account.

Email & Internet Access

With the exception of the Italians, Austrians are the least clued-in western Europeans regarding the Internet. Nevertheless, Vienna has about a dozen institutions offering public access to online services, and many institutions and some hotels now have email addresses. Café Stein (Map 4; ☎ 319 72 411), 09, Währinger Strasse 6, was the first of Vienna's cafés to get on line. The Virgin Megastore (Map 8; ☎ 581 05 00), 06, Mariahilfer Strasse 37-39, charges AS50 for 30 minutes surfing the web, which is fairly typical. Pick up the */@bsurfen ins Internet/* leaflet from Jugend Info (see Other Information Offices earlier in this chapter) for all addresses. The Public Netbase (☎ 522 18 34; email office@t0.or.at) in the Museumsquartier, 07, Museumsplatz 1, has a couple of machines where you can surf for free; it's open weekdays from 2 to 7 pm.

Receiving email is not always possible at Internet access sites. But you can do this at the Nationalbibliothek in the Hofburg (email tief@grill.onb.ac.at) – see Libraries later in this chapter.

INTERNET RESOURCES

For the latest travel information, visit Lonely Planet's web site. The site (www.lonelyplanet.com) contains updates, recent Travellers letters and a Travellers bulletin board.

Many Austrian businesses now have a web page on the net, including the Vienna Tourist Board (www.info.wien.at) as well as ANTO (//austria-tourism.at/). For tips aimed at the English-speaking community in Vienna there's www.austriaguide.com/info, which includes links to various online publications (such as Austria Today's site www.austria-today.com).

For travel information, look for Austrian Railways (www.bahn.at) and Lauda Air (www.laudaair.com), among others. Searching the net under 'Austria' or 'Vienna' will yield lots of other interesting information.

BOOKS

A great deal has been written about Vienna. See the Shopping chapter for information on bookshops in the city; these will have a good selection (especially the British Bookshop) though imported titles will cost more in Schillings than the cover price would imply.

Non-Fiction

Steven Beller's *Vienna and the Jews* (Cambridge University Press) is concerned specifically with the years from 1867 to 1938. The same publisher offers *Austria, Empire and Republic* by Barbara Jelavich. *A History of the Habsburg Empire 1526-1918* (University of California Press) is a large tome by Robert A Kann. Two books you can find in Vienna are *A Brief Survey of Austrian History* and *Music and Musicians in Vienna*, both by Richard Rickett and published by Prachner in hardback.

A number of other books deal with Vienna from the slant of its musical heritage. *Mozart and the Enlightenment* (Faber & Faber paperback), by Nicholas Till, is a scholarly work placing Mozart in his historical context, with detailed analysis of his operatic works. *Mozart and Vienna*, by H C Robbins Landon, focuses on the Vienna years, and successfully evokes the city of the time by quoting extensively from a contemporary work, *Sketch of Vienna* by Johann Pezzl. *Mozart – his Character, his Work* (Oxford University Press, 1945, paperback), by Alfred Einstein, is self-explanatory from the title, as is *Gustav Mahler – Memories and Letters* (Sphere paperback) by Alma Malher. *Freud's Women* (Virago), by Lisa Appignanesi & John Forrester, is a large volume that offers an insight into the psychoanalyst. There's also *The Life and Work of Sigmund Freud* (Penguin) by Ernest Jones.

Fiction

The Third Man (Penguin paperback) is Graham Greene's famous Viennese spy story. John Irving's *Setting Free the Bears* (Black Swan paperback) is a fine tale about a plan to release the animals from the zoo at Schönbrunn. The zoo plot takes place in 1967, yet the book is also very evocative of life in Austria and Vienna before, during and after WWII. Vienna zoo also puts in an appearance in *Invisible Architecture* (Picador paperback), a collection of three stories by Steven Kelly. The architecture in question is more to do with the make-up of the Viennese soul than the buildings in the city.

Mozart & the Wolf Gang, by Anthony Burgess, is a learned but still enjoyable celestial fantasy in which the great composers discourse on music and Mozart. *The Strange Case of Mademoiselle P*, by Brian O'Doherty, is a tale about an attempted medical cure in Maria Theresa's Vienna. It's based on a real incident and provides an insight into the petty power struggles in the imperial court, though it does rather peter out at the end.

See Literature in the Facts about Vienna chapter for fiction by Austrian authors.

Guidebooks

There are dozens of guides to Vienna available internationally.

Check Vienna's bookshops, particularly the British Bookshop, for locally produced guides in English. Lonely Planet publishes *Austria*, which covers places mentioned under the Excursions chapter in more detail, and a German phrasebook. The tongue-in-cheek *Xenophobe's guide to the Austrians* contains some amusing and revealing insights into Austrian people and society.

Falter's Best of Vienna (AS45) is a locally available seasonal magazine giving over 250 current and useful recommendations for eating, drinking, shopping and entertainment. Some categories are typically quirky and playful; past highlights include best wall to lean against, best worker's Beisl with a parrot, best U-Bahn clock, and best wild boar farm in the city. The same publisher releases an annual guide solely dedicated to eating, *Wien, wie es isst* (AS165, 480 pages). Both of these are in German only, which is a pity for monolinguists, as Falter is known for its witty wordplay.

CD ROM

CD ROMs of interest include an alternative guide to Vienna (in English and German, AS480; ☎ 212 50 31; email g.handler@

magnet.at) and an extensive guide to Schloss Belvedere (AS498).

A complete listing of Austrian telephone numbers and at least two Austrian route planners are also available on CD ROM – inquire in the CD ROM outlets mentioned in the shopping chapter.

NEWSPAPERS & MAGAZINES

English-language newspapers are widely available in Vienna, usually on the same day they're published. Prices are between AS20 and AS35. The first to hit the stands are the *Financial Times* and the *International Herald Tribune*. *USA Today*, *Time*, *Newsweek* and most British newspapers are easy to find. The Buch und Presse shop in Westbahnhof (with smaller branches in Südbahnhof and Franz Josefs Bahnhof) stocks many newspapers and magazines from around the world; it's open daily from 6 am to 11 pm (10 pm on Sunday and public holidays).

Of the several German-language daily newspapers available, the magazine-size *Neue Kronen Zeitung* (AS8) has the largest circulation; the tabloid-size *Die Presse* adopts a more serious approach. *Austria Today* is a monthly national newspaper in English (AS25), with several informative sections and a listing of cultural events. *Vienna Reporter*, another English-language monthly (AS25), includes features, reviews of Vienna's restaurants and pubs, and a summary of the month's news.

Austrian newspapers are often dispensed from bags attached to pavement posts, and rely on the honesty of readers to pay for the copies they take. Foreign-language titles are only available from newsstands or pavement sellers.

RADIO & TV

As yet Austria has no commercial TV stations, and commercial radio only started up in the last few years.

State-run national radio channels are Ö1 (87.8 and 92 FM), giving a cultural diet of music, literature and science; Ö2 (89.9 and 95.3 FM in Vienna, 96.06 FM in Lower Austria), broadcasting local and regional news and programmes; and Ö3 (99.9 FM), offering progressive entertainment and topical information. Blue Danube Radio (103.8 FM) is a news and music station, mostly in English but with some French programmes. News is broadcast at 30 minutes past the hour in German and English (sometimes also in French). At 1 pm it has a 'What's on in Vienna' segment.

The two state-run national TV channels are ÖRF1 and ÖRF2. But many homes (and hotels) have satellite or cable and can pick up a whole host of TV channels from Germany and elsewhere, plus MTV, Eurosport, CNN (the 24 hour news network) and NBC (an American general entertainment channel). Local newspapers and events magazines give a full listing of programmes.

PHOTOGRAPHY & VIDEO

Vienna provides numerous photo opportunities. Don't use a camera flash at the opera, theatre or similar event; it's very distracting for the performers, whether they be humans or stallions. Film is widely available and fairly reasonably priced, though developing costs are high. Note that slide film *(Diafilm)* usually excludes mounting and sometimes processing *(Entwicklung)* too.

The Niedermeyer chain store is one of the cheapest places to buy film: a 36-exposure roll costs AS50 for Kodak Gold 100 and AS149 for Kodachrome 64 (including processing, but not mounting). Niedermeyer also has its own make of film that is much cheaper. Some slide film has processing included, but this may entail returning it directly to the shop – check before buying. Photo processing (9cm by 13cm) costs AS35 plus AS2.90 per picture for the three-day service (express service is a shocking AS7.90 per print). Niedermeyer has over 50 branches in Vienna, including a huge one at 09, Alserstrasse 28-30 (☎ 406 06 02), two on Mariahilfer Strasse (Nos 51 and 102), one at 01, Graben 11, and another opposite Franz Josefs Bahnhof. All its stores sell cameras and other electronic gadgets.

Foto Opernhof Lang (Map 8; ☎ 587 26

49), 01, Opernring 3, has good prices for both film purchasing and developing. But the cheapest place we've found for film developing is the larger branches of Libro bookshops, where the per photo price is AS1.90.

Videos purchased in Austria will be recorded using the PAL image system (also used in Britain and Australia), which is incompatible with the NTSC system in use in North America and Japan.

TIME
Austrians use the 24 hour clock for anything written down, instead of dividing the day up into am and pm. Austrian time is GMT/UTC plus one hour. If it's noon in Vienna it is 6 am in New York and Toronto, 3 am in San Francisco, 9 pm in Sydney and 11 pm in Auckland. Clocks go forward one hour on the last Saturday night in March and back again on the last Saturday night in October.

Note that in German *halb* is used to indicate the half hour before the hour, hence *halb acht* means 7.30, not 8.30.

ELECTRICITY
The current used is 220 V, 50Hz AC. Sockets are the round two-pin type, which are standard throughout most of Continental Europe. North American appliances will need a transformer if they don't have built-in voltage adjustment.

LAUNDRY
Look out for *Wäscherei* for self-service *(Selbstbedienung)* or service washes. Many youth hostels have cheaper laundry facilities, and most good hotels have a laundry service, albeit expensive.

Schnell & Sauber Waschcenter (Map 4), 07, Urban Loritz Platz, Westbahnstrasse, is open daily 24 hours, and has instructions in English. It costs AS60 to wash a 6kg load, including powder, plus AS10 to spin, and from AS10 to dry. Another branch is at 09, Nussdorfer Strasse (Map 4; open daily till late).

Miele Selbstbedienung (☎ 405 02 55), 08, Josefstädter Strasse 59, is open Monday to Friday from 7 am to 7.30 pm, and Saturday from 7 am to noon. To wash a 6kg load costs AS80, plus AS25 for powder and AS25 to dry. Dry cleaning is available.

TOILETS
Toilets are found in restaurants, museums and galleries, and these are unattended and free to use. If toilets are attended a small charge is made (eg at train station toilets), or cubicles may be coin-operated (about AS5). There are many public toilets to be found, eg at Graben and Hoher Markt. *Damen* is for women and *Herren* is for men.

WEIGHTS & MEASURES
The metric system is used. Like other Continental Europeans, Austrians indicate decimals with commas and thousands with points. You will sometimes see meat and cheese priced per *dag*, which is an abbreviation referring to 10g (to ask for this quantity say 'deca').

HEALTH
No immunisations are required for entry to Austria, unless you're coming from an infected area. Vienna is a healthy place and if you're healthy when you arrive, there's no reason why you should experience any particular health problems. Even streetside snack stands have adequate sanitary standards. Tap water is perfectly drinkable (except in the rare instance when you'll come across a sign announcing *Kein Trinkwasser*).

Ticks might be a problem in forested areas in east Austria. A very small proportion of ticks carry encephalitis (a cerebral inflammation that can cause death), so if you plan to spend a lot of time in the woods get an encephalitis immunisation before you leave.

If you wear glasses, it's wise to carry a spare pair or a copy of your prescription.

Medical Services
There is a charge for hospital treatment and doctor consultations, so some form of medical insurance is advised (cover provided by normal travel insurance would be sufficient). Get medical treatment at the

general hospital, the Allgemeines Kranken-haus (Map 4; ☎ 404 00) at 09, Währinger Gürtel 18-20. Other hospitals with emergency departments include Lorenz Böhler Unfallkrankenhaus (☎ 331 100), 20, Donaueschingenstrasse 13; Hanusch-Krankenhaus (☎ 910 21), 14, Heinrich Collin Strasse 30; and Krankenhaus Lainz (☎ 801 100), 13, Wolkerbergenstrasse 1.

The University Dental Hospital, Universitäts-Zahnklinik (☎ 401 81), is at 09, Währinger Strasse 25A. For recorded information on out-of-hours dental treatment, call ☎ 512 20 78.

EU and EEA nationals can get free emergency medical treatment, though payment may have to be made for medication, private consultations and for non-urgent treatment. Inquire before leaving home about the documentation required. British people normally need to show an E111 form (available from post offices) to take advantage of reciprocal health agreements in Europe, so it's worth getting one if you're travelling through the Continent. However, in Austria you only need to show a British passport, though if you're staying a long time in Vienna it would facilitate matters if you get a certificate from the health insurance office, the Gebietskrankenkasse (☎ 601 220), 10, Wienerbergstrasse 15-19. This office can also tell you the countries that have reciprocal agreements with Austria (the USA, Canada, Australia and New Zealand don't).

Chemist shops or drugstores (Apotheken) are open normal shop hours, though they operate an out-of-hours service in rotation. Dial ☎ 1550 for recorded information in German.

WOMEN TRAVELLERS

In Vienna, women enjoy equal status and opportunity with men. Although men still predominate in influential and high-ranking posts, the situation is changing, helped by the mayor's campaign to address this inequality. Already there are 34 women in the 100-strong city council, and a (female) councillor has responsibility for women's issues. Women were recently also allowed to join the formerly all-male Vienna Philharmonic Orchestra.

Women travellers should experience no special problems. However, normal caution should be exercised in unfamiliar situations (which occur quite often when travelling). Attacks and verbal harassment are less common than in many countries, though a local reported that 'strange men' are prone to approach women who are relaxing alone on the grassy areas of the Danube Island. There is an emergency, 24 hour hotline for women to report rape and sexual violence; call the Frauenotruf ☎ 71 71 9. The Frauentelefon (☎ 408 70 66) is a non-urgent helpline for women to discuss work, family and social problems; it operates Monday and Wednesday from 8 am to noon, and Thursday from 1 to 5 pm.

GAY & LESBIAN TRAVELLERS

Probably the best organisation to contact is Rosa Lila Villa (Map 6; ☎ 586 81 50; fax 587 17 78; email rosalila.tip@blackbox.at), 06, Linke Wienzeile 102; big letters outside proclaim it's a 'Lesben & Schwulen Haus' (lesbian & gay house). There's telephone counselling, a small library with books in English, and advice and information on what's on offer in the city. Pick up the Gay City Map, identifying gay-friendly hotels, shops, bars, cafés and clubs. Opening hours are Monday to Friday from 5 to 8 pm. On the premises is Café Willendorf, open daily from 7 pm to 2 am (with good food till midnight). The Homosexualle Initiative Wien (HOSI), 02, Novaragasse 40, also has telephone counselling (☎ 216 66 04) on Thursday from 6 to 8 pm and Wednesday and Friday from 7 to 9 pm, and dancing for women only from 7 pm on Friday. It's open to visitors on Tuesday from 8 to 10 pm. The Frauenzentrum (☎ 408 50 57), 09, Währinger Strasse 59 (entry via Prechtlgasse), is a women's centre, dominated by lesbians.

DISABLED TRAVELLERS

There's no national organisation that provides help for the disabled in Austria, but the city of Vienna runs an advice centre for

---

Gay Vienna

Though not as liberal as somewhere like Amsterdam or Berlin, Vienna is reasonably tolerant towards gays and lesbians (more so than the rest of Austria), and the situation is improving all the time. Recently, two of the three federal statutes concerning homosexuality were repealed (these had banned gay meetings and the promoting of homosexuality). The third statute relates to the age of consent – between men this is 18, in contrast to 14 for heterosexuals. There is no set age for lesbian sex, apparently because the legislators got into a lather about the possibility that women might only be washing each other if there was intimate contact between them. While lesbians welcome the lack of legislation, they see this as a typical (male) denial of female sexuality.

Some places popular with gays and lesbians are: *Café Berg* (Map 4), 09, Berggasse 8, open daily from 10 am to 1 am (with a gay bookshop next door); *Café Savoy*, 06, Linke Wienzeile 36, open Monday to Friday from 5 pm to 2 am, and Saturday from 9 am to 6 pm and 9 pm to 2 am; *Why Not?* (Map 8), 01, Tiefer Graben 22, a bar/disco open Friday and Saturday from 11 pm to 5 am, plus Sunday for cabaret and drag queens; and the *Eagle Bar*, 06, Blümelgasse 1, a men's bar with a mostly leather-clad clientele.

Look out for the Regenbogenparade (Rainbow Parade) on the last Saturday in June. Over 20,000 gays and lesbians parade along the Ringstrasse, in an event that has only been fully established since 1996. ■

---

disabled people, the Behindertenberatungsstelle (☎ 531 14-85350), 01, Schottenring 24, open Monday to Friday from 7.30 am to 3.30 pm. The tourist office can also give advice and information. It has a booklet in German, *Wien für Gäste mit Handicaps*, which unfortunately is a little out of date. But it's reasonably easy to follow and gives information on hotels and restaurants with disabled access, plus addresses of hospitals, medical equipment shops, parking places, WCs and much more. The tourist office's Museums and Hotels brochure indicate disabled access; ramps are fairly common but by no means ubiquitous. All stations on the U3 and U6 lines have lifts or ramps, but only about half the others do.

Disabled people often get reduced, concessionary admission prices – look for the word *Behinderte*. Drivers displaying the international handicapped sticker can ignore time restrictions in short parking zones. The two state-run TV channels have a teletext service, and traffic lights 'bleep' when pedestrians are entitled to cross.

SENIOR TRAVELLERS

Senior citizens are often entitled to reduced admission prices; the qualifying age is usually 60 and above for women and 65 and above for men, though the 60 age limit is sometimes good for both sexes. Always carry proof of age. Travel benefits include cheaper flights, rail tickets and discount tickets on Vienna's public transport. Cheaper (and smaller) 'senior' meals are available in some restaurants, though this isn't very common.

The Senioren-Servicetelefon (☎ 4000-8580) can give information on reductions for seniors, plus travel, cultural and leisure-time tips; it's staffed weekdays from 8 am to 4 pm.

VIENNA FOR CHILDREN

It is sometimes said that the Viennese love dogs more than they love children, but children are still fairly well received. There are sometimes special events put on for children – inquire at the tourist office. Children's menus are available in some restaurants. Your hotel should be able to advise you on local babysitting services.

Vienna has museums devoted to teddy bears, dolls and toys, circuses and clowns – all of which children might enjoy; there's even a children's museum, the Kindermuseum ZOOM in the Museumsquartier. Also look out for the puppets in the Marionettentheater at Schönbrunn, and the Niedermair Kindertheater. Schönbrunn zoo has a section where children can stroke the animals. The Volksprater funfair is also ideal for children.

There are lots of enjoyable indoor and outdoor swimming pools in Vienna. City-owned pools offer free entry for children (up to age 15) during the summer school holidays, and perhaps during other school holidays; phone the Bäder information number (see Activities in the Things to See & Do chapter) for the latest information. Children also travel free on public transport during school holidays.

Teenagers can get good information at Jugend Info (see Other Information Offices earlier in this chapter).

LIBRARIES

You need to be a resident (and show the appropriate police stamp to this effect) to borrow books from Vienna's libraries, but anybody is welcome to peruse books on the premises.

The Nationalbibliothek has huge reference and lending sections plus CD ROM, papyrus and musical-scores collections. Upstairs is a room with newspapers such as the *Times* and the *International Herald Tribune*, and magazines and periodicals (many in English) covering all sorts of academic and recreational subjects. The main part of the library is open Monday to Friday from 9 am to 7 pm (to 3.45 pm from 1 July to 31 August) and Saturday to 5 pm.

Libraries are dotted around Vienna. The main branch is the Städtische Hauptbücherei (Map 4; ☎ 4000-84 551), 08, Skodagasse 20, open Monday and Thursday from 10 am to 7.30 pm and Tuesday and Friday from 2 to 7.30 pm. There's also a library on the 2nd floor (the periodicals rooms is on the 1st floor) in the main university building (Map 8) on the corner of Dr Karl Lueger Ring and Universitätsstrasse.

The British Council (☎ 533 26 16-81), 01, Schenkenstrasse 4, has a library, newspapers and magazines in English.

CULTURAL CENTRES

The Museumsquartier (☎ 523 58 81), 07, Museumsplatz 1, is the former imperial bar-

racks. It is being developed as a cultural centre and will have dozens of different organisations based here. Already you can find museums, theatres, exhibitions, galleries, cafés and discussion groups.

Amerika Haus (Map 8; ☎ 405 30 33), 01, Friedrich Schmidt Platz 2, is linked to the US embassy, and has many publications in English about or from the USA. It's geared towards people undertaking research, so you need to make an appointment to visit.

The traditional coffee houses (see the Places to Eat chapter) are the most enjoyable places to go for reading; most carry English-language newspapers.

DANGERS & ANNOYANCES

Emergency telephone numbers in Vienna include:

Ambulance:	☎ 144
Doctor:	☎ 141
Police:	☎ 133
Fire:	☎ 122

Overall, Vienna is a very safe city to visit. Crime rates are low by international standards, but you should still always be security-conscious. Use a moneybelt and make use of hotel safes for your valuables. In hostels, reception staff will usually look after valuables like camera or electronic equipment. If you do get something stolen, get a police report as it will be needed to claim on your travel insurance.

There are police stations all over the place: each district has a head office and branches. The head office for the Innere Stadt (☎ 313 470) is at 01, Deutschmeisterplatz 3, and the police are also in the Stephansplatz and Karlsplatz U-Bahn stations. For other districts, look in the phone book under *Polizei* and the subheading *Bezirkspolizeikommissariate u Wachzimmer*.

Train stations are a habitual haunt of drunks and dropouts who can be annoying and occasionally intimidating. Drug addicts sometimes congregate in the Karlsplatz U-Bahn station near the Secession exit.

LOST PROPERTY

For items lost on Vienna public transport, contact the Zentral Fundstelle (☎ 7909-43500) at U3 Station Erdberg, open daily from 6 am to 10 pm. After a few days, items here end up at the main lost property office, the Polizeifundamt (Map 4), 09, Wasagasse 22; call ☎ 313 44-9214 within two weeks of the loss, thereafter call ☎ 313 44-9211. Unless you're still in Vienna when the item is found they'll usually forward it to your embassy (in the case of the USA they'll post items home). For items lost on Austrian railways call the office in Südbahnhof (☎ 5800-35656).

LEGAL MATTERS

Austria offers the level of civil and legal rights you would expect of any industrialised western nation. If you are arrested, the police must inform you of your rights in a language that you understand.

In Austria, legal offences are divided into two categories: criminal *(Gerichtdelikt)* and administrative *(Verwaltungsübertretung)*. If you are suspected of having committed a criminal offence (such as assault or theft) you can be detained for a maximum of 48 hours before you are committed to trial. If you are arrested for a less serious administrative offence (eg drunk and disorderly, breach of the peace) you will be released within 24 hours. Drink driving is an administrative matter, even if you have an accident, but if someone is hurt in the accident it becomes a criminal offence. Possession of a controlled drug is usually a criminal offence, but if, for example, you have a small amount of dope that is considered to be for personal use only (there's no hard and fast rule on quantity) you will probably be merely cautioned and released without being sent for trial. Prostitution is legal provided prostitutes are registered and have obtained a permit.

If you are arrested, you have the right to make one phone call to a 'person in your confidence' within Austria, and another to inform legal counsel. A legal emergency service is available in Vienna out of normal office hours (the police will give you details). If you can't afford legal representation, you can apply to the judge in writing for legal aid.

Each district has a Bürgerdienst where free advice is given on social and legal matters; in the Innere Stadt it's at 01, Bartensteingasse 13 (☎ 525 50-01). There are also special sessions at district courts (Bezirksgerichte) where you can obtain free legal advice, eg at 01, Riemergasse 7 (☎ 515 28).

As a foreigner, your best bet when encountering legal problems is to contact your national consulate in the first instance. If you have a complaint about the conduct of the Viennese police, contact the Vienna Police Headquarters, the Bundespolizeidirektion (☎ 313 10-0), 01, Schottenring 7-9.

BUSINESS HOURS

Shopping hours have recently been liberalised: shops may stay open till 7.30 pm on weekdays and 5 pm on Saturday, though many close at 6 pm and noon respectively. Business hours for offices and government departments vary, but are usually Monday to Friday from 8 am to 4 or 5 pm. Municipal museums are closed on Monday, though the opening hours for other museums and galleries don't follow any set pattern – some are open daily.

PUBLIC HOLIDAYS & SPECIAL EVENTS

Public holidays are 1 January (New Year's Day), 6 January (Epiphany), Easter Monday *(Ostermontag)*, 1 May (Labour Day), Ascension Day *(Christihimmelfahrt)*, Whit Monday *(Pfingstmontag)*, Corpus Christi *(Fronleichnam)*, 15 August (Assumption), 26 October (National Day), 1 November (All Saints' Day), 8 December (Immaculate Conception), 25 December (Christmas Day – *Weihnachten*) and 26 December (St Stephen's Day). Some people also take a holiday on Good Friday.

The national tourist office compiles a list of annual and one-off events taking place each year in Austria, and the Vienna tourist office releases a monthly listing of events in the city. No matter what time of year you visit Vienna, there will always be something special going on. The cycle of musical events is unceasing. Mozart features heavily, as he had his most productive years in Vienna, from 1781 to 1791, but all varieties of music get a look-in. You may find colourful processions on religious feast days. The following is by no means a complete listing of annual events.

On New Year's Eve various celebrations are arranged in the Innere Stadt, and one of the evening's musical events is relayed onto a giant screen at Stephansplatz. The Opera Ball at the Staatsoper is one of the most lavish of the 300 or so balls put on in January and February. Men wear black tails and women wear white ball gowns. Get tickets from Opernballbüro (☎ 514 44-2606), 01, Goethegasse 1. The Imperial Ball, another sumptuous affair, allows you to see in the New Year at the Hofburg; for tickets (very expensive!) apply to Kongresszentrum Hofburg (☎ 587 36 66-23), A-1014 Wien.

Some districts have events for *Fasching* (Shrovetide carnival) in early February. March sees a Haydn Festival in the Musikverein, and trade fairs. At Easter there's 10 days of classical music in the OsterKlang Festival. On 1 May there's the *Tag der Arbeit* (Day of Work) march along the Ringstrasse, and a festival in the Prater.

The Vienna Festival (from mid-May to mid-June) has a wide-ranging programme of the arts and is considered the highlight of the year. Contact Wiener Festwochen (☎ 589 22-22; fax -49; email festwochen@ festwochen.at), Lehárgasse 11, A-1060 Vienna, for details after December. The same office handles inquiries about a dance festival in the Spring (every one to two years) and a classical music festival in May/June.

Over a weekend in late June there's three days of free rock, jazz and folk concerts, plus general outdoor fun in the Donauinselfest. This event has grown in recent years – some two million visitors pour in nowadays. On 21 June there's Midsummer night's celebrations in the Wachau.

Vienna's Summer of Music (from July to mid-August) fills an otherwise flat spot in the musical calendar, taking place at various venues around town. Contact KlangBoden (☎ 4000-8410), 08, Laudongasse 29, to pay for tickets by credit card after 1 June; the office is expected to move nearer to the Rathaus in 1988, but the phone number won't change. Tickets by cash in person are available from Wien Ticket (☎ 588 85) in the hut by the Oper (no commission charged for most events; open 10 am to 7 pm daily). Reduced student tickets go on sale at the respective venue 10 minutes before the performance. In the first two weeks of July there's the Jazz Festival at the Staatsoper and the Volkstheater; contact the KlangBoden office.

The free open-air Opera Film Festival on Rathausplatz runs throughout July and August. Films of operas, operettas and concerts are shown on a large screen, and hundreds of Viennese turn up in their best evening attire to view the proceedings. Food stands and cafés are erected to take care of bodily needs. The International Dance Festival lasts from mid-July to mid-August. Also in summer, look out for the Volksstimme outdoor festival of music, sports and games.

September is a month of trade fairs, as well as heralding the start of the new opera season. Expect much flag-waving on National Day (26 October). In the second-half of October there's the Viennale Film Festival; ☎ 713 2000 for information.

The Schubertiade in the Musikverein (late November) highlights Franz Schubert's music. In November and December there's the Wien Modern festival, featuring modern classical and avant-garde music, performed in the Musikverein and Konzerthaus. In December there's a Mozart Festival at the Konzerthaus.

Vienna's traditional Christmas market *(Christkindlmarkt)* takes place in front of the City Hall from mid-November to 24 December. Trees are decorated in the Rathaus park, and inside the Rathaus there are free concerts of seasonal music. Other Christmas markets spring up, such as the one on Freyung.

WORK

Job opportunities in Vienna are as varied as

in any other large city. Since January 1993 EU nationals have been able to obtain work in Austria without needing a work permit or residency permit, though as intending residents they need to register with the police within five days of arrival.

Non-EU nationals need both a work permit and a residency permit, and would find it pretty hard to get either. Inquire (in German) about job possibilities via the Arbeitsmarktservice für Wien (☎ 515 25), Weihburggasse 30, A 1011, Vienna. The work permit would need to be applied for by your employer in Austria. Applications for residency permits must be applied for via the Austrian embassy in your home country. In theory a residency permit might be granted without a pre-arranged work permit, but you would need sufficient funds, confirmed accommodation in Austria, and perhaps some form of Austrian sponsorship. Non-EU nationals do not require a residency permit if they are undertaking seasonal work for up to six months.

FACTS FOR THE VISITOR

Getting There & Away

AIR

Air travel can be a bargain if you buy discounted tickets from budget travel agents rather than airlines. Stick to agencies that are bonded or have a protection scheme so your money is safe if they go bust. Buying direct from the airline often means paying full price, though some airlines sell their own discounted tickets. Always be clear about restrictions and conditions before parting with your money, and remember that most airlines require you to confirm return trips at least 72 hours before departure.

High-season varies from airline to airline, but you can expect slightly higher prices from April to October. Youth fares can apply to people up to 30, depending on the airline, though 26 is the usual cut-off age. You may find you have to pay more if you don't stay a Saturday night or if your trip exceeds one month.

Flughafen Wien Schwechat (☎ 7007; 7007-2233 for flight enquiries), Vienna's airport, is 19km east of the city centre; it handles over eight million passengers a year, with more people travelling to/from London than any other city. Schwechat has all the facilities expected of a major airport, such as tourist information, money-exchange counters (high commission rates), a supermarket (open daily) and car rental counters. See the Getting Around chapter for information on transport to the city. There is no departure tax to pay upon departure from Austria as all taxes are included in the ticket price.

Austrian Airlines is the national carrier and has the most extensive services to Vienna. Lauda Air is another home-grown airline.

Europe

There are several daily nonstop flights to all the major European transport hubs from Vienna. STA Travel offers budget and student tickets, and has offices in London (☎ 0171-361 6161) and other British cities. Across Europe many travel agents have ties with STA Travel where STA-issued tickets can be altered (usually for a US$25 fee). Outlets include: Voyages Wasteels (☎ 01 43 43 46 10), 2 Rue Michel Charles, Paris; STA Travel (☎ 069-43 01 91), Berger Strasse 118, Frankfurt; and ISYTS (☎ 01-32 21 267), 2nd floor, 11 Nikis St, Syntagma Square, Athens. Currently there is no travel agent in Austria linked with STA.

Lauda Air Takes Off

Austria's Niki Lauda, three-times Formula One racing world champion, founded Lauda Air in 1979. It initially operated as a charter airline, with Lauda himself, a trained pilot, often taking the controls. In 1985 a long battle to operate scheduled flights began. Partial approval was given in 1987 and Lauda's first scheduled flight took off in May that year.

Lauda Air's struggle to establish itself was made harder by the attitude of the state-owned Austrian Airlines. It halved prices on certain routes, denigrated the fledgling airline in the press and was often uncooperative in air traffic rights negotiations. It took another three years of intensive political and public pressure (greatly aided by Lauda's status as a national hero) before the airline finally received a worldwide concession to operate scheduled flights, in August 1990. Ironically, Austrian Airlines has since purchased a 36% stake in Lauda Air.

Lauda Air currently flies to Europe, the USA, Asia and Australia in aircraft named after the likes of Johann Strauss, Enzo Ferrari, James Dean and Bob Marley. Lauda Air's innovative style has seen it introduce quality in-flight meals (supplied by DO & CO), jeans as part of the staff uniform, and in-flight gambling on the Vienna-Australia route. ■

London is one of the world's major centres for discounted air tickets. London-Vienna return costs upwards of about UK£150, plus around UK£20 tax. The cheapest deals are usually with Lauda Air, or very early morning departures with Austrian Airlines. To Vienna, Lauda Air (☎ 0800-767 737) has a daily flight (except Saturday) from Manchester, and four weekly flights (Tuesday, Saturday, and two on Friday) from Gatwick, London. Austrian Airlines (☎ 0171-434 7300) has daily flights from Heathrow, London. British Airways sells its own discounted tickets, called World Offers (☎ 0345-222 111). It has daily flights from both Gatwick and Heathrow. Mondial Travel (☎ 0181-777 7000), 32 Links Rd, West Wickham, Kent, BR4 0QW, is a specialist in flights to Austria and can arrange fly-drive deals. Other places are Trailfinders in London (☎ 0171-937 5400) and elsewhere, Campus Travel (☎ 0171-730 3402) and Council Travel (0171-437 7767). See Organised Tours at the end of this chapter for other outlets.

Domestic services by Austrian Airlines to and from the rest of Austria are now run jointly with Tyrolean Airlines. There are several flights a day to Graz, Klagenfurt and Innsbruck and at least one a day to Salzburg and Linz. Check schedules as they vary according to the season.

North America

Council Travel (☎ 800-226 8624 toll free) and STA Travel (☎ 800-777 0112 toll free) sell discounted tickets from numerous outlets across the USA. STA branches are in San Francisco (☎ 415-391 8407) and New York (☎ 212-627 3111). An APEX return on a daily Austrian Airlines flight from New York costs around US$776. From Chicago, you can get to Vienna daily with Swissair for around US$450 return. From Los Angeles, Delta flies daily, as does Swissair (via Zürich). Lauda Air (☎ 800-645 3880 toll free) has four flights a week from Miami (via Munich); special promotions have cut this return fare to as low as US$418 in the past.

In Canada look for the budget agency, Travel Cuts. Its head office (☎ 416-977 5228) is at 187 College St, Toronto. From Toronto, daily flights are with Air France (via Paris) and Swissair (via Zürich; about C$985 return).

Australasia

STA Travels has offices at 224 Faraday St, Carlton, Melbourne (☎ 03-9349 2411); 24-30 Springfield Ave, Sydney (☎ 02-9368 1111); and 10 High St, Auckland (☎ 09-309 0458; PO Box 4156). Flight Centres International has offices all over Australia and New Zealand, including at 19 Bourke St, Melbourne (☎ 03-9650 2899; fax 9650 3751) and 205-225 Queen St, Auckland (☎ 09-309 6171).

From Australia, Lauda Air (☎ 1800-642 438) operates the only direct flight to Vienna (via Kuala Lumpur), departing from Melbourne/Sydney on Monday, Wednesday and Saturday; expect to pay around A$2000/1750 in high/low season. From New Zealand, going via the USA or Asia is equally viable, or consider buying a round-the-world ticket.

Airline Offices

Many airline offices in Vienna are on Opernring, opposite the Staatsoper. For a complete listing, look under *Fluggesellschaften* in the Yellow Pages *(Gelbe Seiten)* section of the Wien telephone book. They include:

Aer Lingus
(☎ 369 28 85) 19, Scheibengasse 12
Air Canada
(☎ 712 46 08-412) 01, Schubertring 9
Air France
(☎ 514 18-0) 01, Kärntner Strasse 49
Alitalia
(☎ 505 17 07-0) 01, Kärntner Ring 2
Austrian Airlines
(Map 8; ☎ 505 57 57-0) 01, Kärntner Ring 18
British Airways (BA)
(Map 8; ☎ 505 76 91-0) 01, Kärntner Ring 10
Delta Air Lines
(☎ 512 66 46-0) 01, Kärntner Ring 17

Iberia
(☎ 586 76 36-0) 01, Opernring 11
Japan Airlines (JAL)
(☎ 512 75 22) 01, Kärntner Strasse 11
KLM – Royal Dutch Airlines
(☎ 7007-766) Schwechat World Trade Center Top 326
Lauda Air
(Map 8; ☎ 514 77; tollfree 0660-6655) 01, Opernring 6
Lufthansa Airlines
(☎ 599 11-240) 06, Mariahilfer Strasse 123
MALEV – Hungarian Airlines
(☎ 587 33 18) 01, Opernring 3-5
South African Airways (SAA)
(☎ 587 15 85-0) 01, Opernring 1/R
Swissair
as for Austrian Airlines

BUS
International

Buses are generally slower, cheaper and less comfortable than trains. Europe's biggest network of international buses is provided by a group of companies operating under the name Eurolines. Addresses for Eurolines include: Eurolines UK (☎ 0990-143 219), 52 Grosvenor Gardens, Victoria, London SW1; Eurolines Nederland (☎ 020-627 51 51), Rokin 10, Amsterdam; Eurolines (☎ 01 43 54 11 99), 55 Rue Saint Jacques, Paris; Deutsche Touring (☎ 069-790 32 40), Am Romerhof 17, Frankfurt; and Lazzi Express (☎ 06-88 40 840), via Tagliamento 27R, Rome.

Eurolines in Austria is Blaguss Reisen (☎ 712 04 53), based in Vienna's international Autobusbahnhof (Map 8; bus station) Wien Mitte, next to the train station of the same name. Eurolines tickets must be purchased in person (from the Blaguss Eurolines counters, not from the Blaguss hut) though you can make reservations by telephone. There are bus connections across western and eastern Europe, with reduced prices (of 10% or more, depending on the operator) for people under 26 and over 60.

Eurolines buses to Budapest (3½ hours) depart from Wien Mitte several times daily, starting at 7 am. The fare is AS310 one way or AS440 return. Buses run every two hours or so to Bratislava (Slovakia), via the airport

and Hainburg. The fare is AS110/200 one way/return, but it works out cheaper to buy the return leg in Bratislava.

Eurolines buses to and from London (Victoria Coach Station) operate six days a week (daily in summer). The trip takes 22 hours and costs UK£71/109 single/return, UK£78/119 in July, August and pre-Christmas. Eurolines also has Euro Explorer tickets: a round-trip ticket from London includes stops in Budapest, Vienna and Bratislava, and costs UK£126.

Austrobus (Map 8; ☎ 534 11-123), 01, Dr Karl Lueger Ring 8, has buses to Prague (sometimes continuing to Karlsbad in Germany), leaving Vienna from its stop at 01, Rathausplatz 5. Departures are at 8 am Monday to Thursday and Saturday, and 2 pm Friday and Sunday (AS325; five hours). From Prague, buses leave at 9 am Monday to Thursday and 2 pm Friday to Sunday.

If you want to visit several countries by bus, your first choice should probably be Eurobus, which has set routes across Europe and you can jump on and off as many times as you like within a given period. In Britain, call ☎ 0118-936 2320 for information on Eurobus services. For the northern zone it costs UK£129/149/159 for one/two/four months and UK£119/129/139 for students. Eurobuses set down in Vienna at the Hütteldorf-Hacking hostel. Eurolines UK also has European passes. They're more flexible than those of Eurobus but also more expensive (from UK£159/199 per youth/adult for 30 days).

National

The yellow and orange Bundesbus services are ideal for getting to the more out-of-the-way places. Buses are efficient and usually depart from train stations. Fares work out at around AS130 per 100km, but shorter journeys are proportionately more expensive. Bus timetable information is available on ☎ 711 01 between 7 am and 7 pm. The Bundesbus counters in Wien Mitte are open daily from 6 am to 11.40 am and 12.15 to 5.30 pm (3.30 pm on Saturday and Sunday).

TRAIN
International

Austria benefits from its central location within Europe by having excellent rail connections to all important destinations, and Vienna is the main rail hub in central Europe.

Travellers under 26 can pick up Billet International de Jeunesse (BIJ) tickets that cut fares by up to 30%. Various agents issue BIJ tickets in Europe, eg Campus Travel (☎ 0171-730 3402), 52 Grosvenor Gardens, London SW1, which also sells Eurotrain tickets for people under 26 only, allowing two months travel, stopping off en route. British Rail International (☎ 0990-848 848) and Wasteels (☎ 0171-834 7066), both in London's Victoria station, sell BIJ tickets. From London the cheapest fare to Vienna is via France and costs UK£126/211 single/return and UK£104/183 if under 26.

Express trains can be identified by the symbols EC (EuroCity) or IC (InterCity).

European Rail Passes

These may not work out much more expensive than a straightforward return ticket, and are worth considering if you want to explore a number of destinations en route to Austria. Always study the terms and conditions attached to passes. Buying a circular ticket might be a viable alternative to a full rail pass, such as the 'Explorer' tickets offered by Eurotrain.

Eurail Pass This pass can only be bought by residents of non-European countries. Eurail passes are valid for unlimited travel on national railways and some private lines in Austria, Belgium, Denmark, Finland, France (including Monaco), Germany, Greece, Hungary, Italy, Luxembourg, the Netherlands, Norway, Portugal, Ireland, Spain, Sweden and Switzerland (including Liechtenstein). The UK is not covered. The pass is also valid for free or discounted travel on various international ferries and national lake/river steamers.

A standard **Youthpass** for travellers under 26 is valid for unlimited 2nd-class travel within the given time period, ranging from 15 days (US$376) up to three months (US$1059). The **Youth Flexipass**, also for 2nd class, is valid for freely chosen days within a two-month period: 10 days for US$444 or 15 days for US$585.

The corresponding passes for those aged over 26 are available in 1st class only. The standard Eurail pass costs from US$458 for 15 days up to US$1512 for three months. The Flexipass costs US$634 for 10 days or US$836 for 15 days. Two people travelling together can save around 15% each by buying 'saver' versions of these passes (child fares available). There's also a Euraildrive Pass.

The **Europass** gives five freely chosen days' unlimited travel within two months in France, Germany, Italy, Spain and Switzerland. The youth/adult fare is US$216/326, or US$261/386 including Austria, which is an 'associate' country to the scheme. Extra rail days can be purchased for US$29/42 each (10 maximum). There is a Eurail and Europass Aid Office (☎ 5800-335 98) in Vienna's Westbahnhof station, open Monday to Saturday from 9 am to 4 pm.

Inter-Rail Pass Inter-Rail passes are available in Europe to people who have been resident there for at least six months. The standard Inter-Rail pass is for travellers aged under 26, though older people can get the Inter-Rail 26+ version. The pass divides Europe into eight zones (A to H); Austria is in zone C, along with Denmark, Germany and Switzerland. The standard/26+ fare for any one zone is UK£159/229, valid 22 days. To purchase two/three/all zones (valid one month) costs UK£209/229/259, or UK£279/309/349 for the 26+ version.

The all-zone (global) pass would take you everywhere covered by Eurail, plus to Poland, Czech Republic, Slovakia, Slovenia, Romania, Croatia, Yugoslavia, Bulgaria, Macedonia and Turkey. As with Eurail, the pass gives discounts or free travel on ferry, ship and steamer routes.

Euro-Domino Pass There is a Euro-Domino pass (called a **Freedom Pass** in Britain) for each of the countries covered in the Inter-Rail pass, except for Morocco and some eastern countries. Adults (travelling 1st or 2nd class) and youths (under 26) can choose from three, five, or 10 chosen days within a month. The Domino pass for Austria is a viable alternative to buying one of Austria's national rail passes.

European East Pass This is sold in North America and Australia, and is valid for train travel in Austria, the Czech Republic, Slovakia, Poland and Hungary. The cost is US$185 for five days of travel in one month; extra travel days (five maximum) cost US$22 each. ∎

The French TGV and the German ICE are even faster. Supplements can apply on international and express trains, and it is a good idea (sometimes obligatory) to make seat reservations at peak times and on certain lines.

Europeans over 60 should inquire about the Rail Europe Senior Card, which is good for fare reductions.

National

Austrian trains are efficient and frequent. The country is well covered by the state network, with only a few private lines operating. Eurail and Inter-Rail passes are valid on the former. Many stations have information centres where the staff speak English. In the larger towns, train information can be obtained on ☎ 1717. Tickets can be purchased on the train but they cost AS30 extra. Unless otherwise specified, 2nd class fares are quoted in this book. Reserving train seats usually incurs a AS20 to AS50 fee.

Single tickets over 100km each way are valid for four days, return tickets for two months, and unlike for shorter trips, you can break your journey as many times as you like (warn the conductor of your intentions).

The Bundes-Netzkarte, a one month pass valid on all state railways, including rack railways, costs AS5900 in 1st class and AS4300 in 2nd class.

The Österreich Puzzle is not particularly puzzling – it divides the country into four zones – north, south, east and west. You can buy a pass for each zone for AS1090 (AS660 if under 26) giving you four days' unlimited travel in 10. First class costs 50% more. The north zone covers Vienna, Upper and Lower Austria and Burgenland; east covers Vienna, Lower Austria, Styria and Burgenland. As zone areas overlap you can travel the whole country without actually needing to buy the east zone.

The Kilometerbank allows up to six people to travel on journeys over 51km; the cost is AS2400 for 2000km, AS3540 for 3000km, and AS5850 for 5000km.

Also see the European Rail Passes boxed text for information on the Euro Domino Pass for Austria.

Vienna's Train Stations

Vienna has several train stations and not all destinations are exclusively serviced by one station. Check with train information centres in stations or telephone the 24 hour information line (☎ 1717) to check schedules or to find out the best way to go. Remember to ask about reduced fares if you're under 26. Sometimes there are also cheap fares on international return tickets valid less than four days (eg Budapest return costs AS560 and includes city transport in Budapest). All the following stations (except Meidling) have lockers (from AS30), money exchange (including Bankomat ATMs), and places to eat and buy provisions. Train stations are usually closed from 1 to 4 am.

Westbahnhof Westbahnhof (Map 4) services trains to western and northern Europe and western Austria. There are (approximately) hourly services to Salzburg; some continue to Munich and terminate in Paris Est. Two daytime trains run to Zürich (AS1126); there's also a sleeper service (AS1074, plus charges for fold-down seat/couchette etc) departing at 9.25 pm. A direct train goes to Bucharest; for Athens (AS1833; departure 7 pm) you need to change twice. Eight daily trains go to Budapest (AS368; three to four hours). Westbahnhof is also a U-Bahn station for lines U3 and U6, and many trams stop outside.

Südbahnhof The Südbahnhof (Map 7) station services trains to Italy, the Czech Republic, Slovakia, Hungary and Poland. Trains to Rome (via Venice and Florence) depart at 7.30 am and 7.30 pm. Five trains a day go to Bratislava (AS94); four go to Prague (AS488; five hours), with two continuing to Berlin. Trams D (to the Ring and Franz Josefs Bahnhof) and O (to Wien Mitte and Praterstern) stop outside. The quickest way to transfer to Westbahnhof is to take tram 18, or the S-Bahn to Meidling and then the U6.

Franz Josefs Bahnhof Franz Josefs Bahnhof (Map 4) handles regional and local trains, including trains to Tulln, Krems and the Wachau region. It also has one daily train to Prague (AS432; 5½ hours). From outside, tram D goes to the Ring, and tram No 5 goes to Westbahnhof (via Kaiserstrasse) in one direction and Praterstern (Wien Nord) in the other.

Other Stations Wien Mitte (Map 8) services local trains, and is adjacent to the Landstrasse stop on the U3. Wien Nord (Map 8), at the Praterstern stop on the U1, handles local and regional trains, including the airport service (which also stops at Wien Mitte). Meidling (Map 6) is a stop for most trains going to and from Südbahnhof, and it is linked to the Philadelphiabrücke stop on the U6.

CAR & MOTORCYCLE

By road there are numerous entry points from Germany, the Czech Republic, Slovakia, Hungary, Slovenia, Italy and Switzerland. All main border crossings are open 24 hours a day. To and from Germany and Italy there are no border controls, thanks to the EU Schengen Agreement. Driving into Vienna is straightforward: the A1 from Linz and Salzburg and the A2 from Graz join the Gürtel ring road; the A4 from the airport leads directly to the Ring, and the A22 runs to the city centre along the northern bank of the Danube.

To avoid a long drive, consider a motorail service: many head south from Calais and Paris, and Vienna is linked by a daily motorail to Salzburg, Innsbruck, Feldkirch and Villach.

Paperwork & Preparations

Proof of ownership of a private vehicle should always be carried (Vehicle Registration Document for British-registered cars) when touring Europe. A British (except for the old green version) or other western European driving licence is valid throughout Europe. If you have any other type of licence you should obtain an International Driving

Permit (IDP). Third party insurance is a minimum requirement in Europe, and you'll need proof of this in the form of a Green Card. Taking out a European breakdown assistance policy is a good investment, such as the AA Five Star Service or the RAC Eurocover Motoring Assistance.

Every vehicle travelling across an international border should display a nationality plate of its country of registration. A warning triangle, to be used in the event of breakdown, is compulsory almost everywhere (including Austria). Recommended accessories are a first-aid kit (compulsory in Austria, Slovenia, Croatia, Yugoslavia and Greece), a spare bulb kit and a fire extinguisher. In the UK, contact the RAC (☎ 0800-550055) or the AA (☎ 0990-500600) for more specific information.

Road Rules

Driving is on the right throughout Continental Europe, and priority is usually given to traffic approaching from the right. The RAC annually brings out its *European Motoring Guide*, which gives an excellent summary of regulations in each country, including parking rules. Motoring organisations in other countries have similar publications. Road signs are generally standard throughout Europe. *Umleitung* in German means 'diversion', though in Austria you may see *Ausweiche* instead.

The blood alcohol concentration (BAC) limit when driving is between 0.05% and 0.08%, but in some areas (Gibraltar, eastern Europe, Scandinavia) it can be *zero* per cent. In Austria, the penalty for drink driving is a hefty on-the-spot fine and confiscation of your driving licence.

Crash helmets for motorcyclists and their passengers are compulsory everywhere in Europe. Austria, Belgium, France, Germany, Luxembourg, Portugal, Spain, Scandinavia, Croatia, Yugoslavia and most of eastern Europe also require motorcyclists to use headlights during the day; in other countries it is recommended.

There are toll charges for some of the Alpine tunnels, and some mountain roads and passes are closed in winter. On mountain roads, postbuses always have priority, otherwise priority lies with uphill traffic. Drive in low gear on steep downhill stretches.

Austrian speed limits are 50km/h in towns, 130km/h on motorways and 100km/h on other roads. Cars towing a caravan or trailer are limited to 100km/h on motorways. Snow chains are recommended in winter. Seatbelts must be used, if fitted, and children under 12 should have a special seat or restraint. Austrian police have the authority to impose fines of up to AS500 for various traffic offences. This can be paid on the spot (ask for a receipt) or within two weeks.

Fuel

Leaded petrol is no longer available in Austria, but the brand Super Plus has a special additive that allows it to be used with leaded petrol engines. Prices per litre are about AS12 for Super Plus, which is marginally more than unleaded petrol, and AS9 for diesel. Petrol is cheaper in the Czech Republic, Slovakia and Hungary, similarly priced in Germany and Switzerland and more expensive in Italy. Plan to arrive in the country with a full or empty tank depending on where you're coming from.

Motorway Tax

Tolls were introduced on Austrian motorways in 1997. The annual fee is AS550 for cars (below 3.5 tonnes) and AS220 for motorcycles. Fortunately, unlike in neighbouring Switzerland, tourists have the option of buying short-term passes. The weekly disc costs AS70 for cars and motorcycles and is actually valid for up to 10 days: from Friday to midnight two Sundays hence. The two month disc, valid for consecutive calendar months, costs AS150 for cars and AS80 for motorcycles. The tax doesn't cover the toll fee for other roads and tunnels, but it does give a 15% discount on some.

BICYCLE

Getting to Vienna by bike is certainly possible. A cycle track, for example, runs all the way along the Danube from Donaueschin-

gen in the Black Forest to Vienna and on to Bratislava. If you get weary of pedalling or simply want to skip a boring leg, you can put your feet up on the train. On slower trains, bikes can usually be taken on board as luggage, subject to a small supplementary fee. Fast trains (IC, EC etc) can sometimes accommodate bikes; otherwise, they need to be sent as registered luggage and may end up on a different train from the one you take. British Rail is not part of the European luggage registration scheme, so you have to get to the Continent before you can send your bike in this way. In Austria, it costs AS140 to send a bike as international luggage on the train. Bikes can also be carried by aeroplane, but check with the carrier in advance.

Within Austria, you can get a day card for transporting a bike on a train. It costs AS30, but beware of additional reservation fees (there are no such fees on 'Rad-Tramper' trains, eg trains marked with the bike pictogram from Franz Josefs Bahnhof to St Pölten, Linz and Krems, and from Südbahnhof to Neusiedl am See). See the Getting Around chapter for bicycle hire at train stations.

HITCHING

Hitching is never entirely safe in any country, and we don't recommend it. Travellers who decide to hitch should understand that they are taking a small but potentially serious risk. People who do choose to hitch will be safer if they travel in pairs and let someone know where they are planning to go.

Throughout Europe, hitching is illegal on motorways – stand on the entrance roads, or approach drivers at petrol stations and truck stops. Ferry tickets for vehicles sometimes include a full load of passengers, so hitchers may be able to secure a free passage this way.

Hitching in Austria is not too bad overall. Trying to hitch rides on trucks is often the best bet: check border customs posts and truck stops. *Autohof* indicates a parking place able to accommodate trucks. It is illegal for minors under 16 to hitch in Burgenland, Upper Austria, Styria and Vorarlberg.

Heading west from Vienna, the lay-by across the footbridge from the U4 Unter St Veit stop has been recommended.

A safer way to hitch is to arrange a lift through an organisation that links drivers and hitchers, such as Allostop-Provoya in France and Mitfahrzentrale in Germany. You could also try scanning university notice-boards. In Vienna, Mitfahrzentrale Josefstadt (Map 4; ☎ 408 22 10), 08, Daungasse 1A, is open Monday to Friday from 10 am to 6 pm and Saturday and Sunday from 11 am to 1 pm. Examples of fares are: Salzburg AS210; Innsbruck AS270; Klagenfurt AS190; Vorarlberg AS350; Brussels AS720; Cologne AS580; Frankfurt AS470 and Munich AS310. Lifts across Austria tend to be limited, but there are usually many cars going to Germany. If you're offering a lift, visit the office in person. Drivers get paid the balance of the fees after the office takes its cut.

BOAT

Since the early 1990s the Danube has been connected to the Rhine by the Main-Danube canal in Germany. The *MS Swiss Pearl* does 12-day cruises along this route, from Amsterdam to Vienna, between June and mid-September. It departs monthly in each direction. In Britain, bookings can be made through Noble Caledonia (☎ 0171-409 0376); deck prices start at UK£1780. In the USA, you can book through Uniworld (☎ 800-733 7820).

Several companies run services along the Austrian stretch of the Danube. From Vienna, hydrofoils travel eastwards to Bratislava and Budapest. The trip to Bratislava (once daily, Wednesday to Sunday between 1 May and late October; 1½ or 2½ hours) costs AS230/350 one way/return. Budapest costs AS750/1100 one way/return and takes at least 5½ hours; there's one daily departure from early April to early November, two daily from early July to early September. Bookings can be made through Mahart Tours (Map 5; ☎ 7292-161), 02, Handelskai 265, or DDSG Blue Danube (Map 8; ☎ 588 80; fax -440), 01, Friedrichstrasse 7.

Hydrofoils are more expensive than the bus or the train, but make a pleasant change. Likewise the steamers that ply the Danube west of Vienna to Passau (Germany): these provide an enjoyable excursion, but are rather slow, especially upstream. Yet they're well worth it if you like lounging on deck and having the scenery come to you rather than the other way round. Several operators run boats in the Wachau region (see the Danube Valley section in the Excursions chapter for details), but it is no longer possible to go all the way to and from Vienna and the Wachau by scheduled steamer.

TRAVEL AGENTS

The Österreichisches Komitee für Internationalen Studienaustausch (ÖKISTA), which has its head office (☎ 401 48; fax -6290) at 09, Garnisongasse 7, specialises in student and budget fares. Opening hours are Monday to Friday from 9 am to 5.30 pm. International Student Identity Cards (ISIC) are issued for a AS70 fee, if you can prove your status. Other offices are at 09, Türkenstrasse 6 (Map 4; ☎ 401 48-7000) and 04, Karlsgasse 3 (☎ 505 01 28). ÖS Reisen (☎ 402 15 61), 01, Reichsratsstrasse 13, is linked to ÖKISTA.

Österreichisches Verkehrsbüro (Map 8; ☎ 588 00; fax 586 85 33), 01, Friedrichstrasse 7 and elsewhere, is a major national agency. Cedok (Map 8; ☎ 512 43 72; fax -85), 01, Parkring 10 (entry from Liebenberggasse), is a specialist agency to the Czech Republic.

ORGANISED TOURS

Various packages are available that have a musical theme. Austrian Holidays (☎ 0171-434 7399), the UK tour operator of Austrian Airlines, can do flight-only deals or construct holidays based around tourist sights, winter sights or the opera. Austria Travel (☎ 0171-222 2430), 46 Queen Anne's Gate, London SW1H 9AU, has competitive airfares, and sells 'city breaks' with excursions included.

Young revellers can take bus tours based on hotel or camping accommodation. The

operators in London include Contiki
(☎ 0181-290 6422), Tracks (☎ 0171-937
3028) and Top Deck (☎ 0171-370 6487).

For people over 50, Saga Holidays in
Britain (☎ 0800-300 500), Saga Building,
Middelburg Square, Folkestone, Kent CT20
1AZ, offers a nine night tour of the cities of
the Habsburgs from UK£639, including
return flight from Heathrow. It also does
'city breaks' to Vienna. Saga operates in the
USA as Saga International Holidays (☎ 800-
343 0273), 222 Berkeley St, Boston, MA
02116, and in Australia as Saga Holidays
Australasia (☎ 02-9957 4266), Level One,
110 Pacific Highway, North Sydney.

WARNING
The information in this chapter is particularly vulnerable to change: prices for
international travel are volatile, routes are
introduced and cancelled, schedules change,
special deals come and go, and rules and visa
requirements are amended.

Airlines and governments seem to take a
perverse pleasure in making price structures
and regulations as complicated as possible.
You should check directly with the airline or
a travel agent to make sure you understand
how a fare (and the ticket you might buy)
works. In addition, the travel industry is
highly competitive and there are many lurks
and perks.

The upshot of this is that you should get
opinions, quotes and advice from as many
airlines and travel agents as possible before
you part with your hard-earned cash. The
travel details given in this chapter should
only be regarded as pointers and are not a
substitute for your own careful up-to-date
research.

Getting Around

TO/FROM THE AIRPORT

Wien Schwechat Airport (Map 2; ☎ 7007) is 19km east of the city centre. The cheapest way to get to the airport is by S-Bahn on line S7. The fare is AS34, or AS17 for the supplement if you already have a city pass for the day. Trains leave usually leave at three and 33 minutes past the hour from Wien Nord, calling at Wien Mitte three minutes later. The trip takes about 35 minutes and the first/last train departs at 5.03 am/9.33 pm. In the opposite direction, trains usually depart at 14 and 44 minutes past the hour, with the first/last service at 6.07 am/10.23 pm. (There are earlier trains in both directions on weekdays only.)

Airport buses run from the City Air Terminal (Map 8), at the Hotel Hilton, to the airport every 20 or 30 minutes from 4.30 am (5 am in the opposite direction) to 12.30 am. From late March to late October buses also run hourly during the night. The 20 minute journey costs AS70/130 one way/return, including three pieces of luggage. Buses also run from Westbahnhof between 5.30 am and 11 pm, stopping at Südbahnhof 15 minutes later. The fare is also AS70/130 and departures are every 30 or 60 minutes. For more information on airport bus services, telephone ☎ 5800-2300.

If taking a taxi is the only option, expect to pay around AS400 to AS450; this will be the metered fare plus a AS130 supplement for the driver's return trip to the city. Cityrama (☎ 534 13-13) offers airport transfers for up to four passengers for the fixed price of AS390.

PUBLIC TRANSPORT

Vienna has a comprehensive and unified public transport network that is one of the most efficient in Europe. Flat-fare tickets are valid for trains, trams, buses, the underground (U-Bahn) and the S-Bahn regional trains. Services are frequent, and you rarely have to wait more than five or 10 minutes.

Public transport kicks off around 5 or 6 am. Buses and trams usually finish by midnight, though some S-Bahn and U-Bahn services may continue until 1 am.

Information

Transport routes are given in the free tourist office map, or for a more detailed listing, buy a map (AS15) from a Vienna Line ticket office. These offices are located in many U-Bahn stations. Transport information offices at Karlsplatz, Stephansplatz and Westbahnhof are open Monday to Friday from 6.30 am to 6.30 pm and weekends and holidays from 8.30 am to 4 pm; those at Floridsdorf, Landstrasse, Philadelphiabrücke, Praterstern, Spittelau and Volkstheater are open Monday to Friday from 7 am to 6.30 pm. For public transport information in German call ☎ 7909-105.

Tickets & Passes

Single trip tickets cost AS20 from drivers or ticket machines, or AS17 each in multiples of four (or five from Tabak shops) from ticket offices and ticket machines. You may change lines on the same trip. Single tickets are valid for immediate use; strip tickets have to be validated in the blue boxes (inside buses and trams and beside U-Bahn escalators) before your journey. Some ticket machines don't give change or will only change certain bills – be sure to use the correct money unless you can follow the German instructions.

Daily city passes (Stunden-Netzkarte) are the better deal for extensive sightseeing. Costs are AS50 (valid 24 hours from first use) and AS130 (valid 72 hours). Validate the ticket before your first journey. An eight day, multiple-user pass (Acht-TageStreifenkarte) costs AS265. The validity depends upon the number of people travelling on the same card: one person gets eight days of travel, two people get four days, and so on. Validate the ticket each day (and for each person) at the beginning of your journey.

Weekly passes, valid Monday to Sunday, cost AS142; passes valid for a calendar month cost AS500. Both are transferable, so you can let someone else travel on your ticket or sell any unexpired days. The yearly pass for AS4700 has a photo ID and is not transferable.

Children aged six to 15 travel for half price, or for free on Sunday, public holidays and during Vienna school holidays (photo ID necessary); younger children always travel free. Senior citizens (women aged 60, men aged 65) can buy a ticket for AS23 that is valid for two trips; inquire at transport information offices. Students up to 19 studying in Austria can get cheap deals.

All passes can be purchased at ticket offices and Tabak shops. Ticket inspections are not very frequent, but fare dodgers pay an on-the-spot fine of AS500 plus the fare, if caught. Quite a few Viennese (particularly the young) are prepared to take the risk.

S-Bahn

S-Bahn trains, designated by a number preceded by an 'S', operate from the main train stations, and are mainly used as a service to the suburbs or satellite towns. Inter-Rail, Eurail, and Austrian rail passes are valid on the S-Bahn. Regional trains ('R' services) cover some of the same routes.

U-Bahn

The U-Bahn is a quick and efficient way to get around the city, albeit mostly underground and therefore lacking in visual stimulus. There are five lines, U1 to U6 (there is no U5). Platforms have timetable information and signs showing the different exits and nearby facilities. Station exits are often a fair distance apart, so after disembarking, orientate yourself instead of blindly striking out for the nearest exit. Platforms are often accessible by lift or escalator from street level.

Bus & Tram

Buses and trams are slower than the U-Bahn,

but at least allow you to see the city while you're travelling. Trams are usually numbered but may be lettered instead, and cover the city centre and some suburbs. Buses go everywhere, including inside the Ring (unlike trams). They also cover the suburbs more extensively than trams. Most buses have a number followed by an 'A' or 'B'. Very logically, buses connecting with a tram service often have the same number, eg 38A connects with 38, and 72A continues from the terminus of 72.

Night Bus

There are 22 night bus routes, marked with an 'N' on the buses and bus stops. They run every 30 minutes from 12.30 am to about 5 am, and stretch into all suburbs. Most routes hit the Ringstrasse, with Schwedenplatz, Schottentor and the Oper being the most important intersection points. Vienna Line offices can give you a timetable and route map. The AS25 night bus fare is not covered by daily passes, though possessing a monthly or yearly pass does reduce the fare to AS10. A 10 ride strip ticket saves you 10%.

CAR & MOTORCYCLE

The tourist office encourages visitors to use public transport for sightseeing in Vienna (a tourist office brochure admits that 'the Viennese can be impatient drivers') and it's probably worth heeding this advice. Irrespective of the complications created by one-way streets, you'll find it difficult or expensive to park in the centre.

Take special care if you've never driven in a city with trams before; they always have priority and no matter how much you might swear at them, they're never going to deviate from their tracks just to suit you. Vehicles must wait behind the tram when it stops to pick-up or set down passenger. Parking is not permitted on roads with tram tracks from 10 pm to 5 am between 15 December and 31 March (because of snow-clearing). Use of the horn is prohibited near hospitals.

The evening rush hour starts at about 4 pm. Petrol stations are dotted around the city (eg in the Innere Stadt at Börsegasse and

Schmerlingplatz); some are self-service. Very late at night, you may find the only stations open are near the motorway exits.

Parking

There are many underground parking garages. The Staatsoper garage on Kärntner Strasse charges AS40 per hour, AS450 for the first 24 hours and AS300 for subsequent 24 hour periods. The one in front of the Rathaus is even more expensive. Both are open 24 hours. The one in front of the Museumsquartier charges AS35 per hour and AS245 per day, but it's closed from midnight to 6 am (8 am on weekends and holidays). Garages outside the Innere Stadt are around AS25 per hour. The multi-storey carparks at Südbahnhof and Westbahnhof charge AS20 per hour or AS160 per day (open 24 hours).

All of the Innere Stadt is a short-term parking zone (Kurzparkzone), meaning that on-street parking is limited to a maximum 1½ hours between 9 am and 7 pm from Monday to Friday. Outside these hours there are no parking restrictions. Vouchers (Parkschein) for parking on these streets, designated as blue zones from their blue markings, must be purchased from Tabak shops and displayed on the windscreen. Vouchers cost AS6 per 30 minutes.

On some streets parking may be prohibited altogether (blue sign circled in red with a red cross – Parking Verboten) or only permitted for 10 minutes (blue sign circled in red with a single diagonal line – a Halten area). Plaques under the sign will state any exceptions or specific conditions (eg the 'Halten' sign may also be marked as 'Kurzparkzone', allowing a 1½ hour stop).

Blue zones have gradually crept into the districts bordering the Innere Stadt. The Kurzparkzone restrictions in the 4th, 5th, 6th, 7th, 8th and 9th districts apply on weekdays from 9 am to 8 pm. Much of the 2nd district (not the Prater area) became a short-term parking area in 1998, and the 20th district will probably follow suit. Elsewhere, you can still find white zones where there are no time restrictions on parking. The 1½ hour limit can be ignored upon purchase of a AS50 parking card – inquire at your hotel.

Parking tickets incur a fine of AS300 if you pay within two weeks. Don't assume you can get away with it if you're due to leave the country, as Austria has reciprocal agreements with some countries for the collection of such debts. And don't risk getting towed, as you'll find it expensive (at least AS1000) and inconvenient to retrieve your car.

Car Rental

For the lowest rates, organise car rental before departure. Holiday Autos (☎ 0990-300 400) in the UK charges UK£199 for a Renault Twingo for one week, including airport surcharge, unlimited mileage and collision damage waiver (CDW), and has a lowest price guarantee. It has branches in Europe and its USA office is Kemwel Holiday Autos (☎ 909-949 1737) in Harrison, New York.

Local walk-in rates are pretty expensive. The Europcar office for reservations (☎ 799 61 76) is at 03, Park & Ride U3 Erdberg, Erdbergstrasse 202/1. It has the lowest rates: from AS660 per day for one to three days, AS588 per day for four to six days, and AS516 per day for seven days or more. The rate for a weekend (noon Friday to 9 am Monday) is AS1020 and includes 1000km mileage. Sixt (Map 7; ☎ 503 66 16), in the Südbahnhof Parkhaus, is almost as cheap for daily rates. Budget (Map 8; ☎ 714 65 65), 03, City Air Terminal, has decent rates too; they may look higher, but they include CDW.

Eurodollar (Map 8; ☎ 714 67 17), 01, Schubertring 9, is known in Austria as ARAC Autovermietung and it has the next best daily rates, though the weekend deal is expensive. A little more expensive in normal daily rates is Avis (Map 8; ☎ 587 62 41), 01, Opernring 1. But Avis sometimes has a real bargain: subject to availability (you can't reserve them), it offers Opel Corsa or VW Polo for only AS440 per 24 hours, all inclusive. Avis' normal weekend rate is AS1068. Hertz (Map 8; ☎ 512 86 77; ☎ 795 32 for the central reservations office), 01, Kärntner Ring 17, has marginally higher daily rates.

Quoted rates include 20% MWST (VAT) and are subject to a 1% contract tax, plus AS8.40 per day to cover motorway tax. All the above companies have an airport office, though prices are 11% higher than in city offices.

The minimum age for renting is 19 for small cars and 25 for prestige models. You will need to have held a valid licence for at least a year. CDW is offered for an additional charge of about AS250 per day. Be sure to inquire about all terms and conditions before commencing a rental, such as if you can drive it across the border.

A place offering motorbike rental is 2 Rad-Börse (Map 5; ☎ 214 85 95; fax -26), 02, Praterstern 47. It has various Hondas available, ranging from a 50cc scooter (AS390; AS1.50 per kilometre) to a Goldwing 1500cc (AS2990; AS6 per kilometre). These rates are for 24 hours and include 100km free. The weekend rates (5 pm Friday to 10 am Monday) include 200km and are AS790 and AS6990 respectively. Helmet hire is AS100 a day (AS200 a weekend).

Motoring Organisations

The main national motoring organisation is the Österreichischer Automobil, Motorrad und Touring Club (Map 8; ÖAMTC; ☎ 711 99; fax 713 18 07), 01, Schubertring 1-3. For 24 hour emergency assistance within Austria dial ☎ 120. Assistance is free for ÖAMTC members and for members of motoring clubs in other countries that have reciprocal agreements with ÖAMTC. If you're not entitled to free assistance, call-out charges are AS1066 during the day or AS1366 from 10 pm to 6 am. The ÖAMTC also offers travel agency services.

The other national motoring club, the Auto, Motor und Radfahrerbund Österreichs (ARBÖ; ☎ 891 21), 15, Mariahilfer Strasse 180, offers 24 hour emergency assistance on ☎ 123; call-out charges are similar to those of ÖAMTC for anyone not a member of ARBÖ.

TAXI

Taxis are metered for city journeys. The flag fall starts at AS26 (AS27 on Sunday, holidays and from 11 pm to 6 am). The rate is then about AS14 per kilometre (AS16 on Sunday etc), plus AS2 per 22 seconds of being stuck in traffic. The rate for trips outside the city borders is double, in order to pay for the driver's trip back, though it may be possible to negotiate a fare. Taxis are easily found at train stations and top hotels, or just flag them down in the street. There is an AS26 surcharge for phoning a taxi; numbers to call are ☎ 31 300, ☎ 40 100, ☎ 60 160 and ☎ 81 400.

BICYCLE

There are 480km of bicycle tracks in and around Vienna, including along the banks of the Danube. Pick up the *Nützliche Tips für Radfahrer* booklet from the tourist office. It's in German, but it has maps showing bike tours, eg circular tours through the Prater and along the Old and New Danubes. It also lists bike rental places *(Radverleih)*.

Argus (Map 7; ☎ 505 84 35), 04, Frankenberggasse 11, is an organisation promoting cycling, and has maps and cycling information for Austria. It's open Monday to Friday from 2 to 6 pm.

The cheapest places to rent bikes are at the train stations: Westbahnhof, Südbahnhof, Wien Nord and Floridsdorf. You can return them at a different station, subject to a AS45 fee. Rates are AS150 per day, reduced to AS90 after 3 pm or with that day's train ticket. At Westbahnhof and Südbahnhof you can return them as late as midnight. Bikes can be carried on the S-Bahn and U-Bahn (in a separate carriage on the U6 line) outside rush-hour times, for half the adult fare.

WALKING

The sights in the Innere Stadt can be easily seen on foot; indeed, the main arteries of Kärntner Strasse, Graben and Kohlmarkt are pedestrian only. To visit anything else it's best to buy a transport pass. Be careful not to walk in the cycle lanes that dissect many pavements.

GETTING AROUND

Walking Tours in the city centre are suggested under Innere Stadt in the Things to See & Do chapter; for walks further afield, turn to the Hiking section under Activities later in that chapter.

FIACRES

More of a tourist novelty than a mode of transport, a fiacre *(Fiaker)* is a traditional-style open carriage drawn by a pair of horses. They can be found lined up at Stephansplatz, Albertinaplatz and Heldenplatz at the Hofburg. Commanding AS500 for a 20 minute trot, these horses must be among Vienna's richest inhabitants. Try to bargain. Drivers generally speak English and point out places of interest en route.

ORGANISED TOURS
Bus Tours

Vienna Sightseeing Tours (☎ 712 46 83; fax 714 11 41; email vst@via.at), 03, Stelzhamergasse 4/11, offers a wide variety of tours in English with free hotel pick-up. Several versions of city tours are available; some include performances of the Vienna Boys' Choir (AS640; three hours) and the Lipizzaner stallions (AS590; three or five hours). Tours also run to the Wienerwald, the Danube Valley, Burgenland, Salzburg, Prague and Budapest.

Vienna Cityrama (Map 8; ☎ 534 13; fax -22), 01, Börsegasse 1, offers a similar choice and prices. Both companies allow a child's fare up to age 12.

Reisebuchladen (Map 8; ☎ 317 33 84), 09, Kolingasse 6, conducts an alternative to the normal sightseeing tour, concentrating on 'Red Vienna' buildings like the Karl-Marx-Hof and Art Nouveau sights like Otto Wagner's Kirche am Steinhof. The tour is called 'Traum & Wirklichkeit' (Dream & Reality) and costs AS330 per person. The guide is not afraid to reveal uncomplimentary details about Vienna. Schedules depend upon demand and the tour is in German unless there are enough English speakers.

Boat Tours

These operate from 1 May to late October. DDSG Blue Danube (☎ 588 80-0; fax -440; email ddsg.blue.danube@telecom.at) has a 90 minute 'Hundertwasser Tour', in a boat that's been given the Hundertwasser design treatment. It departs two to four times a day from Schwedenplatz in the Innere Stadt (AS140). There's also the 90 minute 'Danube Tour' that goes from Schwedenplatz to Reichsbrücke (on the Danube River) and costs AS120. Donau Schiffahrt (☎ 715 15 25-20), 03, Marxergasse 19, does similar Danube tours (75 minutes) for AS110, or a full Danube circuit (3½ hours) for AS170.

Other Tours

Pedal Power (Map 5; ☎ 729 72 34; fax 729 72 35; email office@pedalpower.co.at), 02, Ausstellungsstrasse 3, conducts half-day bicycle tours in and around Vienna from 1 May to 31 October. Tours cost AS280 (AS230 for students), or AS180 if you have your own bike.

From May to October you can take a tour of Vienna by 'old-time tram'. The departure point is Karlsplatz and the cost is AS200 (AS70 for children); for information call ☎ 7909-440 26. The tour leaves on Sunday, holidays, and most Saturdays.

GETTING AROUND

Most of Vienna's main sights are in the city centre, called the *Innere Stadt* (inner city, ie the 1st district). Many lesser sights that are not covered in this chapter are mentioned in *Vienna from A to Z*, a 110 page booklet available from the tourist office (AS50) and shops. This outlines over 200 sights, and includes walking-tour suggestions. The tourist office has a useful museums leaflet listing opening times and locations, and another covering *fin de siècle* architecture. Long-term visitors might consider buying a one year pass for state museums costing AS400.

The Vienna Card, which is valid for three days, is available from the tourist office, transport offices and hotels. It's worth getting if you plan on doing a lot of sightseeing in a concentrated period. It costs AS180 and includes a public transport pass (worth AS130) and gives discounts of 10 to 50% on some admission prices (museums, galleries, theatres etc), as well as shopping discounts.

Around the year 2000 Vienna could be a major theme park destination, if the three planned theme parks get built (south of the city and in the Prater).

HIGHLIGHTS

The prime sights in the centre are Stephansdom, the Hofburg, and the Kunsthistoriches Museum. Farther afield, other main attractions are the palaces of Schönbrunn and Belvedere. In addition to exploring these places, visitors might enjoy:

* A tram ride round the Ringstrasse
* The chaos and clutter of the Naschmarkt flea market
* The sights and sounds of Kärntner Strasse and Graben
* People-watching in a traditional coffee house
* A night on the wine in a *Heuriger*
* The elaborate rides and strange sculptures in the Volksprater funfair
* The bizarre waxworks in the Josephinium museum
* The unusual architecture of Friedensreich Hundertwasser
* The fountain and façade of the Parlament
* Art Nouveau creations: the Kirche am Steinhof and the Secession building

Some of these options are covered in the Places to Eat and Entertainment chapters. Overrated attractions include the Lipizzaner stallions in the Spanish Riding School, the 'Bermuda Triangle' drinking area, and touristy 'waltz shows'. A ride around the centre by fiacres *(Fiaker)*, Vienna's horse-drawn carriages, is fun but overpriced.

Innere Stadt

The majestic architecture you see today in the city centre is largely due to the efforts of Emperor Franz Josef I. In 1857 he decided to tear down the redundant military fortifications and exercise grounds that surrounded the Innere Stadt and replace them with grandiose public buildings that would better reflect the power and the wealth of the Habsburg empire. The Ringstrasse, or Ring Boulevard, was laid out between 1858 and 1865, and in the decade that followed most of the impressive edifices that now line this thoroughfare were under construction. Franz Josef had extremely deep pockets to match his elaborate plans; consider this for a shopping list: Staatsoper (built 1861-69), Musikverein (1867-69), Museum für angewandte Kunst (1868-71), Akademie der bildenden Künste (1872-76), Naturhistorisches Museum (1872-81), Rathaus (1872-83), Kunsthistorisches Museum (1872-91), Parlament (1873-83), Universität (1873-84), Burgtheater (1874-88), Justizpalast (1875-81), and the Heldenplatz section of the Neue Burg (1881-1908).

Ironically, WWI intervened and the empire was lost before Franz Josef's grand

Top Left: An accordian player entertains patrons at a Heuriger in Grinzing
Right: Produce at the farmer's market of Naschmarkt includes cheeses and Sturm, a fermenting grape juice drink usually available in autumn
Bottom Left: A cook at the Hotel Sacher shows off some of the hotel's famous Sacher Tortes

MARK HONAN

MARK HONAN

AUSTRIAN NATIONAL TOURIST OFFICE

MARK HONAN

Top: Taking in the day in Volksgarten
Middle Left: Coffee is synonymous with Vienna, and there are plenty of cafés to choose from
Middle Right: A fiacre meanders through Kohlmarkt
Bottom: A tram on Ringstrasse

GLENN BEANLAND

JON DAVISON

JON DAVISON

GLENN BEANLAND

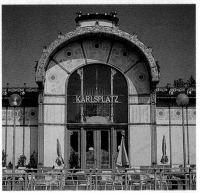

JON DAVISON

Top Left: Naturhistorisches Museum
Top Right: Schloss Schönbrunn
Bottom Left: Athena fountain in front of Parlament
Middle Right: A fiacre driver waits for a client
Bottom Right: Stadt Pavillon, Karlsplatz

AUSTRIAN NATIONAL TOURIST OFFICE

MARK HONAN

TAMSIN WILSON

Left: The giant Risenrad (Ferris wheel) in Volksprater
Top Right: The Lipizzaner horses of the Spanish Riding School
Bottom Right: KunstHausWien, designed by Friedensreich Hundertwasser

scheme was fully realised: a further wing of the Hofburg was planned, and the palace and the giant museums opposite were to be linked by a majestic walkway, rising in arches over the Ringstrasse. Nevertheless, what was achieved is still extremely impressive. To fully appreciate the sheer scale of this endeavour, you should take a tour of at least some of the Ringstrasse by foot. The whole Ring is 4km long, though the grandest section, between the university and the opera, is under 2km. (See the Orientation and Rathaus Park Area walking tours later for sights along this stretch.)

Instead of walking, you can pedal along the bike path on either side of the Ringstrasse, take tram No 1 (clockwise) or No 2 (anticlockwise), drive in a clockwise direction, or even hire a fiacre.

For municipal museums within the Innere Stadt, see the separate heading later in this chapter.

ORIENTATION WALKING TOUR

This walk covers about 2.5km; all the sights are on Map 8.

Kärntner Strasse

From the main tourist office, on Philharmonikerstrasse, walk north up the pedestrian-only Kärntner Strasse, a walkway of plush shops, trees, café tables and street entertainers. The oldest building here is the **Esterházy Palace** at No 41, dating from 1698. It now houses the casino. Detour left down the short Donnergasse to look at the **Donnerbrunnen** (1739) in Neuer Markt. The four naked figures (which were too revealing for Maria Theresa's taste) on this fountain represent the four main tributary rivers to the Danube: the Enns, March, Traun and Ybbs. Across the square is the **Kapuzinerkirche** (Church of the Capuchin Friars) and the **Kaisergruft** (see the Hofburg section later in this chapter for details).

Back on Kärntner Strasse, detour again down the second street on the left, Kärntner Durchgang. Here you'll find the **American Bar** designed by Adolf Loos in 1908. Loos was one of the prime exponents of a func-

tional Art Nouveau style, though the façade here is somewhat garish. Next door is a strip club, **Chez Nous**. The girls who work here may consider themselves artistes, yet in the 1950s it was real artists who undressed here. The premises was the base for the art club of the Wienergruppe (Vienna Group), performance artists and writers who indulged in all sorts of weird and wonderful activities. Events often involved the removal of clothing and the adoption of apparently obscene poses, both of which were guaranteed to enrage the conservative elite of that time. (See Arts in the Facts about Vienna chapter for more information.)

Stephansplatz to Michaelerplatz

From Kärntner Strasse, the street opens out into Stock im Eisen Platz. In the western corner, flush against the building and surrounded by protective perspex, is a nail-studded stump. Nobody quite knows why this 16th century tree trunk acquired its crude metal jacket, but the commonly touted explanation is that each blacksmith who left the city would bang in a nail for luck. Across the square is Stephansplatz and Vienna's prime landmark, **Stephansdom** (see separate heading later). Facing it is the unashamedly modern **Haas Haus**, built by Hans Hollein and opened in 1990. Many Viennese were rather unhappy about this curving silver structure crowding their beloved cathedral, but tourists seem happy enough to snap the spindly reflections of the Stephansdom spire in its rectangular windows.

Leading north-west from Stock im Eisen Platz is the broad pedestrian thoroughfare of **Graben**, another plush shopping street. Like Kärntner Strasse and Stephansplatz, it's a fine place to linger, soak up the atmosphere, and absorb the hubbub of voices and appreciate the musicianship of the buskers. Graben is dominated by the knobbly outline of the **Pestsäule** (Plague Column), completed in 1693 to commemorate the 75,000 or more victims of the Black Plague who perished in Vienna some 20 years earlier. Adolf Loos was also busy in Graben, creating the Schneidersalon Knize at No 10 and, rather appropriately given his surname, the toilets nearby.

Turn left into Kohlmarkt, so named because charcoal was once sold here. At No 14 is one of the most famous of the Konditorei-style cafés in Vienna, **Demel** (see Coffee Houses in the Places to Eat chapter). Just beyond is Michaelerplatz, with the dome of St Michael's Gateway to the **Hofburg** towering above.

The **Loos Haus** on Michaelerplatz (called the Goldman & Salatsch building) is a typical example of the clean lines of Loos' work, and its austere appearance raised eyebrows when it was erected in 1910. It had the opposite effect on Franz Josef's eyebrows, causing him to frown in fury every time he saw it. His complaint? The lintel-less windows seemed to him to be 'windows without eyebrows'. The excavations in the middle of the square are of Roman origin. On the square is **Michaelerkirche**, which betrays five centuries of architectural styles; 1327 (Romanesque chancel) to 1792 (Baroque doorway angels).

Ringstrasse

Pass through St Michael's Gate and the courtyard to find yourself in Heldenplatz, with the vast curve of the new section of the Hofburg (see separate heading later in this chapter) on your left. Walk past the line of fiacres, noting the Gothic spire of **Rathaus** rising above the trees to the right (see the Rathaus Park Area Walking Tour for details). Ahead, on the far side of the Ring, stand the rival identical twins, the **Naturhistorisches Museum** and the **Kunsthistorisches Museum** (see the Museums section later in this chapter). These huge buildings are mirror-images of each other, and were the work of Gottfried Semper and Karl von Hasenauer. Between the museums is a large statue of Maria Theresa, surrounded by key figures of her reign. She sits regally, holding her right hand out, palm upwards, as if in an early version of the 'gimme five' greeting.

Walk anticlockwise round the north side of the Ring and pause for a relaxing meander around the **Burggarten**. This garden was formerly reserved for the pleasure of the imperial family and other high-ranking officials. Statues here include those of Mozart (1896; originally at Albertinaplatz) and of Franz Josef.

Return to the Ring and continue anticlockwise, passing a vast statue of a seated Goethe, until you reach the **Staatsoper** (State Opera). This may appear the equal of any other Ringstrasse edifice, but initial public reaction was so poor Eduard van der Nüll, one of the designers, ended up committing suicide. The building was all but destroyed in WWII and reopened only in 1955. The opulent interior is best explored during the interval of a performance (see the Entertainment chapter), though you can also take a guided tour for AS60 (students AS30, seniors AS45); schedules vary, see the timetable at the window on the Kärntner Strasse side.

Take a left at the near side of the opera to get to **Albertinaplatz**. The south-eastern extremity of the Hofburg is on your left, which usually contains the famous Albertina collection of graphic arts (relocated due to long-term renovations; see separate heading later in the chapter). On the square is a troubling work by Alfred Hrdlicka, created in 1988. This series of pale block-like sculptures commemorates Jews and other victims of war and fascism. The dark, squat shape with the barbed wire is a Jew washing the floor; the greyish block originally came from the Mauthausen concentration camp.

Turn right along Philharmonikerstrasse, passing between the opera and the **Hotel Sacher**, a famous five-star hotel and purveyor of an equally famous cake, the Sacher Torte. Sacher and Demel had a long-running dispute over who was the true creator of the authentic chocolate torte: Sacher was Metternich's cook; while Demel was pastry cook to the Habsburgs. Graham Greene was staying in the Hotel Sacher in 1948 (despite the fact that at the time the hotel was requisitioned solely for the use of British army officers) when he came up with the plot for *The Third Man*.

The Story behind the Story of *The Third Man*

'I had paid my last farewell to Harry a week ago, when his coffin was lowered into the frozen February ground, so that it was with incredulity that I saw him pass by, without a sign of recognition, among the host of strangers in the Strand.' Thus wrote Graham Greene on the back of an envelope. There it stayed, for many years, an idea without a context. Then Sir Alexander Korda asked him to write a film about the four-power occupation of post-war Vienna. The film was to be directed by Carol Reed, who worked with Greene on an earlier film, *The Fallen Idol*.

Greene now had an opening scene and a framework. He still needed a plot. He flew to Vienna in 1948 and roamed the bomb-damaged streets, searching with increasing desperation for inspiration. Nothing came to mind until, with his departure imminent, Greene had lunch with a British intelligence officer. The conversation proved more nourishing than the meal. The officer told him about the underground police who patrolled the huge network of sewers beneath the city. He also waxed on the subject of the black-market trade in penicillin, which the racketeers exploited with no regard for the consequences. Greene put the two ideas together and created his story.

Another chance encounter completed the picture. After filming one night, Carol Reed went drinking in the Heurigen area of Sievering. There he discovered Anton Karas playing a zither and was mesmerised by the hypnotic rhythms the instrument produced. Although Karas could neither read nor write music, Reed flew him to London where he recorded the soundtrack. The bouncing, staggering refrain that became Harry Lime's theme dominated the film, became a chart hit and earned Karas a fortune.

As a final twist of serendipity, the most memorable lines of dialogue came not from the measured pen of Greene, but from the improvising mouth of Orson Welles as Harry Lime. They were delivered in front of the camera in the Prater, under the towering stanchions of the Ferris wheel: 'In Italy for 30 years under the Borgias they had warfare, terror, murder, bloodshed – they produced Michelangelo, Leonardo da Vinci and the Renaissance. In Switzerland they had brotherly love, 500 years of democracy and peace, and what did that produce? The cuckoo clock. So long Holly.'

And in Vienna they had the ideal setting for a classic film. ■

Another few steps will bring you back to Kärntner Strasse, with the tourist office on your left.

RATHAUS PARK AREA – WALKING TOUR

This short walk links several Ringstrasse buildings in the Innere Stadt; all the sights are on Map 8.

Votivkirche

In 1853 Franz Josef survived an assassination attempt when a knife-wielding Hungarian failed to find the emperor's neck through his collar – reports suggested that a metal button deflected the blade. The Votivkirche (Votive Church) was commissioned in thanks at his lucky escape, and is located at 09, Rooseveltplatz. Heinrich von Ferstel designed this twin-towered Gothic construction, which was completed in 1879. The tomb of Count Niklas Salm, one of the architects of the successful defence against the Turks in 1529, is in the Baptismal Chapel. The interior is bedecked in frescoes and bulbous chandeliers. Take note of the interesting stained-glass windows – one to the left of the altar tells of Nazism and the ravages of war. The church is open Tuesday to Saturday from 9 am to 1 pm and 4 to 6.30 pm and Sunday from 9 am to 1 pm.

Rathaus

Walk south past the new university building, constructed in the style of the Italian Renaissance during the Ringstrasse developments. The university itself actually dates from 1365, and the original building still exists at 01, Bäckerstrasse 20.

Next you reach the impressive Rathaus (City Hall), a neo-Gothic structure completed in 1883 and built by Friedrich von Schmidt. The main spire soars to 102m, if you include the pennant held by the knight at the top. It is built around an arcaded courtyard where concerts are sometimes held.

Free guided tours of the building are conducted at 1 pm on Monday, Wednesday and Friday, except when the city council is in session.

Between the Rathaus and the Ring is the Rathaus Park, with fountains, benches and several statues. It is split in two by a wide walkway lined by statues of notable people from Vienna's past.

Burgtheater

The Rathaus Park walkway leads to the Burgtheater (National Theatre), one of the prime theatre venues in the German-speaking world. It was built in Renaissance style to designs by Gottfried Semper and Karl von Hasenauer, and had to be rebuilt after sustaining severe damage in WWII. The interior is equally grand and has stairway frescoes painted by the Klimt brothers, Gustav and Ernst. Guided tours are conducted on Monday, Wednesday and Friday in July and August (the rest of the year on request). The southern side of the building adjoins the Volksgarten.

Churches & Palaces

A short circular detour around the back of the Burgtheater will yield some grand Viennese buildings from an earlier period. Adjoining the Volksgarten is the town palace of the Liechtenstein family. Behind this is the **Minoritenkirche**, a 14th century church that later received a Baroque facelift. Across the square to the south is the **Bundeskanzleramt** (Federal Chancellor's Office), 01, Ballhausplatz 2. It's notable mainly for its historical significance as one of the seats of power since Maria Theresa's time. Prince Metternich had his offices here, and this was where Chancellor Dolfuss was murdered by the Nazis on 25 July 1934.

Take the short Leopold Figl Gasse east, to reach Herrengasse, and then turn left (north). On your right you'll pass **Palais Ferstal**, housing Café Central (see Coffee Houses in the Places to Eat chapter), and the Freyung Passage, an arcade containing elegant shops. On your left, as the road opens out into Freyung, you'll see the classic Baroque façade of **Palais Kinsky**, built by Johann Lukas von Hildebrandt in 1716. Across Freyung is the **Schottenkirche** (Church of the Scots), which had its origins in the 12th century, though the present façade dates from the 19th century. There's an art collection in the adjoining monastery (open Thursday to Sunday; AS50). Turn left down Tienfaltstrasse to return to the Burgtheater.

Volksgarten

The Volksgarten (People's Garden) is attractively laid out, with a riot of rosebushes and several statues (eg to the playwright Franz Grillparzer). There's also the Temple of Theseus, an imitation of the one in Athens. The Volksgarten is open daily from 6 am to 10 pm (8 pm from October to March).

Parlament

The Parlament building is on the opposite side of the Ring to the Volksgarten, and was designed by Theophil Hansen. It has a Greek revival style, with huge pillars and figures lining the roof. The beautiful **Athena Fountain** in the front was sculptured by Karl Kundmann. Grecian architecture was chosen, as Greece was the home of democracy; Athena was the Greek goddess of wisdom. It was hoped that both qualities would be permanent features of Austrian politics.

The Parlament is the seat of the two federal assemblies, the National Council (Bundesrat) and the Federal Council (Nationalrat). Guided tours (except during sessions) are conducted Monday to Friday at 11 am and 3 pm (also at 9 am, 10 am, 1 and 2 pm from mid-July to mid-September).

On its southern side is the German Renaissance Justizpalast (Palace of Justice), home of Austria's Supreme Court.

KARLSPLATZ AREA – WALKING TOUR

This walk takes in both traditional and Art Nouveau architecture; all the sights are on Map 8.

Secession Building

In 1897 the Vienna Secession was formed by 19 progressive artists who had broken away

THINGS TO SEE & DO

from the conservative artistic establishment represented by the Künstlerhaus. Their aim was to present current trends in contemporary art and leave behind the historicism that was then in vogue in Vienna. Among their number were Gustav Klimt, Josef Hoffman, Kolo Moser and Joseph M Olbrich (a former student of Otto Wagner). Olbrich was given the honour of designing the new exhibition centre of the Secessionists. It was erected just a year later at 01, Friedrichstrasse 12, and combined sparse functionality with stylistic motifs.

The building is certainly different from the Ringstrasse architectural throwbacks. Its most striking feature is an enormous golden sphere (a 'golden cabbage head', according to some Viennese) rising from a turret on the roof. Other noteworthy features are the mask-like faces with dangling serpents instead of earlobes that are above the door, the minimalist stone owls gazing down from the walls, and the vast ceramic pots supported by tortoises at the front. The motto above the entrance asserts: *Der Zeit ihre Kunst, der Kunst ihre Freiheit* (To each time its art, to art its freedom).

The 14th exhibition (1902) held in the building featured the famous *Beethoven Frieze* by Klimt. This 34m-long work was only supposed to be a temporary display, little more than an elaborate poster for the main exhibit, Max Klinger's Beethoven monument. Yet it was painstakingly restored and since 1985 has been on display in the basement. The frieze has dense areas of activity punctuated by mostly open spaces, reminiscent of something plastic partially melted and stretched out over a fire. It features willowy women with bounteous hair who jostle for attention with a large gorilla, while slender figures float and a choir sings. Beethoven would no doubt be surprised to learn that it is based on his ninth symphony.

The rest of this so-called 'temple of art' clings true to the original ideal of presenting contemporary art, though it may leave you wondering exactly where the altar is. 'Sometimes people just walk past the art, they think they're in empty rooms,' the lady at the desk

once told us. You have been warned! It's open Tuesday to Friday from 10 am to 6 pm, Saturday and Sunday to 4 pm; entry costs AS60, students AS40. The Secession also has an outside café.

Linke Wienzeile

This runs south-west of the Secession and into the 6th district. Passing the **Theater an der Wien**, you soon get to two Art Nouveau buildings created by Otto Wagner. No 38 features a façade of golden medallions (by Kolo Moser), railings created from metal leaves and a brace of jester figures on the roof who look like they could be shouting abuse at the traditional Viennese buildings nearby. No 40 is known as the **Majolikahaus** (Map 4; 1899) from the majolica tiles Wagner used for the flowing floral motifs on the façade. These buildings overlook the open-air market, the **Naschmarkt**, an interesting place for a wander, especially on Saturday (see Markets in the Shopping chapter).

Treitlstrasse

Returning north-east, turn right from Rechte Wienzeile into Treitlstrasse. On the left is the **Kunsthalle**, a yellow shed that houses contemporary art exhibitions. It looks like a temporary building, but its future is secure till at least 2001; the outside café is a cool place to drink in the summer (open till 2 am).

Across the road, the building with the strange winged cornerpiece (an elongated owl) is the **Technical University Library**. Cross over Wiedner Hauptstrasse for Karlsplatz.

Karlsplatz

Walking north-east across Resselpark, you come to Otto Wagner's **Stadt Pavillons**, station buildings for Vienna's first public transport system, which was built from 1893 to 1902. Wagner was in charge of the overall design for the metro lines, bridges and station buildings. Here he incorporated floral designs and gold trim on a steel and marble structure. When the new U-Bahn transport system was put in place, the west pavilion was used as an exit for the U4 line of the

Karlsplatz station, and now also houses a small municipal museum. The east pavilion is now a café. There is also a municipal museum in Wagner's Stadt Pavillon at Hietzing, near Schönbrunn.

North of the park (east of Akademiestrasse) you can see two traditional Viennese buildings, the white **Künstlerhaus** and the rust-and-white **Musikverein**. Walking southeast through the park, you soon reach Karlskirche, with a Henry Moore sculpture in front, and to the left, the interesting **Historisches Museum der Stadt Wien** (see the separate Municipal Museums section later in this chapter).

Karlskirche
Karlskirche (St Charles' Church) is an imposing creation, built between 1716 and 1739 after a vow by Charles VI at the end of the 1713 plague. It was designed and commenced by Johann Fischer von Erlach and completed by his son, Joseph. Although predominantly Baroque, it combines several architectural styles. The twin columns are modelled on Trajan's Column in Rome, and show scenes from the life of St Charles Borromeo (who helped plague victims in Italy), to whom the church is dedicated. The huge oval dome reaches 72m; the interior of the dome features cloud-bound celestial beings painted by Johann Michael Rottmayr. The altar panel is by Sebastiano Ricci and shows the Assumption of the Virgin.

About 200m north-east of the church is Schwarzenbergplatz. Here is the **Russian Monument**, a reminder that the Russians liberated the city at the end of WWII. It comprises a soldier atop a tall column. In front is a fountain (Hochstrahlbrunnen), and behind stands the Schwarzenberg Palace, co-created by Johann Fischer von Erlach and Johann Lukas von Hildebrandt.

Stadtpark
The Stadtpark (City Park) is about 300m north-east of Schwarzenbergplatz (passing the Konzerthaus on Lothringerstrasse on the way). It was opened in 1862 and is an enjoyable recreation spot for strolling or relaxing

in the sun. It has a pond, winding walkways and several statues. The **Kursalon**, in the south-west corner, hosts waltz concerts in the afternoon and evening from April to 1 November; nearby in the park is the Johann Strauss Denkmal, a golden statue of Johann Strauss under a white arch (this often appears in tourist brochures).

FLEISCHMARKT AREA – WALKING TOUR
The following sights are all within the Ring and can be linked together as a short walking tour, starting in the eastern corner and heading west; all the sights are on Map 8.

Postsparkasse
This celebrated building at Georg Coch Platz, the Post Office Savings Bank, was the work of Otto Wagner between 1904 and 1906 and from 1910 to 1912. The design and choice of materials were both innovative. Inside, note the sci-fi aluminium heating ducts and the naked stanchions – pared down functionality *par excellence*. The main savings hall can be perused during office hours (Monday to Friday from 8 am to 3 pm, Thursday to 5.30 pm), and there is an information counter. Compare the modern appearance of the Postsparkasse with the classical-looking **Kriegsministerium** (Imperial War Ministry) on the Ring opposite, which was built around the same time.

Dominikanerkirche
The Dominikanerkirche (Dominican Church; 1634), Postgasse 4, was built on the site of an earlier church and has a fine Baroque interior, with white stucco, frescoes, and even the imperial double-headed eagle on the ceiling. The Dominicans first came to Vienna in 1226.

Fleischmarkt
This street, formerly a meat market, has a distinctive **Greek Orthodox church** at No 13. Next door is a quaint and famous old tavern, the Griechenbeisl (see the Places to Eat chapter) at No 11. Farther along is a cluster of **Art Nouveau buildings**. No 14,

built by F Dehm and F Olbricht between 1889 and 1899, exhibits gold and stucco embellishments. No 7 (Max Kropf; 1899) now houses an elegant branch of the Julius Meinl supermarket. Arthur Baron was responsible for Nos 1 and 3 (1910), now home to a bank and a Spar supermarket. A few steps to the north of Fleischmarkt is **Ruprechtskirche** (St Rupert's Church), Ruprechtsplatz, the oldest church in Vienna, dating from around the 11th century.

Ankeruhr

The picturesque Art Nouveau Ankeruhr (Anker clock; named after the Anker Insurance Co, who commissioned it) at Hoher Markt 10-11 was created by Franz von Matsch in 1911. Over a 12 hour period, figures slowly pass across the clock face, indicating the time against a static measure showing the minutes. Figures represented range from Marcus Aurelius (the Roman emperor who died in Vienna in 180 AD) to Joseph Haydn, with Eugene of Savoy, Maria Theresa and others in between. Details of who's who are outlined on a plaque on the wall below. Tourists flock here at noon, when all the figures trundle past in succession, and organ music from the appropriate period is piped out.

Peterskirche

Peterskirche (St Peter's Church; 1733), on Petersplatz, is another example of a fine Baroque interior. The fresco in the dome was painted by JM Rottmayr. It is said that Charlemagne founded the first church that stood on this sight, an event depicted in the exterior relief on the south-east side.

Am Hof

The Babenberg rulers of Vienna once had a fortress on this square before moving to the Hofburg, and there are also Roman ruins here. On the north side at No 10 is the former civic armoury (16th century), with an impressively elaborate façade. The Mariensäule column in the centre of the square is dedicated to Mary and was erected in 1667. The **Kirche Am Hof**, on the south-east side, is Baroque, adapted from its fire-damaged Gothic predecessor. Behind the church is Schulhof, where there's the Uhren Museum (see Municipal Museums later in this chapter) and the **Puppen & Spielzeug Museum** (Doll and Toy Museum; AS60; concessions AS30; closed Monday).

Judenplatz

The old Jewish quarter, Judenplatz, is just off the north-east corner of Am Hof. Here you'll find an attractive square and new excavations of an old synagogue (detailed plaques in English). On the north side of Judenplatz is the former Böhmische Hofkanzlei (Bohemian Court Chancery). Walk round to Wipplingerstrasse to see its striking façade by JB Fischer von Erlach; opposite is the plainer **Altes Rathaus**, where there's a museum and a courtyard fountain.

GUIDED WALKING TOURS

Vienna tourist guides conduct around 50 different guided walking tours, covering everything from Art Nouveau to Jewish traditions in Vienna, to palaces and courtyards. The monthly *Walks in Vienna* leaflet from the tourist office details all of these, also giving the various departure points and indicating those conducted in English. Tours last about 1½ hours and cost AS126 (AS63 if aged under 18).

The Third Man Tour, conducted in English by Dr Brigitte Timmermann (☎ 774 89 01), departs at 4 pm, usually on a Friday (except in July and August); the meeting place is the U4 Friedensbrücke exit, and ideally you should bring a torch and a tram ticket. The tour takes in all the main location spots used in the film. That includes the underground sewers, home to 2½ million rats. You'll discover that the sewers are not linked together, so it is impossible to cross the city underground as Harry Lime did in the film. Other places visited include Harry Lime's apartment at Josefsplatz and the doorway on Schrevogelgasse where he was first spotted by Holly Martins.

For information on other organised tours

(by bus, tram and boat), see the Getting Around chapter.

STEPHANSDOM

The latticework spire of this Gothic masterpiece rises high above the city and is a focal point for all visitors.

Stephansdom (St Stephen's Cathedral) was built on the site of a 12th century church, and its remains – the Riesentor (Giant's Gate) and the Heidentürme (Towers of the Heathens) – are incorporated into the present building. Both features are Romanesque in style; the **Riesentor** (so named for the mammoth's tibia, mistaken for a giant's shin, that once hung there) is the main western entrance, and is topped by a tympanum bedecked in statues. The church was recreated in Gothic style at the behest of Habsburg Duke Rudolf IV in 1359, who laid the foundation stone and earned himself the epithet of 'The Founder' in the process.

The dominating feature of the church is

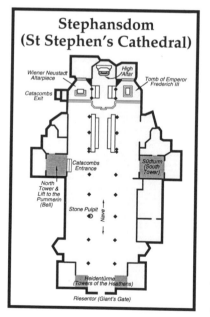

Stephansdom (St Stephen's Cathedral)

Wiener Neustadt Altarpiece · High Altar · Tomb of Emperor Frederich III · Catacombs Exit · Catacombs Entrance · Südturm (South Tower) · North Tower & Lift to the Pummerin (Bell) · Stone Pulpit · Nave · Heidentürme (Towers of the Heathens) · Riesentor (Giant's Gate)

the skeletal **Südturm**, or south tower, nicknamed 'Steffl'. It stands 136.7m high and was completed in 1433 after 75 years of building work. Negotiating the 343 steps will bring you to the viewing platform for an impressive panorama (AS25; open from 9 am to 5.30 pm). It was to be matched by a companion tower on the north side, but the imperial purse withered and the Gothic style went out of fashion, so the half-completed tower was topped off with a Renaissance cupola in 1579. Austria's largest bell, the **Pummerin** ('boomer bell'), was installed here in 1952; it weighs 21 tonnes. Entry to the north tower, accessible by a lift, costs AS40. It's open daily from 8 am to 5 pm; 9 am to 6 pm from 1 April to 30 September.

A striking feature of the exterior is the glorious **tiled roof**, showing dazzling chevrons on one end and the Austrian eagle on the other; a good perspective is gained from the north-east of Stephansplatz. The cathedral suffered severe damage during a fire in 1945, but donations flowed in from all over Austria and the cathedral was completely rebuilt and reopened in just three years.

Interior walls and pillars are decorated with fine statues and side altars. A magnificent Gothic piece is the **stone pulpit**, fashioned in 1515 by Anton Pilgram. The expressive faces of the four fathers of the church (saints Augustine, Ambrose, Gregory and Jerome) are at the centre of the design, yet Pilgram himself can be seen peering out from a window below. The Baroque **high altar** in the main chancel shows the stoning of St Stephen. The left chancel has the winged Wiener Neustadt altarpiece, dating from 1447; the right chancel has the Renaissance red marble tomb of Frederich III. Under his guidance the city became a bishopric (and the church a cathedral) in 1469. Don't forget to study the decorations and statue groups on the outside of the cathedral: at the rear the agony of the Crucifixion is well captured, although some irreverent souls attribute Christ's pained expression to toothache.

The **Katakomben** (catacombs) in the cathedral are open daily, with tours approximately hourly between 10 am and 4.30 pm (AS40; in English if there's sufficient demand). The tour includes viewing a mass grave and a bone house, all that remains of countless plague victims. You also see rows of urns containing the internal organs of the Habsburgs. One of the privileges of being a Habsburg was to be dismembered and dispersed after death: their hearts are in the Augustinerkirche in the Hofburg and the rest of their bits are in the Kaisergruft.

HOFBURG

The huge Hofburg (Imperial Palace) is an impressive repository of culture and heritage. The Habsburgs based themselves here for over six centuries, from the first emperor (Rudolph I in 1279) to the last in 1918 (Charles I). In that time new sections were periodically added, resulting in the current mix of styles and the massive dimensions. The palace now houses the offices of the Austrian president. The Spanish Riding School (see the Entertainment chapter) is also based in the Hofburg.

The oldest part is the **Schweizerhof** (Swiss Courtyard), named after the Swiss guards who used to protect its precincts.

Dating from the 13th century and recently renovated, this small courtyard gives access to the Royal Chapel and the Imperial Treasury. The Renaissance Swiss Gate dates from 1553. It adjoins a much larger courtyard, **In der Burg**, with a large monument to Emperor Franz II at its centre. The buildings around it are all from different eras.

The most active phase of building was carried out from the second half of the 19th century to WWI. Sections created at this time include the impressive St Michael's domed entrance and the Neue Burg, from which Hitler addressed a rally during his triumphant 1938 visit to Vienna after the Anschluss. Plans called for the building of a further wing, the mirror image of this curving façade on Heldenplatz, but the Habsburg era ended before it could be instigated.

Augustinerkirche

The Augustinerkirche (Augustinian Church) is one of the older parts of the Hofburg, dating from the early 14th century. Although Gothic in style, the interior was converted to Baroque in the 17th century, before its original appearance was restored in 1784. Important tombs include that of Archduchess

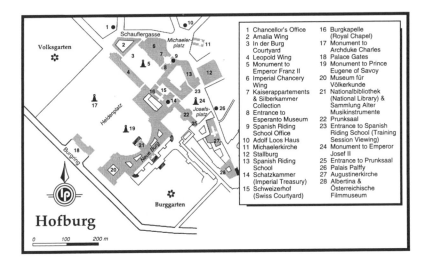

Hofburg

Marie Christina, designed by Canova. In an inner sanctum are the hearts of the Habsburgs, but the room can only be viewed by prior appointment (☎ 533 70 99; not Sunday).

Kaiserappartements

The rooms in the Kaiserappartements (Imperial Apartments) are as opulent as you might expect, with fine furniture, hanging tapestries and bulbous crystal chandeliers. The dining room has a table for 20 laid out in suitably elegant fashion. Rooms in this part of the palace were occupied by Franz Josef I and Empress Elisabeth. Access is by guided tours that are only in German, so you'd probably get more out of a visit to the Schönbrunn Palace's interior finery if your appetite for such things is limited. The tours last 45 minutes and take in 21 rooms.

If royal kitchenware interests you, look to the adjoining Silberkammer collection. Laying a table with some of this silver and porcelain would certainly impress the in-laws; the largest silver service here can take care of 140 dinner guests. A visit to each collection costs AS70 (AS50 for students aged under 26, ISIC card needed; AS35 for children) and opening times are Monday to Saturday from 8.30 am to noon and 12.30 to 4 pm, Sunday and holidays from 8.30 am to 12.30 pm. A combined ticket is AS90 (AS60 students; AS45 children).

Burgkapelle

This Gothic Burgkapelle (Royal Chapel) is where the Vienna Boy's Choir sings at Sunday Mass (see the Entertainment chapter). It has a vaulted roof and rich fittings around the altar, but is not particularly spectacular without the choir. It's open from Tuesday to Friday from 11 am to 1 pm, except July to mid-September (AS15).

Schatzkammer

The Schatzkammer (Imperial Treasury) contains secular and ecclesiastical treasures of great value and splendour. The entry price of AS60 (students and seniors AS50) includes a room-by-room written guide (in English)

and use of a hi-tech personal electronic guide (also in English). Allow anything from 30 minutes to two hours to get around; it's open daily (except Tuesday) from 10 am to 6 pm.

The sheer wealth exhibited in the crown jewels is staggering: Room 7 has a 2860 carat Colombian emerald, a 416 carat balas ruby and a 492 carat aquamarine. The imperial crown (Room 2) dates from the 10th century, and has eight gold plates; precious gems alternate with enamel plaques showing religious scenes. The private crown of Rudolf II (1602) is a more delicate piece, with gems interspersed by four beautifully engraved bas-reliefs in embossed gold. The reliefs show Rudolf in battle and at three of his coronations. Room 5 contains mementoes of Marie Louise, who married Napoleon; the best piece here is the cradle donated by the city of Paris to their son. The golden bees around the sides are a standard motif of Napoleonic state artefacts. Room 8 has two unusual objects formerly owned by Ferdinand I: a 75cm-wide bowl carved from a single piece of agate, and a narwal tusk (243cm long), once claimed to have been a unicorn horn.

The religious relics include fragments of the True Cross, one of the nails from the Crucifixion, and one of the thorns from Christ's crown. Ecclesiastical vestments display delicate and skilled work.

This section also contains some rather more worldly artefacts, like the extremely elaborate Column of the Virgin Mary made from gilded silver, which stands over a metre tall and is encased with 3700 precious stones – a modest conversation piece fit for any mantelpiece.

Prunksaal

This is a Baroque hall of the national library (entrance at Josefsplatz) created by Johann Fischer von Erlach and his son Joseph between 1723 and 1726. It was commissioned by Charles VI; his statue stands under the central church-like dome, which itself has a fresco depicting the emperor's apotheosis (by Daniel Gran). Leather-bound scholarly tomes line the walls, and the upper storey of shelves is flanked by an elegantly curving wood balcony. Rare ancient volumes (mostly 15th century) are stored within glass cabinets, with pages opened to beautifully drawn sections of text. The hall is open Monday to Saturday from 10 am to 4 pm, Sunday and holidays to 1 pm. Entry is AS60, or AS48 for students and senior citizens. The Esperanto Museum for artificial languages is also part of the library (entrance in St Michael's Gate; free).

Sammlung Alter Musikinstrumente

The Sammlung Alter Musikinstrumente (Collection of Old Musical Instruments) is the best part of the three-museums-in-one in the Neue Hofburg. Before you enter the first room, pick up the headphones (free) from the desk. They're activated by infrared as you walk round, giving a relaxing and evocative musical accompaniment to the instruments on display. Instruments of all shapes and sizes are to be found, including horns shaped like serpents, a mini-keyboard disguised as a book, and violins with carved faces. There are some richly ornate pieces, such as the Baroque cabinet incorporating a keyboard from the early 17th century (in Saal XII). Different rooms are dedicated to different composers (eg Haydn, Mozart and Beethoven), and contain instruments played by those notables.

Opening times are Wednesday to Monday from 10 am to 6 pm and admission costs AS30 (children and seniors AS15). This includes entry to two adjoining collections. The **Ephesus Museum** has relief statues and a scale model of the famous archaeological site in Turkey. The **Waffen und Rüstungen** (arms and armour) collection dates mostly from the 15th and 16th centuries and has some fine examples of ancient armour; note the bizarre pumpkin-shaped helmet from the 15th century.

Museum für Völkerkunde

The Museum für Völkerkunde (Ethnological Museum) expounds on non-European cultures, usually with the aid of temporary exhibitions. Its Mexican pre-Colombian

exhibits are important. Admission costs from AS50 (students and seniors AS25) depending upon exhibitions, and it's open Wednesday to Monday from 10 am to 4 pm.

Kaisergruft

Although not part of the Hofburg complex, it's where its residents ended up. The Kaisergruft (Imperial Burial Vault), opened in 1633, is beneath the Kapuzinerkirche (Church of the Capuchin Friars) on Neuer Markt. It was instigated by Empress Anna (1557-1619), and her body and that of her husband, Emperor Matthias (1557-1619), were the first to be placed here. Since then, all but three of the Habsburg dynasty found their way here, the last being Empress Zita in 1989.

It's interesting to observe how fashions change through the ages even in death; tombs range from the unadorned to the ostentatious. By far the most elaborate caskets are those portraying 18th century Baroque pomp, such as the huge double sarcophagus containing Maria Theresa and Francis I, with fine scenes engraved in the metal and plenty of angels and other ornamentation. The tomb of Charles VI is also striking and has been expertly restored. Both of these were the work of Balthasar Moll.

The only non-Habsburg of the 138 people here is the Countess Fuchs, a formative influence on the youthful Maria Theresa. The vault is open daily from 9.30 am to 4 pm and entry costs AS40 (students and seniors AS30).

KUNSTHISTORISCHES MUSEUM

The Kunsthistorisches Museum (Map 8; Museum of Fine Arts) is one of the finest museums in Europe and should not be missed. The Habsburgs were great collectors, and the huge extent of lands under their control led to many important works of art being funnelled back to Vienna.

Rubens was appointed to the service of a Habsburg governor in Brussels, so it is not surprising that the museum has one of the best collections of his works in the world. The collection of paintings by Peter

Brueghel the Elder is also unrivalled. The building itself is delightful and was designed to reflect the works it displays, with older architectural styles faithfully reproduced. No expense was spared in construction and all the marble here is genuine. Ceilings are superbly decorated with murals and stucco embellishments.

The stairway to the 1st floor has Canova's sculpture *Theseus & the Minotaur* halfway up. On the walls above the arches are the portraits of some of the more important artists exhibited in the museum, such as Dürer, Rembrandt and Rafael. The murals between the arches were done by three artists, including a young Gustav Klimt (north wall), painted before he broke with classical tradition.

It's impossible to see the whole museum in one visit, so concentrate on specific areas, but note that the coin collection is closed for renovations until about 1999. Temporary exhibitions sometimes cause reorganisation of rooms, and famous works are occasionally lent to other museums. Various guides and plans are for sale in the shops: a simple guide to the layout of the museum costs AS5 and a guide to '21 Masterpieces' is AS20. Guided tours in English depart at 3 pm (AS30) and provide an interesting analysis of a handful of the main works. The museum is open Tuesday to Sunday from 10 am to 6 pm, with the picture gallery closing at 9 pm on Thursday. Entry to the museum is AS45 (AS30 for students and seniors), or AS95 (AS60) if there's a special exhibition.

Ground Floor

To the right (the west wing) upon entering is the Egyptian collection, including the burial chamber of Prince Kaninisut. Amid the many sarcophagi and statues in this section are the mummified remains of various animals (falcon, baboon, cat etc).

Next come the Greek and Roman collections, including sculptures, urns, vases and Etruscan art. One of the most impressive pieces is the *Gemma Augustea cameo* (Saal XV); made from onyx in 10 AD, delicate white figures have been carved on a bluish-brown background.

The east wing contains a collection of sculpture and decorative arts, covering Austrian high Baroque, Renaissance and mannerist styles, and medieval art. There's some exquisite 17th century glassware and ornaments, and the unbelievably lavish clocks from the 16th and 17th centuries (Saals XXXV and XXXVII) are worth admiring. But the prime item here (Saal XXVII) is the salt cellar (1543) by Benvenuto Cellini, made in gold for Francis I of France. It depicts two naked deities: the goddess of the earth, reclining on elephants, with a small temple by her side where the pepper was kept, and Poseidon, god of the sea, making himself comfortable on a team of sea horses with the salt in a bowl by his trident. Hidden beneath the base are small wheels, so the cellar could be pushed easily around the table. This beautiful work of art begs an envious question: if the humble cruet set looked as good as this, what could the rest of the dining room have looked like?

First Floor

The Gemäldegalerie (picture gallery) on this floor is the most important part of the museum; you could lose yourself for hours wandering round whole rooms devoted to works by Brueghel, Dürer, Rubens, Rembrandt, Van Dyck, Cranach, Caravaggio, Canaletto, Titian and many others. Some rooms have information cards in English giving a critique of particular artists and their work.

East Wing This is devoted to German, Dutch and Flemish paintings. Saal X contains the Brueghel collection, amassed by Rudolf II. A familiar theme in Peter Brueghel the Elder's work is nature, as in his cycle of seasonal scenes, three of which are shown here. *The Hunters in the Snow* (1565) portrays winter; the hunters return towards a Dutch-like frozen lake with frolicking skaters, beyond which rise some very unDutch-looking mountains. The viewer's eye is drawn into the scene by the flow of movement – a device commonly exploited by Brueghel. This is also seen in the atmospheric *The Return of the Herd* (1565), illustrating a glowering autumnal day. Brueghel's peasant scenes are also excellent, such as *The Battle Between Carnival & Lent* (1590), where the centre and foreground are dominated by carnival tomfoolery, with the dour, cowled and caped figures in religious processions pushed to the edges of the scene.

The next gallery (Saal XI), shows Flemish Baroque, in vogue some 80 years later, with warm, larger than life scenes such as *The Feast of the Bean King* by Jacob Jordaens (with the revellers raising their glasses to a motto in Latin that translates as 'None resembles a fool more than the drunkard') and *The Fishmarket* by Frans Snyders.

Albrecht Dürer (1471-1528) is represented in Room 16. His brilliant use of colour is particularly shown in *The Holy Trinity Surrounded by All Saints*, originally an altarpiece. The *Martyrdom of 10,000 Christians* is another fine work.

The paintings by the mannerist Giuseppe Archimboldo in Room 19 use a device well explored by Salvador Dali – familiar objects arranged to appear as something else. The difference being that Archimboldo did it nearly 400 years earlier! His series of four composite pictures *Summer, Winter, Water* and *Fire* (1563-66) cleverly show faces composed of objects related to those particular themes.

Peter Paul Rubens (1577-1640) was a very influential figure because of his synthesis of northern and Italian traditions. His works can be seen in Saals XIII and XIV and in Room 20. Try to spot the difference between those he painted completely himself (eg note the open brushwork and diaphanous quality of the fur in *Indefonso Altar)* and those that he planned and finished but were mostly executed by his students (like the vivid but more rigid *Miracle of Ignatius Loyola*, a dramatic Baroque picture displayed along with Rubens' initial study for the scene).

Rembrandt has several self-portraits in Saal XV. Vermeer's *The Allegory of Painting* (1665-66) is in Room 24. It's a strangely static scene of an artist in his studio, but one that transcends the mundane by its composition and use of light.

West Wing Saal I has some evocative works by Titian, of the Venetian school. He uses colour and broad brushstrokes to create character and mood, rather than distinct outlines. In Room 2 is *The Three Philosophers* (1508), one of the few authenticated works by Giorgione.

In Room 4 is Rafael's harmonious and idealised portrait, *Madonna in the Meadow* (1505). The triangular composition and the complementary colours are typical features of the Florentine high Renaissance. Compare this to Caravaggio's *Madonna of the Rosary* (1606) in Saal V, an example of new realism in early Baroque; note the dirty soles on the feet of the supplicants. Caravaggio emphasises movement in this picture by a subtle deployment of light and shadow.

Susanna at her Bath (1555) by Tintoretto can be found in Saal III. It recreates the Old Testament tale of Susanna being surprised at her ablutions by two old men. The picture successfully portrays both serenity and implicit menace. Tintoretto employs mannerist devices (contrasting light, extremes of facial features) to achieve his effect.

Saal VII has paintings by Bernado Bellotto (1721-80), Canaletto's nephew. He was commissioned by Maria Theresa to paint scenes of Vienna, and several are shown here. Note the way landmarks are sometimes compressed to create a more satisfying composition; the view from the Belvedere is not a faithful reproduction. The pastoral view of Schönbrunn is in stark contrast to its urban situation today.

Room 10 has portraits of the Habsburgs. Juan Carreño's portrait of Charles II of Spain really shows the characteristic Habsburg features: a distended lower lip and jaw and a nose that better belongs in an aviary. Most of the young women in Diego Velázquez's royal portraits are wearing dresses broad enough to fit around a horse, but the artist still manages to make the subjects come to life.

NATURHISTORISCHES MUSEUM

The Naturhistorisches Museum (Map 8; Museum of Natural History) is the scientific counterpart of the Kunsthistorisches Museum (Museum of Fine Arts). The building is as grand but the exhibits aren't quite in the same league. There are still plenty of interesting things to see, though, particularly along the lines of minerals, meteorites and assorted animal remains in jars. Zoology and anthropology are covered in detail and there's a children's corner. A replica of the 25,000-year-old statuette of Willendorf is here (see the Danube Valley in the Excursions chapter), and there are some good dinosaur exhibits. The museum also puts on special exhibitions. Opening hours are Wednesday to Monday from 9 am to 6 pm. In winter it's only open to 3 pm and the geological and palaeontological collections are closed. Admission usually costs AS30 (students AS15).

MUSEUM FÜR ANGEWANDTE KUNST

The Museum für angewandte Kunst (Map 8; MAK; Museum of Applied Arts), 01, Stubenring 5, provides a large amount of display space for its permanent collection and temporary exhibitions, as well as having a popular café and a garden. The 1871 high Renaissance-style building offers some fine features in its own right, especially the ceilings. There are two main parts to the permanent collection: the exhibition rooms and the Study Collection.

Each of the **exhibition rooms** is devoted to a different style, eg Renaissance, Baroque, orient, historicism, empire, Art Deco, and the distinctive metalwork of the Wiener Werkstätte. Rooms are presented in an interesting way: the layout of each was the responsibility of a specific artist, and their reason for displaying the exhibits in a particular manner are explained; their justifications are sometimes pretentious but invariably illuminating. In the Biedermeier room, Jenny Holzer placed electronic signs near the ceiling so 'they can be ignored'; the aluminium sofa here is fun. A famous room is Barbara Bloom's display of Art Nouveau chairs; they're all back-lit and presented behind translucent white screens. There's a Klimt frieze upstairs, and some interesting pieces in the 20th century Design & Architecture room (like Frank Gehry's cardboard chair). Objects exhibited in these rooms encompass tapestries, lace, furniture, glassware and ornaments.

In the basement is the **Study Collection**, which groups exhibits according to the type of materials used: glass and ceramics, metal, wood and textiles. Actual objects range from ancient oriental statues to modern sofas. There are some particularly good porcelain and glassware pieces, with casts showing how they're put together.

MAK (☎ 711 36) is open daily except Monday from 10 am to 6 pm (9 pm Thursday). Admission costs AS90 (AS30 if no special exhibitions) for adults, AS45 (AS15) for students and senior citizens, or AS150 (AS50) for a family ticket. Entry is free on 14 April, 26 October and 4 November.

AKADEMIE DER BILDENDEN KÜNSTE

The Akademie der Bildenden Künste (Map 8; Academy of Fine Arts), 01, Schillerplatz 3, has a smallish picture gallery, which is open Tuesday, Thursday and Friday from 10 am to 2 pm, Wednesday from 10 am to 1 pm and 3 to 6 pm, and weekends from 9 am to 1 pm. Hieronymus Bosch's impressive *The Last Judgement* altarpiece is here, as well as works by Guardi (scenes of 18th century Venice), Cranach the Elder, Titian and Rembrandt. Flemish painters are well represented, particularly Rubens. Van Dyck and Jordaens also get a look-in. Admission costs AS30 (concession AS15). The building itself has an attractive façade and was designed by Theophil Hansen. It was this academy that turned down would-be artist Adolf Hitler, forcing him to find a new career. In front there's a statue of Schiller.

JÜDISHES MUSEUM

The newly refurbished Jüdishes Museum (Map 8; Jewish Museum) at 01, Dorotheergasse 11 documents the history of the Jews in Vienna, from the first settlements at

Hitler's Vienna

Born in Braunau am Inn, Upper Austria, in 1899, Adolf Hitler moved to Vienna when he was just 17. Six unsettled, unsuccessful, poverty-stricken years later he abandoned the city to make a name for himself in Germany. He later wrote in *Mein Kampf* that his Vienna years were 'a time of the greatest transformation which I have ever been through. From a weak citizen of the world I became a fanatical anti-Semite.' Hitler briefly returned in 1938 at the head of the German army, to be greeted by enthusiastic crowds.

Although Vienna would be happy for the world to forget about its association with Hitler, an increasing number of tourists are retracing the Vienna footsteps of the infamous fascist. He spent

several years living in a small, dimly lit apartment at Stumpergasse 31, in the 6th district. It's a private block, but frequent visits by curious tourists have prompted plans to turn the apartment into a museum.

Hitler was a regular visitor to the opera, and despite his penury, preferred to pay extra to stand in sections that were barred to women. Café Sperl (see coffee houses in the Places to Eat chapter) is another address on the Hitler itinerary: here he would noisily express his views on race and other matters. Among his gripes was probably the nearby Akademie der Bildenden Künste (Academy of Fine Arts), which twice rejected an application by the would-be artist, dismissing his work as 'inadequate'. Although convinced that proper training would have made him into a very successful artist, these rejections made Hitler write to a friend that perhaps fate may have reserved for him 'some other purpose'. ∎

Judenplatz in the 13th century up to the present. Relations between the Jews and the Viennese have not always been tranquil. Jews were first expelled in 1420 (the 300 who remained were burned to death in 1421) and again in 1670. The darkest chapter in the story came with the arrival of the Nazis in 1938 and the consequent curtailment of Jewish civil rights and persecution. Violence exploded on the night of 9 November 1938, known as the *Reichskristallnacht*. All the synagogues except the Stadttempel (01, Seitenstettengasse 4) were destroyed, and 7000 Jews were arrested and sent to concentration camps. Jews in Vienna now number 12,000, compared to 185,000 before 1938. The museum is open daily, except Saturday, from 10 am to 6 pm (9 pm Thursday) and entry costs AS70 (AS40 concessions).

ALBERTINA

The Albertina is a famous and extensive collection of graphic arts, comprising some 40,000 drawings. Only part of the collection is ever on display at one time. Its premises in the Hofburg are being renovated (or will be, once the money is found). In the meantime, the Albertina is putting on a series of temporary exhibitions at the **Akademiehof**, 01, Markatgasse 3; this is expected to continue into the 21st century. Opening times are Tuesday to Friday from 10 am to 6 pm and weekends from 10 am to 4 pm; admission costs AS45 (concessions AS20).

LIPIZZANER MUSEUM

This new museum at 01, Reitschulestrasse 2 will show you everything you might want to know about Lipizzaner stallions and the antics they get up to in the Spanish Riding School. It includes special display windows directly overlooking the stallion stables. Entry costs AS50 (AS35 concessions) and it's open daily from 9 am to 6 pm.

Other Districts

SCHLOSS BELVEDERE

This splendid Baroque palace (Map 7) was built for Prince Eugene of Savoy, conqueror of the Turks in 1718 and hero of many other conflicts. It was designed by Johann Lukas von Hildebrandt. The Unteres (Lower) Belvedere was built first (1714-16), with an Orangery attached, and was the prince's summer residence. Connected to it by a long, landscaped garden is the Oberes (Upper) Belvedere (1721-23), the venue for the prince's banquets and other festivities.

Considered together, the Belvedere residences were at the time almost more magnificent than the imperial residence, the Hofburg. This was something of an irritation to the Habsburgs, especially as the prince was able to look down onto the city from the elevated vantage point of the Oberes Belvedere. It was therefore with some satisfaction that Maria Theresa was able to purchase the Belvedere after the prince's death. It then became a Habsburg residence, most recently occupied by the Archduke Franz Ferdinand who started a court there to rival his uncle's (Franz Josef) in the Hofburg. Ferdinand was assassinated in 1914, an event that sparked off WWI.

The Belvedere is now home to the **Österreische Galerie** (Austrian Gallery); the Baroque section is in the Unteres Belvedere (entrance via 04, Rennweg 6A; take tram No 71) and 19th and 20th century art is in the Oberes Belvedere (entrance via 04, Prinz Eugen Strasse 27; take tram D). Opening hours are Tuesday to Sunday from 10 am to 5 pm; entry for both is AS60, or AS30 for students and senior citizens. You don't have to visit both parts on the same day, and the

---

Prince Eugene

One of Austria's greatest military heroes wasn't even a native of the country. Prince Eugene of Savoy (1663-1736) was born in Paris. After being informed he was too short to be accepted into the French army he left France in 1683 to join the Habsburg forces. Eugene was just in time to help beat off the Turkish forces besieging Vienna. He was given his own regiment and within 10 years was promoted to field marshal. His skills as a military strategist were evident in his victories against the Turks at Zenta in 1697, and during the campaign in the Balkans from 1714 to 1718, which finally succeeded in driving the Turks out of all but a small corner of Europe. His capture of the fortress at Belgrade in 1718 was instrumental in concluding that war. Prince Eugene's skills as a statesman were also employed in the War of the Spanish Succession, where he negotiated with his former homeland. ■

---

ticket is also good for entry to the Gustinus Ambrosi Museum at 02, Scherzergasse 1A.

Oberes Belvedere

This houses the most important collection. You can rent headphones and a two hour commentary in English for AS40. The Baroque interior provides a diverting setting for the drift into modern art. An elaborate fresco depicts the apotheosis of Prince Eugene, and there are Herculean figures supporting columns in the entrance lobby.

The 1st floor has turn-of-the-century paintings, particularly the work of Hans Makart (1840-84) and Anton Romako (1832-89), who both influenced the later Viennese Art Nouveau artists. But the 20th century section of this floor has the gallery's best exhibits. Gustav Klimt (1862-1918) was one of the founders of the Secessionist Art Nouveau school. His later pictures (such as the two portraits of Adele Bloch-Bauer) employ a harmonious but ostentatious use of background colour (much metallic gold and silver) to evoke or symbolise the emotions of the main figures. One of the best known but also one of the most intriguing works here is Klimt's *The Kiss* (1908). It shows a couple

ALL PHOTOS BY MARK HONAN

A	
B	D
C	
E	

A: Majolica House, by Otto Wagner
B: Detail on the Secession Building
C: Schloss Schönbrunn
D: The gardens of Schloss Belvedere
E: Statuary on Kaiserappartements, Hofburg

GLENN BEANLAND

GLENN BEANLAND

JON DAVISON

AUSTRIAN NATIONAL TOURIST OFFICE (WIESENHOFER)

Top Left: The intricate glazed tiled roof of the Stephansdom
Top Right: Statue of Archduke Karl in Heldenplatz, Hofburg
Bottom Left: The twin columns and dome of Karlskirche
Bottom Right: Hundertwasserhaus

embracing within what looks like a yellow overcoat, surrounded by the usual Klimt circles and rectangles. The man's neck is twisted unnaturally as he strains towards her; her face is half turned away and enclosed within his hands. Nobody knows quite how to interpret this scene: is she demurely and willingly proffering her cheek, or is she trying to avoid his advances? Some of Klimt's impressionist landscapes are also on display.

Egon Schiele (1890-1918) produced intense, melancholic work. See the hypnotic and bulging eyes on the portrait of his friend, *Eduard Kosmack* (1910). Schiele's bold, brooding colours and unforgiving outlines are in complete contrast to Klimt's golden tapestries and idealised forms. He lived with one of Klimt's models for a while – Schiele's portraits of her were very explicit, bordering on the pornographic. Critics are fond of trying to explain his obsessions with sex and desperate subjects by looking at Schiele's upbringing: his father went insane from syphilis and destroyed the family's stocks and bonds in a fire. Schiele's last work is *The Family*. He added the child between the woman's legs when he found out his own wife was pregnant; however, she died of Egyptian flu before the child was born. Schiele died of the same illness before this painting was completely finished (look closely and you'll see the imprecision of the male's left hand).

Other artists represented include Herbert Boeckl, Anton Hanak, Arnulf Rainer and Fritz Wotruba. There are several examples of the output of the influential expressionist, Oskar Kokoschka (1886-1980). The gallery also has some exhibits from non-Austrian artists such as Munch, Monet, Van Gogh, Renoir and Cézanne.

The top (2nd) floor has a display of 19th century paintings from the Romantic, classical and Biedermeier periods, which was only recently opened (1997). In particular, this section has work by the Biedermeier painter Georg Waldmüller, showing to very good effect his very precise portraits and rural scenes.

Unteres Belvedere

The Baroque section offers some good statuary, such as the originals from Donner's Neuer Markt fountain, and especially the apotheosis of Prince Eugene. Eugene was presumably suffering delusions of grandeur by this time, for he commissioned the latter work himself; the artist, not to be outdone, depicted himself at the prince's feet. Paintings include those of Maria Theresa and her husband, François of Lorraine. A room is devoted to the vibrant paintings by Franz Anton Maulbertsch (1724-96).

The **Orangery** has the collection of Austrian Medieval Art. This comprises religious scenes, altarpieces and statues. There are several impressive works by Michael Pacher (1440-98), a Tirolean artist who was influenced by both early Low-Countries art and the early Renaissance of northern Italy.

Gardens

The long garden between the two Belvederes was laid out in classical French style and has sphinxes and other mythical beasts along its borders. South of the Oberes Belvedere is a small **Alpine Garden**, which has 3500 plant species and a bonsai section. It's open daily during the flowering season (April to July) from 10 am (9 am weekends) and entry costs AS35 or AS20 for students under age 27. Running north from here is the much larger **Botanic Gardens** belonging to the Vienna University. These are open daily from April to October from 9 am to one hour before dusk and admission is free.

SCHLOSS SCHÖNBRUNN

It may not look a modest dwelling, but this Baroque palace (Map 6) is a much diminished version of the grandiose imperial centrepiece that was first planned. The name comes from the beautiful fountain (Schöner Brunnen) built around a spring that Emperor Matthias (1557-1619) found while hunting. A pleasure palace was built here by Ferdinand II in 1637, but this was razed by the Turks in 1683. Soon after, Leopold I commissioned Johann Fischer von Erlach to build a more luxurious summer palace.

Fischer von Erlach came up with hugely ambitious plans to site a palace to dwarf Versailles on the hill where the Gloriette Monument now stands. However, the imperial purse felt unworthy of the venture and a 'less elaborate' building was constructed. It was finished in 1700.

Maria Theresa, upon her accession to the throne in 1740, chose Schönbrunn as the base for her family and her court. The young architect Nikolaus Pacassi was commissioned to renovate and extend the palace to meet the new requirements. Work was carried out from 1744 to 1749. The interior was fitted out in rococo style, and the palace then had some 2000 rooms, as well as a chapel and a theatre. Like all the imperial buildings associated with Maria Theresa, the exterior was painted a rich yellow, her favourite colour.

Napoleon lived in the palace in 1805 and 1809. In 1918 the last Habsburg emperor, Charles I, abdicated in the Blue Chinese Salon, after which the palace became the property of the new republic. Bomb damage was suffered during WWII, and restoration was completed in 1955. In 1992 the palace administration was transferred to private hands, which caused an immediate change in policy. Admission prices jumped and renovations commenced, and ways of presenting Schönbrunn in a more commercial manner were explored. It's one of Vienna's most popular attractions: annually, 1.3 million people tour the palace and a further 5.2 million visit the various attractions in the grounds.

The palace can be reached by the U4 line; 'Schönbrunn' is the closest stop, though 'Hietzing' is better for the zoo and the western part of the gardens. There are restaurants and snack bars within the complex.

The Palace

The interior can be visited daily. Opening times are 8.30 am to 5 pm (4.30 pm from 1 November to 31 March). There are two self-guided tours, each including a personal audio guide in English. The Imperial Tour gives access to 22 rooms for AS90 (students

under 26 AS80, children A45); allow 45-60 minutes. The Grand Tour includes 40 rooms and costs AS120 (students AS105, children AS60); allow up to 1½ hours. Tickets are stamped with a departure time, and there may be time-lag before you're allowed to set off in summer, so buy your ticket straight away and then explore the gardens. On the Grand Tour you have the option of paying an extra AS25 for an English-speaking guide, but you have to hurry to the guide's schedule. Special guided tours are available for children on weekends and holidays (in German).

The interior of the palace is suitably majestic with frescoed ceilings, crystal chandeliers and gilded ornaments. However, the endless stucco and gold twirls can seem overdone at times. Franz Josef evidently thought so too, for he had the rococo excesses stripped from his personal bedchamber in 1854.

The pinnacle of finery is reached in the **Great Gallery**. Gilded scrolls, ceiling frescoes, chandeliers and huge crystal mirrors create the effect. Numerous sumptuous balls were held here, including one for the delegates at the Congress of Vienna (1814-15).

The **Mirror Room** is where Mozart (then six) played his first royal concert (1762) in the presence of Maria Theresa and the royal family. His father revealed in a letter that afterwards young Wolfgang leapt onto the lap of the empress and kissed her. The **Round Chinese Room** is over-the-top but rather ingenious too. Maria Theresa held secret consultations here: a secret doorway led to her adviser's apartments and a fully laden table could be drawn up through the floor so the dignitaries could dine without being disturbed by servants.

The **Million Gulden Room** is so called because that's the sum that Maria Theresa paid for the decorations, comprising Persian miniatures set on rosewood panels and framed with gilded rocaille frames. The **Gobelin Salon** is named after its 17th century Gobelin tapestries. An unusual item in the **Napoleon Room** is a stuffed crested lark, the favourite childhood bird of Napoleon's son, who died in this room.

The Porcelain Room and the Miniatures Room both display drawings by members of the imperial family. In the Breakfast Room the walls are decorated with embroideries made by Maria Theresa and her daughters.

The **Bergl Rooms** are not part of the guided tours and can only be visited by appointment (☎ 811 13-239). They were painted by Johann Wenzl Bergl (1718-89); his exotic depictions of flora and fauna attempt to bring the ambience of the gardens inside.

Wagenburg

This is the Imperial Coach Collection of the Kunsthistorisches Museum, situated across the courtyard to the west of the palace. The horse-drawn carriages on display range from tiny children's wagons to great vehicles of state. The most ornate is the imperial coach of the court, built for Maria Theresa around 1765. It's extreme Baroque on wheels, with fussy gold ornamentation and painted cherubs. Allow around 30 minutes to look round; it's open daily from 9 am to 6 pm, but closes at 4 pm on Monday from 1 November to 31 March (AS30, students and senior citizens AS15).

Gardens

The beautifully tended formal gardens, arranged in the French style, are a symphony of colour in the summer. The extensive grounds have many attractions hidden away in the tree-lined avenues, arranged according to a grid and star-shaped system between 1750 and 1755. From 1772 to 1780 Ferdinand Hetzendorf added the Roman Ruins (now the site of summer concerts), the Neptune Fountain (a riotous ensemble from Greek mythology), and the crowning glory, the **Gloriette Monument**, standing tall on the hill overlooking the gardens. The view from up here, looking back towards the palace with Vienna shimmering in the distance, is excellent. It's possible to go on the roof of the Gloriette (entry AS20; May to October only), but the view is only marginally superior. The palace grounds are open from 6 am until sunset.

On the west side of the grounds are the **Palmenhaus** (Palm House) and the **Schmetterlinghaus** (Butterfly House). Entry for either costs AS45 (AS30 for students under 28) or it's AS75 (AS45) for a combined ticket. The butterfly house is the more interesting, with many butterflies fluttering about, or coming to rest on the fake flowers that have been sprayed with honey.

The attractively laid-out **Tiergarten** (zoo) is the oldest zoo in the world, dating from 1752. The once-cramped animal cages have now (mostly) been improved. Walkways radiate out from a central pavilion, painted in Maria Theresa-yellow. Admission costs AS90 (AS70 seniors, AS40 for students under 28, AS25 children). Opening times are 9 am to 4.30 pm (November to January), to 5 pm (February and October), 5.30 pm (March), 6 pm (April) and 6.30 pm (May to September). Feeding times vary for the different animals; sea lions dine at 10.30 am and 3.30 pm, 'land' lions have to wait until one hour before closing time.

VOLKSPRATER

This large amusement park (Map 5), also known as the Wurstelprater, is dominated by the giant **Riesenrad** (Ferris wheel) built in 1897. This achieved celluloid fame in *The Third Man* in the scene where Holly Martins confronted Harry Lime. The wheel rises to almost 65m and has a total weight of 430 tonnes. It rotates slowly, allowing plenty of time to enjoy the view from the top during the 10 minute ride. The wheel operates as late as 11.40 pm in the summer (AS50).

The amusement park has all sorts of funfair rides, ranging from gentle children's merry-go-rounds to stomach-twisting big dippers. There are also bumper cars, go-karts, haunted houses, games rooms, mini golf, a mini train and plenty of places to eat and drink. Rides cost AS10 to AS50.

Even if you don't like fairground rides, it's a great place just to wander and soak up the atmosphere. As you walk, you're liable to bump into one of the colourful metal sculptures depicting humans caught up in strange hallucinogenic happenings. Some are rather

THINGS TO SEE & DO

witty, and seem inspired by the Beatles' animated film *Yellow Submarine*. Look for them on Rondeau and Calafattiplatz.

The park also has a **Planetarium** (AS40, closed August to mid-September), and a municipal museum (closed Monday) that traces the history of the Wurstelprater and its woodland neighbour, the Grüner Prater. Joseph II first opened up the Prater (former royal hunting grounds) to the public in 1766.

CEMETERIES
Numerous famous composers have memorial tombs in the **Zentralfriedhof** (Map 2; Central Cemetery), 11, Simmeringer Hauptstrasse 232-244, including Gluck, Beethoven, Schubert, Brahms and Schönberg. Mozart also has a monument here, but he was actually buried in an unmarked mass grave in the **St Marxer Friedhof** (Map 7; Cemetery of St Mark), 03, Leberstrasse 6-8. Nobody quite knows where. His wife, Constanze, searched in vain to locate the exact location some years later. A poignant memorial (Mozartgrab) made from a broken pillar and a discarded stone angel marks the most likely area where he was buried. For St Mark's, take tram No 71 to Landstrasser Hauptstrasse then follow the signs (10 minutes).

From the Landstrasser Hauptstrasse stop you can take either tram No 71 or 72 on to the Central Cemetery. Get off at gate (Tor) two for the graves of the composers and other famous Viennese figures. There's a cemetery plan at the gate. Post-war Austrian presidents are entombed in front of the memorial church. Behind the church, at the far end of the cemetery, are the simple plaques devoted to those who fell in the world wars. These are in contrast to the ostentatious displays of wealth exhibited in the mausoleums of the rich, who couldn't take it with them but certainly tried. Most graves are neat and well tended and garlanded with fresh flowers. For a further contrast, wander around the old Jewish section.

A visit to the **Namenlosen** cemetery can be poignant. It contains unidentified, 'nameless' corpses washed up on the shores of the Danube. It's south-east of the city at 11, Alberner Hafen, and is reached by bus No 6A, but only some of the buses go that far.

KIRCHE AM STEINHOF
This distinctive Art Nouveau creation (Map 2) was the work of Otto Wagner from 1904 to 1907. Kolo Moser chipped in with the mosaic windows. The roof is topped by a

Corpse Disposal, Viennese Style
It is said that nowhere else are people so obsessed with death as in Vienna. Songs performed in wine taverns often deal with the subject, and the city has a unique museum dealing with coffins and the undertakers' craft (the Bestattungsmuseum, 04, Goldeggasse 19; visits by arrangement only, ☎ 501 95-227). The country as a whole has the highest suicide rate in the world. Being able to afford a lavish funeral at death is a lifetime ambition for many Viennese. Joseph II caused outrage in the 1780s with his scheme to introduce false-bottomed, reusable coffins.

In 1784 the huge Central Cemetery was opened as there was simply no more space in the city cemeteries. To try to entice the populace to believe that their future dear departed would rest better in this new location, they shipped out the coffins of the famous composers where they now rest together in group 32A. An unusual method was contemplated for transporting bodies to the suburban site: engineers drew up plans for a tube, many kilometres long, down which coffins would be fired using compressed air. However, the high cost of this scheme (one million florins) led to its abandonment.

At dawn, before the public are admitted to the Central Cemetery, special hunters are employed to shoot male pheasants, hares and wild rabbits. The reason is that these inconsiderate creatures have a tendency to eat or disturb the carefully arranged flowers around the graves. Meanwhile, you won't find any cemeteries for pets in Vienna. Animals are expressly forbidden from being buried in the soil, as the high water table might be contaminated by seepage of chemicals used in inoculations and putting the pets down. Pet cremations are now big business, although they are strictly controlled. ■

Otto Wagner

Along with Adolf Loos, Otto Wagner (1841-1918) was one of the most influential *fin de siècle* Viennese architects. He was trained in the classical tradition, and became a professor at the Akademie der Bildenden Künste (Academy of Fine Arts). His early work was in keeping with his education, and he was responsible for some neo-Renaissance buildings along the Ringstrasse. But as the new century approached he developed an Art Nouveau style, with flowing lines and decorative motifs. Wagner joined the Secession in 1899 and attracted public criticism in the process, one of the reasons why his creative designs for Vienna's Historical Museum were never adopted. In 1905 Wagner, Klimt and others split from the Secession. Wagner began to strip away the more decorative aspects of his designs, concentrating instead on presenting the functional features of buildings in a creative way. ■

MARK HONAN

One of Wagner's Art Nouveau buildings on Linke Wienzeile

copper-covered dome that earned the nickname *Limoniberg* (lemon mountain) from its original golden colour (now turned green but soon to be restored to its original sheen). The design illustrates the victory of function over ornamentation prevalent in much of Wagner's work, even down to the sloping floor to allow good drainage. It's at 14, Baumgartner Höhe 1, near the end of bus No 48A. The church is on the grounds of the Psychiatric Hospital of the City of Vienna, and the interior can be seen on Saturday at 3 pm (AS40).

About 2km west is Hüttelbergstrasse. Here you will find two **villas**, at Nos 26 and 28, designed by Wagner. The most unusual (No 26) was built in 1888 and is now the Ernst Fuchs private museum (entry by arrangement from Tuesday to Saturday; call ☎ 914 85 75). In the gardens (visible from the road) are some interesting statues, ceramics and the ornate Brunnenhaus created by Fuchs. The villas are near the Wien West campsite (take bus No 148 or 152).

KIRCHE ZUR HEILIGSTEN DREIFALTIGKEIT

The remarkable Kirche zur Heiligsten Dreifaltigkeit (Map 2; Holy Trinity Church), sometimes called the Wotrubakirche, looks like a collection of concrete blocks haphazardly stacked together. It was designed by Fritz Wotruba and completed in 1976. It's a long way to the south-west of the city, at the intersection of Georgsgasse and Rysergasse in district 23, near the Kaserngasse stop of bus No 60A.

DONAUTURM

The Donauturm (Map 5; Danube Tower) is the tallest structure in Vienna. Two revolving restaurants (at 170 and 160m) allow you to enjoy a fine panorama. Go up to watch the sun set behind the Wienerwald. Meals in the restaurants cost AS75 to AS300. Admission costs AS65 (AS45 for children). It stands in the Donaupark on Danube Island. Also in Donaupark is **UNO City**, home to international organisations and a conference centre.

KUNSTHAUSWIEN

This art gallery (Map 7) at 03, Untere Weissgerberstrasse 13 looks like something out of a toyshop. It was designed by Friedensreich Hundertwasser; his innovative buildings feature coloured ceramics, uneven floors, patchwork paintwork, irregular corners and grass and trees on the roof.

The contents of the KunstHausWien are

Peace Empire & a Hundred Waters

Friedensreich Hundertwasser was born as Friedrich Stowasser on 15 December 1928. In 1943, 69 of his Jewish relatives on his mother's side were deported to eastern Europe and killed.

In 1948, he spent three months at the Akademie der Bildenden Künste (Academy of Fine Arts) in Vienna, and the following year adopted his new name, meaning 'peace empire' and 'a hundred waters'. Environmental themes were present even in his early work, eg People (Complement to Trees) from 1950, now displayed in the KunstHausWien. His paintings employ vivid colours, metallic silver and spirals (sometimes reminiscent of Gustav Klimt's ornamental backgrounds).

Hundertwasser feels that 'the straight line is Godless'. He faithfully adheres to this principle in all his building projects, proclaiming that his uneven floors 'become a symphony, a melody for the feet and bring back natural vibrations to man'. His belief is that cities should be more harmonious with their

Spittelau incinerator

MARK HONAN

surrounding (natural) environment: buildings should be semisubmerged under undulating meadows, homes should have 'tree tenants' that pay rent in environmental currency.

Hundertwasser has always been something of an oddity to the Viennese establishment. He complains that they won't allow him to put into practice his more radical building projects. Nevertheless, he was commissioned to recreate the façade of the Spittelau incinerator. This was opened in 1992; it's the most unindustrial-looking heating plant you'll ever see (it's just north of Franz Josefs Bahnhof: take U3 to Spittelau). Hundertwasser has stated that man is shielded from nature by three levels of insulation: cities, houses and clothes. He has tried to limit the effect of the first two levels with his building projects. His proposed solution to the third is to go naked (he did make a couple of public speeches in the nude in the 1960s).

Hundertwasser remains one of Vienna's most idiosyncratic inhabitants. Whether he's organising a campaign to retain Austria's traditional car number plates, designing postage stamps, redesigning national flags, or simply painting pictures, he's always passionate, sometimes irritating and usually challenging established thinking. ■

something of a paean in honour of Hundertwasser himself, presenting his paintings, graphics, tapestry, philosophy, ecology and architecture. His vivid paintings are as distinctive as his diverse building projects. Hundertwasser's quotes are everywhere; some of his pronouncements are annoyingly didactic or smack of old hippiedom ('each raindrop is a kiss from heaven'), but they're often thought-provoking. There are even a couple of films of him. The gallery also puts on quality temporary exhibitions featuring other artists. Entry costs AS90 (concessions AS50) for the Hundertwasser collection, and the same again for the exhibitions, with a combination ticket costing AS140 (AS100).

Though this is expensive, Monday is half-price day (unless it's a holiday). Opening hours are daily from 10 am to 7 pm; the café around the back is open daily from 10 am to midnight.

When you are in the area, walk down the road to see the **Hundertwasserhaus** (Map 7), a block of residential flats designed by Hundertwasser on the corner of Löwengasse and Kegelgasse. It is now one of Vienna's most prestigious addresses, even though it only provides rented accommodation and is owned by the city of Vienna. Opposite is the **Kalke Village**, also Hundertwasser's handiwork, created from an old Michelin factory. It contains a café, souvenir shops and art shops, all with Hundertwasser's trademark uneven surfaces and colourful ceramics. It's open daily from 9 am to 5 pm (7 pm in summer).

MUSEUM MODERNER KUNST

The Museum moderner Kunst (Museum of Modern Art), or the Museum moderner Kunst Stiftung Ludwig Wien, is based at two locations: 09, Fürstengasse 1, in the Baroque setting of the Liechtenstein Palace (Map 4), and the modern exhibition space of the 20er Haus (Map 7), 03, Arsenalstrasse 1. In the former, the classical frescoes and stucco embellishments contrast well with the modern exhibits. Rooms are devoted to various movements in 20th century art: expressionism, cubism, futurism, constructivism, surrealism, pop art, photo-realism, and Viennese Actionism. Well-known artists represented include Picasso, Klee, Warhol, Magritte, Ernst and Giacometti. Many Viennese are indifferent to modern art, and the coverage here is a little brief by international standards. Yoko Ono is represented by an all-white chess set (and you thought she could only sing badly!). Special exhibitions are held periodically and there are sculptures dotted around the garden. On the ground floor is a café with inside and garden seating

where you can browse through the art catalogues. The entry to the grounds is from Alserbachstrasse, on the north side.

The 20er Haus has conceptual art, minimal art and installations ranging from about 1950 to the present, created by Austrian and international artists. Signs are in English. It also has temporary exhibitions and a sculpture garden (with work by Henry Moore, Alberto Giacometti and others). Admission for each venue costs AS45 (AS25 for students and seniors), or a combined ticket is AS60 (AS30) – you don't have to visit both on the same day. Both are open daily, except Monday, from 10 am to 6 pm. The collection is expected to move to the Museumsquartier one day.

WIENER KRIMINALMUSEUM

The Wiener Kriminalmuseum (Map 5; Crime Museum), 02, Grosse Sperlgasse 24, gives a prurient, tabloid-style look at crimes and criminals in Austria. It dwells with particularly grisly relish on murders in the last 100 years or so, though there are skulls of earlier criminals, and even an 18th century head pickled in a jar. There is lots of accompanying text, but it's only in German, and the displays could do with updating (the murderers mentioned in The Good-Hearted Widow

---

The Good-Hearted Widow & the Witch of Lainz

Elfriede Blauensteiner, blonde, bespectacled and apparently respectable, placed a string of Lonely Hearts advertisements, each time seeking an elderly man with whom to share the autumn years. She typically described herself as a 'Widow, no attachments, early sixties, good-hearted'. When she found her man she would get him to alter his will in her favour, then poison him. Police suspect she has murdered up to 12 wealthy old men since 1986; she initially confessed to five, but later pleaded not guilty at her trial in Krems in 1997. She was sentenced to life imprisonment.

Described as the 'Black Widow' by the media, Blauensteiner grew up in a cramped, working-class Viennese home and in her later years became a familiar figure at the gaming tables in the Vienna and Baden casinos. This 'nurse and faithful companion' (her own words) had around AS120 million in her bank account when she was arrested. As she departed from the funeral of her last victim, she was already drafting her next advertisement – using the back of the obituary notice.

Equally notorious was Waltraud Wagner, dubbed the 'Witch of Lainz' by the tabloids, who confessed to 22 murders at Lainz General Hospital in 1989. She and three other nurses had between them murdered over 48 (the exact figure was never established) elderly patients by administering drug overdoses, or most inhumanely, by forcing water down their throats until they drowned. The crimes were often provoked by trivial incidents, such as the patient being irritating or unpleasant during the nightshift! ■

boxed text don't appear yet). Opening times are Tuesday to Sunday from 10 am to 5 pm. Entry costs AS60 (AS50 for students and senior citizens, AS30 for kids). Axe murderers get in free (as an exhibit rather than as a visitor).

JOSEPHINIUM

The Josephinium (Map 4), 09, Währinger Strasse 25, is also known as the Museum of Medical History. Go to the 1st floor in the right-hand wing. Opening hours are Monday to Friday (not public holidays) from 9 am to 3 pm and admission costs AS10 (free for students). It's a small museum but still fascinating, and a little bizarre.

The prime exhibits are the ceroplastic and wax specimen models of the human frame, created over 200 years ago by Felice Fontana and Paolo Mascagni. They were used in the Academy of Medico-Surgery, instigated by Joseph II in 1785 to try to improve the skills of army surgeons who lacked medical qualifications. These models, showing the make up of the body under the skin, were intended to give the students a three-dimensional understanding of the organs, bones, veins and muscles. Three rooms of this gory lot will make you feel like you've wandered onto the set of a tacky horror movie. One strange touch is the necklace they've put on the female model lying down in the first room. Why this ornamentation? She's hardly dressed for a sophisticated night out, as half her torso is missing.

The rest of the museum contains cases of arcane medical instruments, photos of past practitioners, accounts of unpleasant-looking operations, and some texts (one book is thoughtfully left open on a page dealing with the dissection of eyeballs).

SIGMUND FREUD MUSEUM

Sigmund Freud is perhaps Vienna's most famous Jew. This museum (Map 4) is housed at 09, Berggasse 19, in the apartments where he lived and psychoanalysed from 1891 to 1938 (until he fled from the Nazis). It contains furniture, Freud's possessions (such as his case embossed with the initials SF),

letters, documents and photographs; very detailed notes (in English) illuminate the offerings. Students and Freud freaks could spend a while here; most casual observers would just skim through the three main rooms and wonder what on earth Freud wanted with that terracotta votive offering of male genitals (exhibit 24). There's also a fairly dull home movie of Freud, narrated by his daughter, Anna. The museum is open daily from 9 am to 4 pm (6 pm in summer) and costs AS60 (AS40 for students and senior citizens).

Municipal Museums

There are 20 municipal museums run by the city of Vienna, if you include the always accessible Roman ruins (free) on Michaelerplatz. A free booklet is available describing them.

Entry for the Historisches Museum der Stadt Wien, the Uhren Museum and the Hermesvilla cost AS50 (students AS20); all the rest cost AS25 (students AS10). A book of 10 entry tickets costs AS160. All municipal museums are free for visits before noon on Friday.

The **Historisches Museum der Stadt Wien** (Map 8; Historical Museum of the City of Vienna) is the best of the municipal museums. It gives a detailed rundown on the development of Vienna from prehistory to the present day, and does a good job of putting the city and its personalities in context, without needing words. Exhibits occupy three floors and include maps and plans, artefacts, many paintings (eg by Klimt, Schiele, and Biedermeier painters like Waldmüller) and reconstructed rooms from the homes of Adolf Loos and Franz Grillparzer. Two models (on the 1st and 2nd floors) of the Innere Stadt show the impact of the Ringstrasse developments, and there are some good period photographs. The museum is at 04, Karlsplatz 5, by Karlskirche, and it's open daily (except Monday) from 9 am to 4.30 pm.

The **Uhren Museum** (Map 8; Clock Museum), 01, Schulhof 2, on three floors (no lift), displays 1200 clocks and watches, ranging from the 15th century to a 1989 computer clock. The **Hermesvilla** (Map 2) is in the Lainzer Tiergarten (see Hiking under Activities later in this chapter); this former hunting lodge features the private apartments of Franz Josef and Empress Elisabeth.

Several municipal museums are based in the former residences of the great composers, and generally contain assorted memorabilia and furniture of their exalted former inhabitants. Most of the museums are open daily (except Monday) from 9 am to 12.15 pm and 1 to 4.30 pm. A visit may take up to 30 minutes. Locations include:

Eroica House (Map 3), 19, Döblinger Hauptstrasse 92 – this house was named after Beethoven's symphony No 3, which was written here
Haydn Museum (Map 6), 06, Haydngasse 19 – Haydn lived here for 12 years and composed most of the oratorios *The Creation* and *The Seasons*. He died here in 1809. The museum also has rooms devoted to Brahms.
Johann Strauss Residence (Map 5), 02, Praterstrasse 54 – Strauss composed the *Blue Danube Waltz* here
Mozart's Apartment (Map 8; Figaro House), 01, Domgasse 5 – Mozart spent 2½ productive years here and his work included writing *The Marriage of Figaro*
Pasqualati House (Map 8), 01, Mölker Bastei 8 – Beethoven lived on the 4th floor of this house from 1804 to 1814
Schubert Commemorative Rooms (Map 8), 04, Kettenbrückengasse 6 – Schubert lived here briefly before his death in 1828. You can see his birth house (Map 4) at 09, Nussdorfer Strasse 54.

Activities

There are plenty of opportunities for visitors to participate in sporting activities such as basketball, tennis, squash, sailing, swimming, judo, ice hockey etc. However, apart from a couple of leaflets listing city-owned indoor and outdoor swimming pools (Bäder), neither the tourist office nor the city information desk in the Rathaus has any

sports information. The best place to contact is the Sportamt (Map 7; ☎ 4000-84111), Ernst Happel Stadion, 02, Meiereistasse 7. In addition, good hotels will be able to tell you about local facilities, or you can check the newspapers, or get addresses from the phone book. Get information on city-owned Bäder on ☎ 60112-8044, weekdays from 7.30 am to 3.30 pm.

The Prater, a large area between the Danube and the Danube Canal, is an important location for sports. It has tennis courts, a bowling alley (Map 7; 02, Hauptallee 124), horse riding, sports stadia and swimming pools. A more compact sports complex is the Stadthalle (Map 4; ☎ 98 100), 15, Vogelweidplatz 15, which has a swimming pool, ice rink and bowling alley.

HIKING
To the west of the city, the rolling hills and marked trails of the Wienerwald (Vienna Woods) are perfect for walkers. The Prater also has a wood with walking trails. The *Wander bares Wien* leaflet from the Sportamt has maps of trails close to the city and explains how to get there by public transport (city travel passes are valid).

A good trail to try is the one starting in Nussdorf (take tram D from the Ring) and reaching **Kahlenberg** for a fine view over the city. On your return to Nussdorf you can undo all that exercise by imbibing a few at a Heuriger. The round trip is an 11km hike, or you can save your legs by taking the Nussdorf-Kahlenberg 38A bus in one or both directions.

For information on parts of the Wienerwald farther afield, turn to the Excursions chapter.

Another place to roam around is the **Lainzer Tiergarten** animal preserve, open from late March to 31 October between 8 am and dusk. Get there by Tram No 62 to Hermesstrasse and then bus No 60B to the last station.

CYCLING
Cycling is a pleasant and popular activity, especially along the banks of the Danube.

See the Getting Around chapter for more information.

SWIMMING POOLS

Pools are usually open daily. Entry costs about AS50, with reduced admission prices after midday and perhaps also 4 pm. In the city-owned pools, kids under six get free entry; those aged six to 15 get free entry during the summer holidays.

Many places are open-air and open only from May to mid-September, such as the Stadionbad (Map 7; ☎ 720 21 02), a large privately owned complex of pools in the Prater. Bus No 80B runs there from the U3 stop Schlachthausgasse. Other outdoor pools include the city-owned Krapfenwaldbad (Map 3; ☎ 32 15 01), 19, Krapfenwaldgasse 65-73, in the north (bus 38A), a small pool with a view of the city, and the privately owned Schönbrunner Bad (Map 6; ☎ 815 01 32), on the east side of the palace park.

Some swimming baths also have sauna facilities (in which senior citizens get reductions), such as Ottakringer Bad (Map 4; ☎ 914 81 06), 16, Johann Staud Strasse 11, and Amalienbad (Map 2; ☎ 607 47 47), 10, Reumannplatz 23. Both of these city-owned places are open year-round.

BEACHES

There are swimming spots (easy access to the water, no charges) on both banks of the New Danube (Neue Donau); some of these are for nude bathing, are marked FKK (Freikörperkultur) on maps and signs (these are mostly near the edge of the city).

The Old Danube (Alte Donau) also has various places where you can just jump in. Its water has been a little murky and slimy with algae in the past (the water was safe for swimming, but not so pleasant), though recent measures have been taken that have improved water quality. A day ticket for the specific bathing complexes costs AS50 with a locker or AS70 with a cabin (reductions after noon), and these are open approximately from May to September. Places on the south bank (Map 5) are Angelibad, Arbeiterstrandbad and Strandbad Alte

Donau. All these city-owned complexes provide beaches on the Old Danube but only the last has separate outdoor swimming pools. Gänsehäufel (Map 5; on an island, connected to the Danube Park by a bridge) is the biggest bathing complex. It is also city-owned, and has a nude section.

WATER SPORTS

Both the Old Danube and the New Danube provide opportunities for sailing, boating, windsurfing and waterskiing. On the east bank of the New Danube by the Reichsbrücke bridge (U3 to Donauinsel) there's sailing, rowing and sailboard hire.

The Old Danube is the favoured area for sailing. Hofbauer (☎ 204 34 35; fax -36), 22, Obere Alte Donau 186, rents sailing boats and also has a branch on the New Danube at the Reichsbrücke bridge. For more outlets look in the Yellow pages under Boote/Vermietung or contact the Austrian Sailing Federation: Österreichischer Segel-Verband (☎ 587 86 88; fax 586 61 71), 04, Grosse Neugasse 8.

Language Courses

Many places offer German language courses, and a wide selection are listed in Young Vienna Scene from the tourist office; the Jugend Info office also has information. ÖKISTA (Map 4; ☎ 401 48-8820; fax -8800; email german.course@oekista.co.at), 09, Türkenstrasse 8, 1st floor, Door 11, has a standard/intensive course beginning every Monday, with 20/30 lessons per week. It costs AS5200/7300 for a minimum of two weeks and thereafter AS1360/2200 per week, with a maximum of 15/six students per class. It also offers individual tuition.

Inlingua Sprachschule (Map 8; ☎ 512 22 25); fax 512 94 99) 01, Neuer Markt 1, charges AS2850 per week (20 lessons) for a minimum two weeks, with monthly starts and an eight students per class limit. It also does individual tuition and evening classes. The Internationales Kulturinstitut (Map 8;

☎ 586 73 21; fax 586 29 93), 01, Opernring 7, has intensive courses (15 hours per week, AS4400 for four weeks; monthly starts) and evening classes (five hours per week, AS4400 for 10 weeks; starting in January, April and October). There are 10 to 16 students per class. All three schools can arrange accommodation.

Places to Stay

TYPES OF ACCOMMODATION

As in the rest of Austria, there has been a general move towards providing higher quality accommodation at higher prices (eg rooms where guests use hall showers are gradually being upgraded and fitted with private showers). This makes life more difficult for budget travellers, who increasingly will have to rely on hostels.

🐾 🐾 🐾 🐾 🐾 🐾 🐾 🐾 🐾

Problems with Numbers

In a Vienna address, the number of a building within a street *follows* the street name. Any number *before* the street name denotes the district.

In this book fax numbers are presented as extensions (eg fax -30) of the phone numbers that they follow. To send a fax dial the main phone number and add the fax extension.

Throughout Vienna you'll also see telephone numbers presented with extensions. For an explanation of this system see the Post & Communications section in the Facts for the Visitor chapter. ■

🐾 🐾 🐾 🐾 🐾 🐾 🐾 🐾 🐾

Breakfast is included in hostels, pensions and hotels listed in this chapter, unless stated otherwise; in the more expensive places this will be a substantial breakfast buffet instead of a continental breakfast. Prices quoted here are summer prices; most mid-range and top-end hotels reduce prices in winter. Instant hotel reservations can be made from Britain via Austria On-line (☎ 0171-434 7390).

Hostels

Vienna offers a choice of private hostels and hostels affiliated with Hostelling International (HI). Membership cards are always required except in a few private hostels. Non-members pay a guest surcharge of AS40 per night for a guest card; after six nights the guest card counts as a full membership card.

The name for youth hostel in German is *Jugendherberge*. Austria has two youth hostel organisations. Hostels affiliated with the worldwide HI network are linked to one or the other; this is something of a historical legacy and makes no difference to how the hostels are run. Either head office can give information on all HI hostels. The Öster-reichischer Jugendherbergsverband (☎ 533 53 53; fax 535 08 61) is on the corner of 01, Gonzagagasse 22 and 01, Schottenring 28; either address is OK for post. The Öster-reichischer Jugendherbergswerk (☎ 533 18 33; fax -85) is at 01, Helfersdorferstrasse 4, and has a travel arm called Supertramp (☎ 533 51 37) and a hiking shop on the premises.

Most hostels accept reservations by telephone, and in two of them (Myrthengasse and Brigittenau) you can prebook via the worldwide computer reservations system. Hostel prices are around AS160 per night. Unless otherwise stated, hostel prices are quoted per bed. Vienna's HI hostels may impose a three to eight night maximum stay in busy times.

Hotels & Pensions

Hotels and pensions are rated from one to five stars depending on the facilities they offer, though as respective criteria vary you can't assume a three-star pension is equivalent to a three-star hotel. Pensions tend to be smaller than hotels, and usually provide a more personal service and less standardised fixtures and fittings; often they're located on a few floors of an apartment block. Pensions generally offer a better size and quality of room for the price than hotels. Where they usually can't compete is in back-up services (eg room service, laundry service) and on-site facilities (eg private parking, bar and/or restaurant). If none of that matters to you, stick with the pensions.

With very few exceptions, rooms are clean and adequately appointed. Expect to pay a minimum of around AS300/550 for a single/ double with hall shower or AS400/650 with private shower. In budget accommodation, a room with a private shower may mean a room with a shower cubicle rather than with a proper *en suite* bathroom.

If business is slow, mid-range and top-end hotels (and, to a lesser extent, pensions) are willing to negotiate on prices. It's always worth asking for a special deal as prices can come down quite substantially. Some places (especially the five-star hotels) offer special weekend rates, or 'two nights for the price of one' packages. Even in budget places, ask for a special price if you're planning to stay for more than a few days. Cheaper places rarely accept credit cards, and some may close for a few months in winter.

Other Types of Accommodation

Vienna has five camping grounds, mostly in the western and southern suburbs. They all take caravans. From July to September student residences are converted to hotels, giving a much-needed boost to beds at the lower end of the market. A few rooms in private homes are on offer, mostly in the suburbs, but economic affluence over recent years has suppressed the supply of these; expect a three day minimum stay. Apartments are available through accommodation agencies, and hotels sometimes have self-contained apartment rooms.

FINDING SOMEWHERE TO STAY

Vienna can be a nightmare for budget backpackers who arrive without reservations. Even those who can afford to consider a range of options may find their choices full, especially in summer. Book ahead, especially at Christmas and Easter and between June and September. Reservations are binding on either side and compensation may be claimed by the hotel if you do not take a reserved room, or by you if the room is unavailable.

Accommodation Agencies

Several agencies can help with accommodation. Tourist offices (see the Facts for the Visitor chapter) charge a commission of AS40 per reservation, irrespective of the number of rooms being booked. They can help find private rooms but don't have lists to give out. What they can give you instead is the useful *Jugendherbergen* pamphlet detailing youth hostels and camping grounds, and a booklet of hotels and pensions, revised annually.

ÖKISTA (☎ 401 48), 09, Türkenstrasse 8, Door 11, charges AS150 to find hotel rooms (three-star and above) for a minimum of three nights. For stays of at least two weeks it can find a room in a family house from AS180 per night B&B (AS700 commission). The Odyssee Mitwohnzentrale (☎ 402 60 61, fax -11; mitwohnzentrale@odyssee .vienna.at), 08, Laudongasse 8, can find private rooms from AS250/320 a single/ double, or apartments from AS6000 per month (AS4000 in summer); in either case, a minimum stay of three days is usual. The office is open Monday to Friday from 10 am to 2 pm and 3 to 6 pm and commission is 24% of the rent (reduced for stays exceeding one month).

Choosing a Location

Staying within the Innere Stadt is convenient for the sights, though inevitably you have to pay more for what you get. Most hotels and pensions are between the Ring and the Gürtel; these are better value and still within easy striking distance of the centre. Places in the suburbs have the lowest prices, though they have a cost in terms of accessibility; these are more of a viable option if you're not too bothered about late-night attractions in the city. Businesspeople may need to attend conferences at the Austria Center Vienna on Danube Island; there's only one hotel nearby, but the site is easily accessible on the U1 line.

If you have a car, staying in the city centre becomes even more expensive; parking is restricted in the Innere Stadt and most adjoining districts, meaning you will end up paying high parking fees (AS200 to AS400 for 24 hours, whether in public or hotel garages). A better option would be to find

PLACES TO STAY

somewhere farther out where you can safely leave your car, and then rely on public transport. Even if you want a late night and have to take a taxi home, the taxi fare will still be less than a day's garage fees. Hotels outside the Innere Stadt with private garages charge around AS100 to AS250 for 24 hours; the farther from the centre the cheaper it gets. Street parking is no problem in the suburbs.

PLACES TO STAY – BUDGET
Camping
Camping Wien West (Map 2; ☎ 914 23 14), 14, Hüttelbergstrasse 80, is open all year except February. It costs AS63/35 per adult/tent, or AS69/40 in July and August. Four-bed bungalows are AS415. To get there, take U4 or the S-Bahn to Hütteldorf, then bus No 148 or 152. *Aktiv Camping Neue Donau* (Map 2; ☎ /fax 202 40 10), 22, Am Kleehäufel, is the same price and is open from early May to mid-September. It's the closest site to the city centre and the only one east of the Danube. Take U1 to Kaisermühlen, then the No 91A bus.

Camping Wien Süd (Map 2; ☎ 865 92 18), 23, Breitenfurter Strasse 269, costs AS63/35 per adult/tent and is only open from early July to late August. Take bus No 62A from the U4 Philadelphiabrücke stop.

Schwimmbad Camping Rodaun (Map 2; ☎ 888 41 54), 23, An der Au 2, is open from late March to mid-November and charges AS65/50 per adult/tent. Take S1 or S2 to Liesing then bus No 60A. Beyond the city to the south is the largest site, *Campingplatz Schloss Laxenburg* (☎ 02236-713 33) on Münchendorfer Strasse. It has a swimming pool and boat rental and costs AS63/35 for an adult/tent, or AS69/40 in July and August (open 1 April to 31 October).

Hostels
Near the Centre No hostels invade the imperial elegance of the Innere Stadt. The nearest are two linked HI *Jugendherbergen* (Map 4; ☎ 523 63 16; fax 523 58 49), at 07, Myrthengasse 7 and around the corner at 07, Neustiftgasse 85. Both are well run with newish facilities and helpful staff. All rooms

have private shower. Beds (each with bedside light) are AS165 in six or four-bed dorms, or AS195 in double rooms. Lunch or dinner is AS60 and laundry is AS50 per load. Curfew is 1 am. You can check in for either hostel any time during the day at Myrthengasse, but Neustiftgasse closes from 11.15 am to 3.45 pm. Telephone reservations are accepted and strongly advised.

Believe it or Not (Map 4; ☎ 526 46 58), 07, Apartment 14, Myrthengasse 10, is a small, private hostel opposite the Myrthengasse hostel. The only sign outside is on the doorbell. It has a friendly atmosphere, but one room has triple bunks and can get hot in summer. There's no breakfast; use the kitchen facilities instead. Beds are AS160 in summer or AS110 in winter (November to Easter), and you get your own key so there's no curfew. *Panda Hostel* (Map 4; ☎ 524 78 88), 07, 3rd floor, Kaiserstrasse 77, has the same prices and a similar set-up, with a TV in every room and at least 20 beds. It's linked to the Lauria Hostel (see under Budget Hotels & Pensions).

Hostel Zöhrer (Map 4; ☎ 406 07 30; fax 408 04 09), 08, Skodagasse 26, is a private hostel close to the Ring, and is reasonable value. Four to six-bed dorms are AS170 and doubles (bunk beds) are AS460; all rooms have a private shower. There's a kitchen, courtyard and you get your own key. Reception is open from 7.30 am to 10 pm but there's no curfew and the doors aren't shut during the day.

Turmherberge Don Bosco (Map 7; ☎ 713 14 94), 03, Lechnerstrasse 12, south-east of the Ring in a church tower, has the cheapest beds in town; AS75 plus AS25 for sheets if required. However, the place hasn't been modernised since the 1950s – some rooms are cramped and have few lockers (no locks). Breakfast is not included though there are basic kitchen facilities. It has 50 beds and is open from 1 March to 31 November. Curfew is 11.45 pm; reception closes at noon but you can only check in once it reopens at 5 pm (telephone reservations accepted).

Near Westbahnhof, *Hostel Ruthensteiner* (Map 6; ☎ 893 42 02; fax 893 27 96), 15,

Robert Hamerling Gasse 24, is open 24 hours. Ten-bed dorms are AS129 (own sheets needed; they sell sheets for AS120). Sheets are provided with the basic singles/doubles for AS239/450 and the three to five-bed rooms (AS159 per person). Breakfast costs AS25 and there's a kitchen and shady rear courtyard.

The very modern *Kolpingsfamilie Meidling* (Map 6; ☎ 813 54 87; fax 812 21 30), 12, Bendlgasse 10-12, is near the U6 stop 'Niederhofstrasse', south of Westbahnhof. Beds cost from AS100 (eight to 10-bed dorms) to AS155 (four-bed dorms). All dorms have private shower, and some have a WC; the four-bed dorms have a balcony. There are lockers but no keys, and there is a patio round the back. Non-HI members pay AS20 extra, which is a bit of a cheek as they don't provide the guest card stamp. Breakfast costs AS45 and sheets (if required) are AS65. Curfew is at midnight, though reception is open 24 hours.

In the Suburbs *Brigittenau* (Map 5; ☎ 332 82 940; fax 330 83 79), 20, Friedrich Engels Platz 24, is an HI hostel with 334 beds in a modern, multi-storey building just a couple of minutes' walk from the Danube (trams N31 and N33 stop outside). Four-bed dorms cost AS165 and doubles with private shower are AS195 per person. Dinners are AS60, and there's also a café, games room and garden. Reception is open 24 hours though dorms are closed from 9 am to 1 pm. Curfew is 1 am but you can be let in on the hour after that.

Hütteldorf-Hacking (Map 2; ☎ 877 15 01; fax 877 02 63-2), 13, Schlossberggasse 8, a HI hostel it has different-sized dorms for AS156 (AS30 surcharge for single occupancy), and a total of 271 beds. Meals are AS62 or AS72, and laundry costs AS70. There's a lounge with various games, and doors are locked from 9.30 am to 3 pm. Curfew is 11.45 pm but you can buy a key card (AS25) for late entry. It's far from the centre of town, but only a five minute walk from both the U4 Hütteldorf station and the N49 nightbus route.

Another HI hostel is the *Schlossherberge*

am Wilhelminenberg (Map 2; ☎ 485 85 03-700; fax -702) at 16, Savoyenstrasse 2, in the grounds of the Schloss Wilhelminenberg. Four-bed dorms with shower and WC are AS220 per person and a double room is AS500. Reception is open through the day but the dorms are locked from 9 am to 2 pm. Curfew is 11.45 pm, or a key card (AS25) gives late entry. The great view includes Vienna and some vineyards but it's a long way from the centre: bus Nos 46B and 146B link to city-bound trams J, 44 and 46.

Student Residences

These *Studentenheime* are available to tourists from 1 July to 30 September, while the students are on holiday. In their student incarnation they usually have a kitchen and dining room on each floor, but when they reinvent themselves as seasonal hotels these useful facilities generally remain locked. Rooms are perfectly OK but nothing fancy. Expect single beds (though beds might be placed together in doubles), a work desk, a wardrobe. Cheaper places have institutional-style ablutions blocks; pricier places offer private shower and WC. Most are outside the Innere Stadt but are still reasonably convenient for the centre.

Some more expensive places not listed below appear in the tourist office's *Hotels and Pensionen* brochure.

Auge Gottes (Map 4; ☎ 319 44 88-10; fax -11), 09, Nussdorfer Strasse 75, has singles/doubles from AS270/470 with hall shower. Doubles with shower start at AS570, and triples/quads from AS630/840.

Auersperg (Map 4; ☎ 406 23 40), 08, Auersperg-strasse 9, has singles/doubles from AS355/580, or AS500/820 with private shower and WC. It's near the Ring and has 24 hour reception. Advance reservations must be made via Albertina Hotels Austria (☎ 512 74 93; fax 512 19 68), 01, Führichgasse 10.

Haus Döbling (Map 3; ☎ 34 76 31; fax -25), 19, Gymnasiumstrasse 85, has over 300 beds. Singles/doubles with private shower and hall WC and 'hostel service' costs AS270/340, whereas 'hotel service' (bathroom towels, beds made up, etc) costs AS300/400.

Gästehaus Pfeilgasse (Map 4; ☎ 401 74; fax 401 76-20), 08, Pfeilgasse 4-6, has singles/doubles/ triples for AS270/480/600 with shower and WC in the corridor. Reception is at the Hotel Avis (open 24 hours), which can also tell you about *Academia*, a more expensive place across the road with private shower and WC.

Katholisches Studentenhaus (Map 3; ☎ 34 92 64), 19, Peter Jordan Strasse 29, has singles/doubles with hall shower and toilet for AS235/340 without breakfast.

Music Academy (Map 8; ☎ 514 84-48; fax -49), 01, Johannesgasse 8, is central but only available from July to September. It has singles/doubles from AS480/960 with private bath and WC, or AS410/740 with hall facilities, while triples/ quads AS780/960 with sink. All rooms have a fridge, and a phone for incoming calls. Prices are reduced for students in September. It also has a washing machine, 24 hour reception, and one room and one apartment (inexpensive) are available year-round.

Porzellaneum (Map 4; ☎ 317 72 82), 09, Porzellangasse 30, has singles and doubles (hall showers) for only AS175 per person without breakfast. Reception open 24 hours.

Ruddfinum (Map 7; ☎ 505 53 84), 04, Mayerhofgasse 3, has singles/doubles/triples with hall showers starting at AS280/500/650. There's also a cable TV lounge, and reception is open 24 hours.

Hotels & Pensions

Near the Centre *Kolping-Gästehaus* (Map 8; ☎ 587 56 31-119; fax 586 36 30), at 06, Gumpendorfer Strasse 39, has its entrance on Stiegengasse. It has singles with/without shower for AS550/250. Doubles with shower are AS800, or AS940 with WC also. Triples are available. Rooms are OK, and there are kitchen facilities, but it's a newish building with an institutionalised aura (students stay here long-term). Book well ahead.

Auer (Map 4; ☎ 406 21 21; fax -4), 09, Lazarettgasse 3, is friendly, pleasant and feels very Viennese. Singles/doubles start from AS370/540 with hall shower; doubles with private shower are AS610. This pension has 14 rooms and reception is on the 1st floor (no lift).

Pension Wild (Map 4; ☎ 406 51 74; fax 402 21 68), 08, Langegasse 10, is quieter than the name suggests and very close to the Ring. Singles/doubles/triples are AS450/ 590/860; add AS100 per room for private

shower. An apartment is AS790/1250 for two/four people. It's run by an elderly Frau who speaks a quirky combination of English and German. Reception is open 24 hours and the kitchen on each floor is a bonus. A massage/sauna health centre shares the building.

Lauria (Map 4; ☎ 522 25 55), 07, 3rd floor, Kaiserstrasse 77, has clean, well decorated rooms, some with large pictorial scenes and homey touches; all have TV, and there are communal kitchens (no breakfast provided). Doubles are AS530 (AS480 with bunk beds), or AS700 with private shower. Triples (AS700) and quads (AS850) are also available, as are fully equipped apartments (AS1400/1600 for four/six people). There may be a two day minimum stay for reservations, and credit cards are accepted. The place is close to the centre, and well situated for transport and local shops.

Hotel Westend (Map 6; ☎ 597 67 29; fax -27), 06, Fügergasse 3, is close to Westbahnhof and has reasonable singles/doubles for AS340/610 (AS390/730 with shower) in a typical building, which has large plants gracing the stairway. Reception is open 24 hours.

Pension Kraml (Map 6; ☎ 587 85 88; fax 586 75 73) is nearby at 06, Brauergasse 5. Small, friendly and family run, it has singles/ doubles for AS310/620 and large doubles with private shower for AS700, or AS820 with WC also. Triples start at AS810, and there's also family apartments from AS1020. Unusually for a budget place, breakfast is buffet style.

Pension Falstaff (Map 4; ☎ 317 91 86; fax -4), 09, Müllnergasse 5, has singles/doubles for AS370/620 (with an irksome fee of AS30 to use the hall shower) or AS490/740 with private shower. Prices are around AS100 lower in winter. The rooms are long but some lack width; fittings are ageing but adequate. It's convenient to tram D to the Ring and Nussdorf.

Praterstern (Map 5; ☎ 214 01 23; fax 214 78 80; email 113052.3725@compuserve .com), 02, Mayergasse 6, east of the Ring, has singles/doubles for AS290/545. Rooms with private shower are AS385/655, or

ALL PHOTOS BY MARK HONAN

Top Left: The most significant stage in the German-speaking world, the Burgtheater
Top Right: A fiacre driver
Bottom Left: Old world Vienna meets the new
Middle Right: A street performer on Graben, but which one lives in the suitcase?
Bottom Right: Street vendors selling hot chestnuts

GLENN BEANLAND

JON DAVISON

MARK HONAN

MARK HONAN

Top Left: Shop fronts blend with Vienna's historic architecture
Top Right: VW Beetle struggling with its passenger
Bottom Left: A creative shop display on Rathauzplatz, Melk
Bottom Right: There are many surprises at Naschmarkt, Vienna

AS425/685 with toilet also. Cheaper rates are possible excluding breakfast in low season. There's also a pleasant rear garden.

Close to the centre is *Quisisana* (Map 8; ☎ 587 71 55; fax 587 71 56-33), 06, Windmühlgasse 6, with a café-restaurant on site. It charges from AS380/600 for rooms with shower or AS330/520 without. Rooms vary in size and quality but are good value.

A 10 minute walk from Südbahnhof is *Hotel Kolbeck* (Map 7; ☎ 604 17 73; fax 602 94 86), 10, Laxenburger Strasse 19. Rooms with hall shower are AS400/750; those with private shower, WC and cable TV are AS600/1000. The patterned floor tiles in the corridor are typically Viennese. Reception is open 24 hours.

Down the road at No 14 is *Cyrus* (Map 7; ☎ /fax 604 42 88), with a range of rooms, all with shower and cable TV. Singles are AS300 to AS450 and doubles are AS500 to AS800, depending on the size, furnishings, and whether they have private toilet.

Nearby is *Pension Caroline* (Map 7; ☎ 604 80 70; fax 602 77 67), 10, Gudrunstrasse 138, convenient for local transport. Attractive, renovated rooms with shower, WC and satellite TV are AS520/820; it's on the 4th floor (there's a lift).

Pension Ani (Map 4; ☎ 408 10 60; fax 408 10 82), 09, Kinderspitalgasse 1, costs from AS400/650 for rooms with shower, cable TV and phone, or you can pay more for bigger rooms with WC. It's good value anyway, but the owner will give a discount to students and young people, and prices seem to be negotiable for everyone.

Pension Esterházy (Map 4; ☎ 587 51 59), 04, Nelkengasse 3, just off Mariahilfer Strasse, has decent-sized rooms (many singles) for AS320/490 without breakfast. Showers and toilets are down the hall, though a couple of rooms with private facilities are being built.

Pension Hargita (Map 4; ☎ 526 19 28; fax 526 04 92), 07, Andreagasse 1, has just 10 rooms with/without shower – the doubles for AS550/650 are better value than the singles (AS400/450). Breakfast is AS40.

Fünfhaus (Map 6; ☎ 892 35 45), 15, Sperr-gasse 12, near Westbahnhof, has a range of rooms and prices (English not spoken; closed in winter). Simple, clean rooms are AS390/590, or AS470/680 with shower; there's also triples and apartments. Breakfast is AS35, and parking costs AS50.

Pension Bosch (Map 7; ☎ 798 61 79; fax 799 17 18), 03, Keilgasse 13, is in a traditional building in a residential street. Rooms (AS380/650 using hall shower, AS530/720 with shower, AS600/860 with shower and WC) have personal touches and satellite TV; most have old-fashioned furnishings. Reception is on the 1st floor (there's a lift).

Goldenes Einhorn (Map 6; ☎ 544 47 55), 05, Am Hundsturm 5, is a small, simple place opposite a post office and a new underground carpark. Singles/doubles with hall shower and no breakfast cost from AS270/480; doubles with shower are AS520. Phone ahead in low season as reception hours may be irregular; it's closed in February.

In the Suburbs *Zum Goldenen Stern Gasthof* (Map 6; ☎ 804 13 82), 12, Breitenfurter Strasse 94, has simple singles/doubles with hall shower for AS250/440 (12 beds in total), not including breakfast. The place is perfectly adequate, though the tourist office considers it too basic to make it into its accommodation booklet. Bus 62A from Meidling goes there.

Matauschek (Map 4; ☎ /fax 982 35 32), 14, Breitenseer Strasse 14, is by the new Hütteldorfer Strasse U3 stop and has 25 fairly basic rooms. It costs AS330/560 with hall shower, or AS620 for a double with private shower. The simple restaurant is closed on Wednesday and Thursday.

Rustler (Map 6; ☎ /fax 982 01 62), 14, Linzer Strasse 43, is an efficiently run place close to Schönbrunn (or take tram No 52 from Westbahnhof). It has a pretty garden (complete with garden gnomes), double glazing and a small bar-breakfast room. Singles/doubles are AS330/600, triples AS810; add about AS160 per room for private shower and the same again for private WC. It's closed from December to Easter, except over New Years.

Waldandacht (Map 2; ☎ 979 16 50), 14, Wurzbachtalgasse 23, is as far as you can get into the Wienerwald without crossing into Lower Austria, and has 10 doubles with hall shower for AS500. Take the S50 to Weidlingau-Wurzbachtal.

PLACES TO STAY – MIDDLE
Innere Stadt
Unless otherwise noted the following can all be found on Map 8.

Pension Nossek (☎ 533 70 41; fax 535 36 46), Graben 17, is good value considering its ideal situation. Clean, comfortable singles (AS650 to AS800) and doubles (AS1100 to AS1500) are individually priced depending on the size, view and private facilities. Book weeks ahead during high season. Around the corner at Dorotheergasse 6-8 is *Pension Aclon* (☎ 512 79 40-0; fax 513 87 51), which has rooms with satellite TV but without shower for AS520/880. Those rooms for AS720/1220 are better all round and have a private shower.

Schweizer Pension Solderer (☎ 533 81 56; fax 535 64 69), Heinrichsgasse 2, is very clean and run by Swiss sisters. It has singles/doubles from AS450/580 with hall shower, AS650/860 with private shower, and AS700/980 with shower and WC. Most rooms have cable TV and ornamental ceramic stoves. You get a key to operate the old-fashioned lift, and there's street parking for AS70.

Pension Am Operneck (☎ 512 93 10), Kärntner Strasse 47, opposite the tourist office, has big rooms with private shower, toilet and TV for AS620/900. It's usually booked up months ahead.

Hotel Orient (☎ 533 73 07; fax 535 03 40), Tiefer Graben 30, has a fin-de-siècle hallway and façade, and rooms decked out in a variety of interesting styles. Scenes from the movie 'The Third Man' were shot here. Singles/doubles with private shower start at AS700/850, while singles with hall shower (AS20 to use it) are AS450. Some rooms are rented by the hour for discrete liaisons, but it's by no means a seedy place.

Hotel Post (☎ 51 583 -0), Fleischmarkt

24, has pricey rooms with shower and WC for AS900/1140; rooms without shower are a better deal from AS500/770. All rooms have satellite TV. *Hotel Wandl* (☎ 534 55-0), Petersplatz 9, is a family run hotel with many of its 138 rooms arranged around inner courtyards. Renovated singles/doubles start at AS900/1410 with shower or AS700/1100 without.

Near the Centre
Alla Lenz (Map 4; ☎ 523 69 89; fax -55), 07, Halbgasse 3-5, is an excellent, top-of-the-range pension with a rooftop swimming pool (free to guests), a café, and a garage next door (AS150 per day). Doubles start at AS980 (lower in winter, and for stays of two nights or more) and have air-con, private shower and WC, telephone and cable TV. There singles, which aren't such a good deal at AS900, and apartments too.

Nearby, *Pension Atrium* (Map 4; ☎ 523 31 14; fax -9), 07, Burggasse 118, has clean, renovated rooms from AS590/720 with shower, WC and TV, plus one apartment for AS980. Also close by is *Pension Carantania* (Map 4; ☎ 526 73 40; fax -6), 07, Kandlgasse 35-7. Big singles/doubles with shower, WC and cable TV are AS615/920 and most have old-style furnishings.

Altwienerhof (Map 6; ☎ 892 60 00; fax -8), 15, Herklotzgasse 6, is a small, family run hotel offering good-value, decent-sized rooms, and a quality restaurant. Stylish singles/doubles are AS700/1080 and have a shower, WC, TV and phone. Half or full board is possible.

Pension Continental (Map 4; ☎ 523 24 18; fax 523 26 30), 07, Kirchengasse 1, has variable rooms starting at AS700/950 with bath or shower, WC and cable TV. It enjoys a convenient location overlooking Mariahilfer Strasse and has private parking for AS80.

Hotel Cryston (Map 6; ☎ 813 56 82; fax 812 37 01-70; email hotel.cryston@netway.at), 12, Gaudenzdorfer Gürtel 63, has good rooms from AS700/1180 with shower, WC, satellite TV and double glazed windows. There's also free private parking and a breakfast buffet. Rooms for AS420/650 have a sink but don't have TV, shower or WC. There's an AS10 charge to use the hall showers.

Hotel Fürstenhof (Map 6; ☎ 523 32 67; fax -26; fuerst@ping.at), 07, Neubaugürtel 4, opposite Westbahnhof, is a typical Viennese family run hotel. Rooms (with TV) are AS880/1260 with shower and WC or AS500/800 without. Inquire about any discounts that may be available.

Rooms in all the following places have shower and WC, cable or satellite TV, and other amenities. *Hotel Am Schottenpoint* (Map 4; ☎ 310 87 87; fax -4; email schott@treangeli.at) is at 09, Währinger Strasse 22. The entrance is through a small, fading gallery with frescoes and a stucco ceiling, but the rest of it is in a more modern style. Singles/doubles are AS980/1400, or AS890/1180 in winter.

Attache (Map 7; ☎ 505 18 17; fax 505 18 17-232), 04, Wiedner Hauptstrasse 71, has 23 rooms from AS790/1090; most have period furniture, some are in Art Nouveau style. *Hotel Adlon* (Map 5; ☎ 216 67 88; fax -116), 02, Hofenedergasse 4, has a relaxing ambience, and white rooms with fake flowers for AS850/1250. There's a sauna (AS100, including a drink).

Hotel Congress (Map 7; ☎ 505 55 06; fax 505 23 40), 04, Wiedner Gürtel 34-36, has rather characterless rooms for AS890/1090, but it's convenient to Südbahnhof. In *Hotel Alpha* (Map 4; ☎ 319 16 46; fax 319 42 16), 09, Boltzmanngasse 8, rooms (from AS795/1160) are similarly nondescript, but reasonably equipped.

Hotel Donauwalzer (Map 4; ☎ 405 76 45; 408 60 73) is at 17, Ottakringer Strasse 5. Its rooms, from AS590/790, are reasonable value though they vary in quality. The dimly lit café has live dancing music (waltzes etc) on Friday and Saturday.

In the Suburbs

Hotel Victoria (Map 6) is next to the plush Parkhotel Schönbrunn (see Top End) where it has its reception. It's an excellent deal as guests can use all the top facilities at the

Schönbrunn. Singles/doubles start at AS775/1100 and have shower, WC, TV and telephone; a few small singles without shower start at AS455.

West of the city in the Wienerwald is *Sophienalpe* (Map 2; ☎ 486 24 32; fax 485 16 55 12; sophienalpe@hotels.or.at), 14, Sofienalpenstrasse 13, with an indoor swimming pool and a restaurant. The yellow Bundesbus from the end of tram No 43 passes near the hotel, but as it doesn't run in the evening you really need a car to stay here. Singles/doubles with private shower and WC are AS350/700; rising to AS500/900 for bigger rooms. It's closed from 1 November to 31 March.

Schloss Wilhelminenberg (Map 2; ☎ 485 85 03; fax 485 48 76), 16, Savoyenstrasse 2, is also convenient for the Wienerwald and has a big garden, stately appearance and fine views from the terrace café. Prices start at AS850/1270 for rooms with very high ceilings, cable TV, shower and WC. Bus Nos 46B and 146B stop outside and link to citybound trams J, 44 and 46. There's plenty of parking.

Beyond the central cemetery, near the terminus of tram No 71, is *Weber Gasthof* (Map 2; ☎ 769 10 82; fax -40), 11, Kaiserebersdorfer Strasse 283C, with singles/doubles with shower, WC and cable TV for 720/980. There's lots of parking.

There are few places east of the Danube. One is *Landgasthof Müllner* (Map 2; ☎ 774 27 26; fax -21), 22, Esslinger Hauptstrasse 82; it's a small place and good value. Renovated singles/doubles with shower, WC and cable TV are AS480/900. Phone ahead if arriving on Monday, Tuesday and after 3 pm on Sunday as the restaurant is closed. There's free parking, otherwise you need to take the U1 to Kagran and then a 20 minute trip on bus No 26A.

Just east of the Alte Donau, a five minute walk from the U1 line, is the hotel-restaurant *Zur Kagraner Brück* (Map 5; ☎ 203 12 95; fax -16), 22, Wagramer Strasse 52. It offers large singles/doubles with shower and WC for AS660/980. There's free parking round the back.

PLACES TO STAY – TOP END

All rooms in this category should have, as a minimum, private shower or bath, WC, cable TV, direct-dial phone, mini-bar and radio. These hotels will have all the facilities business visitors might require.

Innere Stadt

Unless otherwise noted the following can all be found on Map 8.

The *Hotel am Schubertring* (☎ 717 02 -0; fax 713 99 66), Schubertring 11, is a good choice. Maze-like corridors lead to well-equipped singles/doubles (from AS1350/1850; less in winter) with Biedermeier or Art Nouveau furniture.

Hotel Austria (☎ 515 23; fax -506; email hotelaus@ping.at), Am Fleischmarkt 20, is down a quiet cul-de-sac, and offers good value. Pleasantly furnished rooms start at AS1160/1690 with private shower and WC or AS770/1110 without.

Appartement Pension Riemergasse (☎ 512 72 200; fax 513 77 78; email otto@otto.co.at), Riemergasse 8, can arrange parking for AS90 a day. A variety of apartments are available, all with kitchenette, cable TV and bath or WC. Prices for the smallest apartments range from AS920 a single to AS1960 for four, and breakfast costs AS66. Larger apartments sleep up to seven people. Credit cards are not accepted.

Hotel zur Wiener Staatsoper (☎ 513 12 74; fax -15), Krugerstrasse 11, has an attractive stuccoed façade. Rooms (AS1000/1400) are quiet and have white fittings, but are perhaps a little too compact for comfort. Garage parking is discounted to AS200 per day. The plain frontage of *Hotel Kaiserin Elisabeth* (☎ 515 26; fax -7), Weihburggasse 3, belies its pleasant interior and long history (Mozart stayed here). Nicely decorated rooms are AS1450/2450 with bath and WC, and there are a few smaller rooms for AS950/1900 with shower and WC.

Hotel am Stephansplatz (☎ 53 405-0; fax -711), Stephansplatz 9, is the closest you can sleep to Stephansdom without building a nest in the belfry. Comfortable, sizeable singles/doubles cost AS1560/2360 or less.

Near the Centre

Hotel Maté (Map 4; ☎ 404 55; fax -888), 17, Ottakringer Strasse 34-36, has standard four-star rooms but the hotel has five-star facilities, including a swimming pool, solarium, sauna and fitness room (all free for guests). Prices start at AS1080/1780, or AS960/1280 in winter.

Thüringer Hof (Map 4; ☎ 401 79; fax -600; email thuehof@atnet.at), 18, Jörgerstrasse 4-8, has a variety of rooms from AS850/1290; some are very spacious. There's parking for AS50 and a rooftop terrace.

Hotel Arkadenhof (Map 4; ☎ 310 08 37; fax 310 76 86), 09, Viriotgasse 5, is a comfortable, stylish, small hotel that opened in 1992. Rooms have all the facilities (including air-con) and cost AS1380/1880 (AS200/300 less in winter). A comparable if larger place is the *Theater-Hotel* (Map 4; ☎ 405 36 48; fax 405 14 06), 80, Josefstädter Strasse 22, with an Art Nouveau aura. Rooms cost AS1600/2510; 20% less in winter.

Located in a typically grand Viennese building, the *Hotel Atlanta* (Map 4; ☎ 405 12 30; fax 405 53 75), 09, Währinger Strasse 33, is a good four-star hotel. Rooms are reasonably spacious and well furnished with elegant touches. Singles/doubles are AS1020/1500 and triples are AS1800. From November to March prices are reduced by about AS200 per person.

Close to the Theater an der Wien, the theatrical connection of *Hotel-Pension Schneider* (Map 8; ☎ 588 38-0; fax -212), 06, Getreidemarkt 5, is obvious when you enter the lobby and see the signed photos of the actors and opera stars who have stayed here. Singles are AS880 to AS1380, doubles are AS1700, and there are excellent self-contained two-person apartments for AS2180. Prices are slightly lower in the winter.

Aphrodite (Map 8; ☎ 211 48; fax -15), 02, Praterstrasse 28, is a four-star hotel with a unique extra: beauty treatments for both men and women (eg a three day program costs AS4830). You'll be dazzled by the many mirrors in the rooms, presumably there so you can admire your progress. There's also a rooftop terrace, swimming pool, sauna and fitness room, all of which are free to guests. Singles/doubles are AS1650/2250.

Other four-star hotels include:

Albatros (Map 4; ☎ 317 35 08; fax -85; email albatros@atnet.at), 09, Liechtensteinstrasse 89, is a modern hotel with single/double rooms from AS1320/1740. There's also a sauna/solarium on site.

Artis (Map 7; ☎ 713 25 21; fax 714 59 30), 03, Rennweg 51, has standardised rooms for AS1300/1890, and an underground carpark (AS100).

Favorita (Map 7; ☎ 601 46-0; fax -720; email favorita@trendhotels.at), 10, Laxenburger Strasse 8-10, is a modern hotel with good facilities for businesspeople. It has rooms from AS1320/1700, and a sauna/steam bath (free for guests).

Reither (Map 6; ☎ 893 68 41; fax 893 68 35), 15, Graumanngasse 16, is a Best Western B&B hotel, with rooms from AS1000/1640. It also has a sauna and indoor swimming pool (free for guests).

Tyrol (Map 8; ☎ 587 46 06; fax -66), 06, Mariahilfer Strasse 15, is a smallish hotel with rooms from AS900/1280, some with large, oval baths. The entrance is around the side.

In the Suburbs

Celtes (Map 3; ☎ 440 41 51; fax -116), 19, Celtesgasse 1, is in the Neustift am Walde Heurigen area (take bus No 35 from the centre). It's good value for a four-star place at AS850/1400 for singles/doubles. There's a bar, garden and gym. A higher standard is offered at *Clima Villenhotel* (Map 3; ☎ 37 15 16; fax 37 13 92), 19, Nussberggasse 2C, also in a Heurigen area and close to Nussdorf station. It has covered parking, an indoor swimming pool and sauna, a restaurant and garden; rooms start at AS1300/1900, reducing in low season.

Parkhotel Schönbrunn (Map 6; ☎ 87 804; fax -3220; parkhotel@austria-hotels.co.at), 13, Hietzinger Hauptstrasse 10-20, is easily accessible from the centre by U4 (get off at the Hietzing stop). It was built partially with money from Emperor Franz Josef who considered it his guesthouse. The lobby and grand ballroom all have the majesty of a five-star place, and the rooms surround a large garden with sun lounges, trees and grass. There's also a 12m swimming pool

(free for guests), and AS140 gives you entry to the fitness room and sauna. The best rooms are in the older part, but they're more expensive. Singles/doubles with bath and WC start at AS1385/1780; there are a few cheaper, smaller singles.

PLACES TO STAY – OVER THE TOP

Vienna has 13 five-star hotels; all but one are within or adjoining the Innere Stadt. Standard or 'economy' (something of a misnomer in this category) rooms are comfortable and with all the expected fittings and facilities, but they're not necessarily much better than those in a good four-star hotel. You're really paying the premium for the ambience, reputation, better service levels and the grandeur of the reception and lobby areas. All also offer 'superior' rooms and suites, as well as facilities for businesspeople. Breakfast generally costs extra, but may be included in special, lower weekend rates.

At the *Hotel Sacher* (Map 8; ☎ 51 456; fax -810; email hotel@sacher.com), 01, Philharmonikerstrasse 4, elegance and tradition go hand in hand. Rooms with Baroque furnishings and genuine 19th century oil paintings start at AS2500/4200.

Hotel Imperial (Map 8; ☎ 501 10-0; fax -410), 01, Kärntner Ring 16, is a truly palatial and expensive period hotel (singles/doubles from AS4200/5300). Similarly impressive is *Hotel Bristol* (Map 8; ☎ 51 516-0; fax -550), 01, Kärntner Ring 1, where rooms start at AS3500/5900.

The *Inter-Continental* (Map 8; ☎ 711 22-0; fax 713 44 89; email vienna@interconti .com), 03, Johannesgasse 28, has a huge stylish lobby and ballroom, and rooms from AS2850/3190 with traditional furnishings. The solarium, sauna and fitness room are free for guests.

Hotel Marriott (Map 8; ☎ 515 18-0; fax -6736) is at 01, Parkring 12A. Its harmonious, galleried lobby shelters shops, cafés and fake pink flamingos. Large, renovated rooms are AS2800 (single or double), and excellent hotel facilities such as fitness room, sauna and 13m swimming pool are free for guests.

Schwarzenberg (Map 7; ☎ 798 45 15; fax

798 47 14; email palais@schwarzenberg
.via.at), 03, Schwarzenbergplatz 9, is a small
hotel in the Schwarzenberg Palais with
extensive private grounds and tennis courts;
rooms with period furniture start at AS2900/
3300, and there's free parking.

Renaissance (Map 6; ☎ 85 04-0 fax -100),
15, Ullmannstrasse 71, by the Schönbrunn
U3 station, is a modern hotel with a rooftop
swimming pool, where rooms start at
AS1900/2200.

Other possibilities include the *Ana Grand*
(Map 8; ☎ 515 80-0; fax 515 13 13), 01,
Kärntner Ring 9, recently rebuilt and charging AS3700/4700; or the *Hotel Ambassador*
(☎ 514 66; fax 513 29 99; email sales@
anagrand.com), 01, Kärntner Strasse 22,
bang in the centre with relatively affordable
singles for AS1800 (AS1200 in low season).

LONG-TERM ACCOMMODATION
Viennese looking for accommodation turn to
Bazar magazine (AS20). It's packed with
advertisements for all sorts of things, including ads placed by people seeking or offering
houses or flats to share. It's free to place ads.
The time scale of places on offer may range
from indefinite rental, to occupation of a flat
for a month or so while the resident is on
holiday abroad. *Findegrube* is a similar publication. The *Falter* events magazine also
carries accommodation ads.

The accommodation agencies mentioned
earlier under Finding Somewhere to Stay can
arrange long-term accommodation, either in
apartments or private rooms. Another approach is to ask around the universities, and
check university noticeboards – those in the
main university building and in the technical
university are good bets. There's quite a
swift turnover of student-type accommodation so you'll be able to find something.
Prices start at about AS3000/6000 per month
for rooms/ apartments.

Contact the student dorms listed earlier
under Student Residences to see if they have
places; even if they don't, they may be able
to put you on to something. *Kolping-
Gästehaus* (see Hotels & Pensions in the
Budget category) charges AS3690/5980 per
month for a single/double with hall shower,
or AS4570/7740 in a new room with private
shower and WC, telephone and cable TV;
doubles with shower are AS6860. These
prices are for B&B; add AS745 for half board
and a further AS285 for full board. Rooms
are mainly occupied by students, but you
don't have to be one to stay here.

Places to Eat

There are thousands of restaurants to choose from in Vienna, covering all budgets and all styles of cuisine. Coffee houses and wine taverns are almost a defining characteristic of Vienna, and are great places to eat. *Beisl* is a common Viennese name for a small tavern or restaurant. If you haven't the time or the money for a sit-down meal, there are many takeaway places, including the Würstel stands that are another characteristic institution of Vienna; they provide a quick snack of sausage and bread for about AS20 to AS35.

The main meal is taken at midday. Most restaurants have a set meal or menu of the day (*Tagesteller* or *Tagesmenu*) that gives the best value for money: a lunch menu with soup can sometimes cost as little as AS55 to AS70. Chinese restaurants are particularly good value in this respect. For reasons of space only a few have been mentioned in this chapter, but they're well worth looking out for. Pizzerias are numerous and also offer good value.

The cheapest sit-down food is generally in the university restaurants (*Mensas*). These are open to everyone, though they usually only serve weekday lunches. Expect to find two or three different daily specials, including a vegetarian choice. Students may be able to get a discount of AS4 or so if they show an ISIC card. Mensas are good places to meet students (who usually speak English well) and find out about the new 'in' places round town. The main train stations all have several options for a cheap meal. Branches of the Wienerwald chain of restaurants offer unremarkable but reasonably priced chicken dishes, either on an eat-in or takeaway basis. Nordsee is its fishy equivalent. The Schnitzelhaus chain is an excellent place for fast food on a schnitzel theme. Prices are low: a schnitzel with fries or potato salad costs AS45, a schnitzel burger is AS25, and large cans of beer are AS22. There are nearly 30 branches round town, and all are open daily

from 10 am to 10 pm. It's rather like an Austrian version of McDonald's but without the clown with pink hair. (Plenty of McDonald's are scattered round Vienna, too.)

For expensive dining, five-star hotels invariably have a gourmet restaurant. Pricier restaurants usually add a cover charge (*Gedeck*), typically around AS25 at lunch and AS45 in the evening.

VIENNESE CUISINE

Traditional Viennese food is generally quite heavy and hearty with meat strongly emphasised. Even so, many places now offer at least one vegetarian dish, and there has been a noticeable move towards providing light, healthy meals (eg a *Fitnessteller*), especially in the summer.

Wiener Schnitzel is Vienna's best known culinary concoction, and is consumed everywhere. It's a cutlet covered in a coating of

---

A Culinary Institution

The Würstel Stand (sausage stand) is a familiar Viennese institution and may sell up to a dozen types of sausage. Each comes with a chunk of bread and a big dollop of mustard (*Senf*) – which can be sweet (*süss* or *Kremser Senf*) or hot (*scharf*). Tomato ketchup and mayonnaise can be requested. The thinner sausages are served two at a time, except in the less expensive 'hot dog' version, when the sausage is placed in a bread stick.

Types of sausage include: the *Frankfurter*, a standard thin, boiled sausage; the *Bratwurst*, a fat, fried sausage; and *Burenwurst*, the boiled equivalent of Bratwurst. *Debreziner* is a thin, spicy sausage from Hungary. *Currywurst* is Burenwurst with a curry flavour, and *Käsekrainer* is a sausage infused with cheese. *Tiroler Wurst* is a smoked sausage. If you want to surprise and perhaps impress the server, use the following Viennese slang to ask for a Burenwurst with sweet mustard and a crust of bread: 'A Hasse mit an Sóassn und an Scherzl, bitte'. But you probably won't get it – crusts are reserved for regular customers. ∎

---

egg and breadcrumbs and fried. The cutlet is veal *(Kalb)* or, less expensively, pork *(Schwein)*; occasionally you can get variations like turkey *(Puten)*.

Goulash *(Gulasch)* is also very popular. It's a beef stew with a rich sauce flavoured with paprika. Paprika pops up in various other dishes too, though note that *Gefüllte Paprika* is a bell pepper (capsicum) stuffed with rice and meat. Dumplings *(Knödel)* are an element of many meals, and can appear in soups and desserts as well as main courses. *Nockerl* is a home-made pasta with a similar taste to Knödel. Chicken may be called variously *Geflügel* (poultry), *Huhn* (hen) or *Hähnchen* (small cock). A great variety of sausage *(Wurst)* is available, and not only at the takeaway stands. Beef *(Rindfleisch)*, lamb *(Lamm)* and liver *(Leber)* are mainstays of many menus.

Potato will usually appear as French fries, boiled, roasted, or as *Geröstete*, sliced small and sautéed. Tagliatelli-like pasta *(Nudeln)* is a common substitute. *Sauerkraut* is sour-tasting cabbage. You can sometimes find regional Austrian dishes such as *Tiroler Bauernschmaus*, a selection of meats served with sauerkraut, potatoes and dumplings.

The most famous Austrian dessert is the *Strudel*, baked dough filled with a variety of fruits – usually apple *(Apfel)* with a few raisins and cinnamon. *Salzburger Nockerl* (an egg, flour and sugar pudding), although a Salzburg speciality, also makes an appearance on menus. Pancakes are another popular dessert. Vienna is renowned for its excellent pastries and cakes, which are very effective at transferring bulk from your money belt to your waistline.

DRINKS
Nonalcoholic Drinks
Coffee is the preferred hot beverage, rather than tea. Mineral or soda water is widely available, though tap water is fine to drink (Vienna's water comes from the Alps via 100km-long pipes). Apple juice *(Apfelsaft)* is also popular. *Almdudler* is a soft drink found all over Austria; it's a sort of cross between ginger ale and lemonade. Non-

alcholic drinks are generally expensive – taking a water bottle with you while sightseeing could help your budget.

Alcohol
Austrian wine comes in various categories that designate quality and legal requirements in the production, starting with the humble Tafelwein, through to Landwein, Qualitätswein, and Prädikatswein; the latter two also have subgroups. See the Heurigen section later in this chapter for more information on wine.

Austria is also known for its beer; some well known makes include Gösser, Schwechater, Stiegl and Zipfer. It is usually a light, golden colour *(hell)*, though you can sometimes get a dark *(dunkel)* version too. *Weizenbier* (wheat beer), or *Weissbier*, has a distinctive taste. It can be light or dark, clear or cloudy, and is usually served with a slice of lemon straddling the glass rim. Draught beer *(vom Fass)* comes in a 500mL or 300mL glass, called respectively a *Krügerl* (sometimes spelled *Krügel*) and a *Seidel*. A *Pfiff* is ⅛ of a litre (125mL).

Austria produces several types of rum. Obstler is a spirit created from a mixture of fruits, and Sturm is made from fermenting grapes. Schnapps is also a popular spirit.

An Explosive Hangover
The reputation of Austrian wine has fully recovered from the 'anti-freeze scandal' that hit the fan in 1985. In that year Burgenland growers were arrested and convicted for contaminating their wine with illegal additives. Bottles were seized that actually contained chemicals used in the manufacture of explosives. Austrian wines were removed from supermarket shelves around the world and exports plummeted (though one Asian nation mistakenly banned Australian wine instead!). The federal government moved quickly to introduce tough new legislation that tightened controls considerably. Austrian wines have received good press in recent years and exports have now clawed their way back to pre-scandal levels. ■

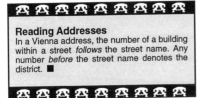

Reading Addresses
In a Vienna address, the number of a building within a street *follows* the street name. Any number *before* the street name denotes the district. ■

SELF-CATERING

Supermarkets are dotted around the city. Only a few have been marked on maps in this book, but anywhere you stay you should be reasonably close to one. Hofer supermarkets are acknowledged as the cheapest; Billa, Konsum, Spar, Löwa and Mondo sometimes have discounted ranges; Julius Meinl is more expensive. Typical opening hours are Monday to Friday from 7.30 or 8 am to 6 or 7.30 pm, and Saturday to noon or 5 pm.

Outside normal shopping hours you can stock up with groceries at the main train stations, though prices are considerably higher. Westbahnhof has a *large shop* (with alcohol) in the main hall, open daily from 6 am to 10.50 pm. Shops in Südbahnhof and Franz Josefs Bahnhof are only *tiny kiosks*, but they're open daily until late. Wien Nord station has a *Billa supermarket* open Monday to Saturday from 7 am to 6.30 pm (8 pm Friday, 2 pm Saturday), and several small provision shops open from 5.30 am to 9 pm daily. Wien Mitte has a large *Interspar supermarket* (standard hours) and a reasonably sized *provisions store* open from 5.30 am to 9.50 pm daily. Near the S-Bahn exit in the airport is a *Billa supermarket*, open daily from 7.30 am to 10 pm.

See the Shopping chapter for information on markets.

INNERE STADT

Unless otherwise noted the following can all be found on Map 8.

Self-Service & Budget Restaurants

If you only want a snack, try one of the many Würstel stands, or there's always *McDonald's* (eg on Johannesgasse and Singerstrasse).

Nordsee has a branch at Kärntner Strasse 25. *Schnitzelhaus* is at Krugerstrasse 6.

The *University Mensa*, Universitätsstrasse 7, has dishes from a mere AS36. Take the continuous lift to the 6th floor then walk up one storey. The café adjoining the Mensa has the same meals and longer hours (weekdays from 8 am to 6 pm), and it stays open over summer. In the next block on Universitätsstrasse is *Café Bierkeller Zwillings Gewölb*, also popular with students. It features daily specials from about AS55 in the maze of subterranean rooms. It's open Monday to Friday from 8 am to 1 am and Saturday from 9.30 am to 2 am.

Close by, the *Katholisches Studenthaus Mensa*, Ebendorferstrasse 8, is open Monday to Friday from 11.30 am to 2 pm (closed August to mid-September). Main courses are just AS35 or AS44, and there's a salad buffet. The *Academy of Applied Art Cafeteria*, Oskar Kokoschka Platz 2, open weekdays from 9 am to 6 pm (3 pm Friday), is where you can get cheap snacks and light meals. A small *Mensa* is at the Academy of Fine Arts, Schillerplatz 3, open weekdays from 8.30 am to 7 pm (closed July to September).

The most central university cafeteria is the *Music Academy Mensa*, Johannesgasse 8. Lunches are served Monday to Friday between 11 am and 2 pm (daily to 1.30 pm during the summer holidays), though you can also have coffee and snacks weekdays from 7.30 am to 3 pm. Main meals cost AS48 to AS55 and the salad buffet is AS24/48 for a small/large bowl. Nearby at No 3 is *Zur Fischerin Capua*, with fishing trophies on the walls and good weekday menus (to about 6 pm) for around AS78 including soup. There are tables on the 1st floor above the small bar area (open daily, except Sunday lunch time).

Trzesniewski, Dorotheergasse 1, is open Monday to Friday from 8.30 am to 7.30 pm and Saturday from 9 am to 1 pm. It's a basic deli bar where you stand in line to choose your food from the counter. Open sandwiches with a variety of toppings are about AS9 each; they're quite tiny (two bites and they're gone), but this is a famous Viennese institution and you may want to sample a few, if only to follow in Kafka's mouthfuls (he was a regular here). Beer comes in tiny Pfiff (125mL) measures.

Rosenberger Markt Restaurant is at Maysedergasse 2. This downstairs buffet place offers a fine array of meats, drinks and desserts to enable you to compile a meal for around AS100, but watch out for extras (like bread and butter) that can be pricey. If you really want to save Schillings, concentrate on the salad or vegetable buffet: some people unashamedly pile a Stephansdom spire-shaped food tower on small plates (AS29) for a filling feast. It's open daily from 10.30 am to 11 pm, and has free lockers for your bags.

Restaurant Marché Movenpick is in the Ringstrassen Galerien shopping complex, Kärntner Ring 5-7. It's almost the same as Rosenberger except the small salad/vegetable bowls are only AS26. Another good feature is the pizza for AS57, available most days, where you can help yourself to a variety of toppings. It's open Monday to Saturday from 9 am to 11 pm, and Sunday and holidays from 11 am to 11 pm.

Sushi bars have sprung up in Vienna in recent years. *Akakiko*, Singerstrasse 4, has sushi from AS20 per piece, or complete lunchboxes from AS88; it's open daily from 10.30 am to 10.30 pm. Pizzerias are scattered around too, and are generally reasonable value. *Pizza Bizi*, Rotenturmstrasse 4, is a convenient self-service place open daily from 11 am to 11.30 pm. Pasta with a choice of sauces is AS65, pizzas are AS60 to AS75 (or AS28 for a slice) and there are salad and vegetable buffets. Pizza Bizi also has a takeaway counter at Franz Josefs Kai 21.

Brezel Gwölb, Ledererhof 9, offers Austrian food from AS80 to AS175 in a cobbled courtyard or an atmospheric, cellar-like interior, complete with background classical music. It's open daily from 11.30 am to 1 am.

China Restaurant Turandot, Vorlaufstrasse 2, is open daily. The three course weekday lunch specials are AS68, or there's also an all-you-can-eat lunch buffet for AS79 (AS129 on weekends and weekday evenings). Weekday Chinese lunches start at AS57 at *Restaurant Siam*, at Rotenturmstrasse 11.

Naschmarkt is a buffet-style restaurant chain, offering a good choice of meals, including a three course lunch menu for AS67 (AS77 on weekends). There's a branch at Schottengasse 1, and another (with an outside terrace) at Schwarzenbergplatz 16. It's open daily.

An unconnected place, also called *Naschmarkt* (Map 8), is on the corner of Ebendorferstrasse and Felderstrasse. It has two parts. The self-service section has menus with soup for AS54 and AS59 and is open weekdays from 11 am to 2 pm. The cosier Stüberl, with outside tables, is open weekdays from 6.30 am to 2.30 pm and has similar food, plus breakfasts.

Restaurant Smutny, Elisabethstrasse 8, serves typical Viennese food in a room with wall tiles and colourful lightshades. Dishes are filling and reasonably priced (from AS80) and it's open daily from 10 am to midnight. A simpler 'Schwemme' section is next door.

Mid-Range Restaurants

La Crêperie (☎ 512 56 87), Grünangergasse 10, has different rooms with varied and creative décor, ranging from arty odds and ends and ancient books, to a pseudo circus tent complete with clowns' faces. Meat and fish dishes are AS145 to AS245, beer is AS40 a Krügerl (500mL) and wine is AS24 an Achterl (125mL). If you stick to its speciality, crêpes, a light meal can be inexpensive. These are available with sweet or savoury fillings; the Florentine (AS98) is a good combination of spinach, ham, cheese and egg with a dollop of sour cream. It has outside seating down the side street (Nikolaigasse) and is open daily from 11.30 am to midnight.

Zu den 3 Hacken (☎ 512 58 95), Singerstrasse 28, is a down to earth place with outside tables and a small room devoted to Schubert (despite the anachronistic WWII radio). It serves typical Austrian food for around AS90 to AS220, and opens Monday to Saturday from 9 am to midnight.

Wrenkh (☎ 533 15 26), Bauernmarkt 10, is a fairly upmarket specialist vegetarian restaurant, open daily (except Sunday) till midnight. Meticulously prepared dishes are AS88 to AS125, with a three course menu for AS175. It has a bar next door serving the same meals. Wrenkh has a simpler Gasthaus (☎ 892 33 56), 15, Hollergasse 9, which also serves vegetarian food.

Definitely not for squeamish vegetarians is *Zum Weissen Rauchfangkehrer* (☎ 512 34 71), Weihburggasse 4, because of the many hunting trophies on the wall. Meat specialities are served up for around AS100 to AS230 (plus a AS30 cover charge). It's an atmospheric place, mostly partitioned into small booths, and has live piano music nightly from 7 pm (open daily).

Griechenbeisl (☎ 533 19 77), Fleischmarkt 11, is a famous old tavern once frequented by the likes of Beethoven, Schubert and Brahms. Choose from the many different vaulted rooms pierced by hanging antlers, or sit in the plant-fringed front garden. Viennese main dishes are in the range of AS165 to AS230, and it's open daily from 11 am to 1 am.

Figlmüller, Wollzeile 5, is a well known place for eating schnitzels (AS156), but it's generally packed (open daily; closed August). *Grotta Azzurra* (☎ 586 10 44-0), Babenburgerstrasse 5, open daily, provides good Italian food, with most dishes above AS160 (plus AS35 cover charge). A popular starter is the antipasto buffet (AS135/165 a small/large plate), which is selected by the server.

Wiener Rathauskeller (☎ 405 12 19), Rathausplatz 1, is in the Rathaus, and the entrance is on the north-east corner. Enjoy the atmosphere in the arcaded Rittersaal, where the walls are filled with murals and floral designs; live harp music (after 7 pm, extra charge of AS15) adds to the ambience. Down the corridor, the *Grinzinger Keller* is similar if barer; from 1 April to 31 October, Tuesday to Saturday, it puts on a dinner show for AS395, comprising music, waltzing and

a three course meal. Otherwise, the same Viennese and international dishes are offered in both halls; most choices are above AS145 (open 11.30 am to 3 pm and 6 to 11.30 pm, closed Sunday).

Situated in the modern building right by Stephansdom, *DO & CO* (☎ 535 39 69), Stephansplatz 12, provides a good view of the cathedral. It serves international and oriental dishes for around the AS200 mark; the food is superb – gourmet quality – but it's so busy the service can be a little tardy (book ahead). It is open daily from noon to 3 pm and 6 pm to midnight, and there's an adjoining café-bar (9 am to 2 am). DO & CO also has a restaurant (Map 6; ☎ 811 18) in Schloss Schönbrunn.

Top-End Restaurants
Zum Kuckuck (☎ 512 84 70), Himmelpfortgasse 15, is a tiny one room place with a vaulted ceiling. Viennese dishes are above AS200 or you can opt for multi-course gourmet menus. The kitchen is open Monday to Friday from noon to 2 pm and 6 to 11 pm.

For Japanese food, try *Yugetsu Saryo* (☎ 512 27 20), Führichgasse 10. On the ground floor is a sushi bar, or go upstairs to have the food cooked in front of you on a large hotplate built into the table. Lunch menus start at AS120, otherwise expect to pay above AS200 per person, plus drinks. Evening set menus start at AS320. The kitchen is open from noon to 2.30 pm and 6 pm to 11 pm (closed Sunday).

Korso (☎ 515 16-546), Mahlerstrasse 2, features wood-panelled elegance and opulent chandeliers. Viennese and international specialities are AS290 to AS420 and there's a vast wine cellar. Its proximity to the opera prompts it to offer a light three course meal (AS630) for those who are replete with culture but depleted of cuisine. Opening hours are noon to 3 pm and 7 pm to 1 am, though it's closed at lunch time on Saturday and on Sundays in July and August.

Drei Husaren (☎ 512 10 92-0), Weihburggasse 4, is in the same price range and is similarly formal and elegant, with soothing live piano music to aid digestion. There's a huge selection of excellent hors d'oeuvres, which are priced according to season and selection. This traditional Viennese restaurant is open daily from noon to 3 pm and 6 pm to midnight.

THE NORTH-WEST
Self-Service & Budget Restaurants
There are numerous inexpensive places to eat to the north and west of the university. The Afro-Asiatisches Institut (Map 4; AAI), 09, Türkenstrasse 3, has a *Mensa* with meals for about AS45, and courtyard eating in the summer. It's open weekdays from 11.30 am to 7 pm (1.30 pm from July to September). The café on the 1st floor is open daily and carries Newsweek magazine.

Tunnel (Map 4; ☎ 405 34 65), 08, Florianigasse 39, is another student haunt, open daily from 9 am to 2 am. The food is satisfying and easy on the pocket: breakfast is AS29, lunch specials start at AS45, spaghetti is from AS38, big pizzas from AS60 and salads from AS20. Bottled beer costs from AS25 for 500mL. The Tunnel also has a cellar bar with live music (see the Entertainment chapter).

Vegi Rant (Map 4; ☎ 425 06 54), 09, Währinger Strasse 57, has a three course daily menu for AS102, and dishes like cheese schnitzel for AS79; it's open from 11.30 am to 2.30 pm Sunday to Friday. Next door is a health food shop. Good vegetarian lunches (AS70) are also available at *Kräuterdrogerie* (Map 4; ☎ 405 45 22), 08, Kochgasse 34, a health food and Ayurvedic remedies shop.

Laudon Stüberl (Map 4), 08, Laudongasse 16, is open weekdays from 9 am to 6 pm. Lunch menus (to 3 pm) with soup are AS50 or AS58. A block east on Laudongasse is *Beislbar Geralala*, with similarly-priced food till the early hours.

Middle & Top-End Restaurants
For Thai food, try *Thai Haus* (Map 4; ☎ 405 71 56), 17, Hernalser Hauptstrasse 21. Main courses are AS88 to AS195, plus AS18 to AS40 for garnishes like rice and noodles. All dishes can be mild or hot (scharf) – as in

Thailand, hot means hot! It's open from 6 pm to midnight, except on Tuesday.

Fromme Helene (Map 4; ☎ 406 91 44), 08, Josefstädter Strasse 53, is a small place with a cluttered salon look and good Viennese food. Midday dining is not too expensive (menus from AS75 with soup) though evening dishes are above AS155. It's open weekdays from 11 am to 2.30 pm and 6 pm to midnight, and Saturday from 6 pm to midnight.

Restaurant Sailer (Map 4; ☎ 479 21 21-0), 18, Gersthofer Strasse 14, serves traditional Viennese dishes for around the AS180 mark, but with refined touches. The quality and service are exceptional for the price. There's a garden, and a cellar area serving snacks, perhaps to musical accompaniment. It's open daily.

Casa Culinaria (Map 3; ☎ 328 70 30), 19, Sieveringer Strasse 4, attached to the four-star hotel Kaiser Franz Joseph, is a quality Italian restaurant. Main courses are above AS170 (plus cover charge) and it's open daily; on Tuesday and Wednesday nights a pianist tinkles tunes by the aquarium.

Feuervogel (Map 4; ☎ 317 53 91), 09, Alserbachstrasse 21, is a Russian restaurant that has been run by the same family of Ukrainians for over 75 years. The colourful décor matches the conversational gambits (in English) of the surviving generations. The food is hearty rather than refined, but tasty nonetheless. Main courses are from AS150 up to AS635 (for caviar) and there's sometimes live music on the weekend. It's open from 6 pm to 2 am, but closed Sunday and mid-July to mid-August.

THE SOUTH-WEST
Self-Service & Budget Restaurants
Würstel stands are all over the place, but if you're in the area, wander down to the Ring end of Mariahilfer Strasse to choose between two cheap, adjacent ones engaged in cut-throat competition. The sign on one proclaims *mein Kunde ist König* (my customer is king); the other counters with *mein Kunde ist Kaiser* (my customer is emperor). The nearby *Naschmarkt* has plenty of places to

eat. The Turkish influence is very evident in this market nowadays, with Turkish breads and cheeses for sale; filling kebabs for around AS35 are a popular choice for lunch.

The *Technical University Mensa* (Map 8) is at 04, Resselgasse 7-9; once in the building, find the yellow area and then go upstairs to the 1st floor. Good weekday lunches (11 am to 2.30 pm) are only AS30 to AS55, with several choices. There are *Schnitzelhaus* branches at 06, Otto Bauer Gasse 24 (Map 4), and 05, Kettenbrückengasse 19 (Map 6).

Schnitzelwirt Schmidt (Map 4; ☎ 523 37 71), 07, Neubaugasse 52, is the best place for schnitzels and prides itself on its enormous portions (from AS64). This informal, often hectic place is something of an institution among travellers – you really have to visit to see the size of these things. Unless you have a huge appetite, share one (they're used to supplying two plates) and just get extra garnishes (around AS22 each). Many variations on the basic schnitzel are offered: the Schnitzel Don Carlos (AS101) is a good choice, it comes with a piled serving of rice, capsicums and ham. They can wrap leftovers to take away. Service is sometimes sloppy; get your drinks order in first (these are from a different server) – it's no fun chomping through a mountain of schnitzel with a parched throat. Opening hours are 11 am to 10 pm (closed Sunday and holidays).

A good pizzeria is *Il Mare* (Map 4), 07, Zieglergasse 15. It's open to 11 pm (closed Sunday and holidays). The pictures on the wall betray a definite fondness for nautical themes, as befits the name. Pizzas are thin but with tasty toppings (AS60 to AS130, most are around AS85).

Gaunkerl (Map 4), 07, Kaiserstrasse 50, serves typical food, from about AS65 (closed Sunday). The décor in the front room creates the illusion that you're sitting outside, complete with glowing stars and witches on broomsticks flying overhead. The illusion becomes more convincing after a couple of beers. Around the corner is *Burg-Keller*, 07, Burggasse 115. It's a quiet, relaxing place with tasty Austrian cooking priced from AS65 to AS150. Weekday lunch specials are

excellent value – three courses from about AS60 (open daily from 10 am to midnight). There are English menus.

Amerlingbeisl (Map 4), 07, Stiftgasse 8, attracts mainly young people, both as an eating (AS58 to AS115) and a drinking (beer AS36 a Krügerl) venue. It's open daily from 9 am to 2 am. In summer people flock into the rear courtyard. Nearby, on Gutenburggasse, there's a cheap pizzeria, *La Gondola* (open daily), and *La Bodega de Fito*, a Latin American place with live music on Friday nights and food for around AS90 (closed Sunday). These three places are in the Spittelberg quarter, an historic area with restored Biedermeier houses and various interesting shops and bars.

K & K Bierkanzlei (Map 8), 06, Windmühlgasse 20, is small, cheap and typically Viennese. Filling and straightforward daily menus cost from AS59 (several choices, with soup). Opening hours are 8 am to 6 pm. There are many images of Franz Josef and Elisabeth – their faces even appear on the salt and pepper pots. The K & K in the name, incidentally, which you'll come across elsewhere, stands for 'König und Kaiser' (king and emperor), and refers to the Austro-Hungarian dual monarchy.

Pulkautaler Weinhaus (Map 4), 15, Felberstrasse 2, near Westbahnhof, is a simple place with good food (AS40 to AS115; English menus). There's also a bar area with several different beers (AS32 a Krügerl), and it's open daily from 9 am to 10 pm.

Middle & Top-End Restaurants

Ungar-Grill (Map 4; ☎ 523 62 09), 07, Burggasse 97, is a Hungarian restaurant with a patio area and live Gypsy music every night. Fish, chicken, grills and other dishes are AS85 to AS180, and there's a AS11 cover charge. Opening hours are Monday to Saturday from 6 pm to midnight. Reserve ahead as it's popular with tour groups. Another place to try nearby is *Sobieski* (Map 4; ☎ 523 13 96), 07, Burggasse 83A, a small restaurant serving Polish and Austrian food above AS88 (closed weekends and holidays).

Glacisbeisl (Map 4) is in the middle of the

Museumsquartier. It feels miles away from the centre of the city. Ascend the path up to garden tables surrounded by trees, a trellis and vines. Vegetarian and Austrian food are in the AS90 to AS225 range (open daily from 10 am to midnight).

The attentive *Beim Novak* (Map 4; ☎ 523 32 44), 07, Richtergasse 12, has traditional Austrian food (AS85 to AS255) with good explanations of each dish in the English menu. Speciality of the house is Überbackene Fledermaus (bat au gratin) for AS160 – the 'bat wings' are actually cuts of beef. It's closed Saturday evening, Sunday, and mid-July to mid-August.

The *Hotel Altwienerhof* (☎ 892 60 00), 15, Herklotzgasse 6, has an elegant restaurant serving quality French and international cuisine for around AS300. It also has a huge wine cellar.

WESTERN SUBURBS

Schutzhaus am Ameisbach (Map 4), 14, Braillegasse 1, is great value, and has many tables in a large garden, plus a play area for kids. A popular choice is spare ribs: the full serving for AS140, including sauces and baked potato, will feed two (a half portion is AS80). Take bus No 51A from Hietzing to Braillegasse. It's open from 9 am (3 pm Tuesday) to midnight (11 pm Sunday) though the kitchen closes at 9.30 pm, or 9 pm on Sunday. It's closed Monday and throughout February.

Prilisauer (Map 2; ☎ 979 32 28), 14, Linzer Strasse 423, is a typical Viennese Gasthaus, with meals starting at about AS85. There's a garden and several beers on tap. It is by the last stop on tram No 49; it's closed on Monday and until 4 pm on Tuesday. From here, you could take bus No 150 or 151 to the Badgasse stop, where you'll find *Hawei* (Map 2) at 14, Hauptstrasse 62. This place has good food and a garden, but its main novelty is that the beer prices fluctuate according to demand – monitor the price on screens above the bar. It calls itself the 'Erste Wiener Bierbörse' (Vienna's first beer stock exchange) and it's open daily from 4 pm (11 am on Sunday) to 2 am.

THE SOUTH

On Wiedner Gürtel opposite Südbahnhof are several inexpensive places to eat – all can be found on Map 7. They include a branch of *Wienerwald*, the fried chicken chain (open 8 am to 12.30 am daily), and *China Restaurant Phoenix*, with weekday lunch menus for AS56 including soup or a spring roll. A few doors down at No 4 is *Kristall*, open daily from 7 am to 4 am. Meals start at about AS60 (English menu); the food is surprisingly good for the price and there's plenty of it.

Mona Lisa, 10, Gudrunstrasse 136, has cheap pizzas, including special lunch-time deals (closed Sunday).

Oxen Steak, 04, Prinz Eugen Strasse 2, is carnivore territory, with ox skulls on the walls and schnitzels, steaks, grills and spare ribs (AS85 to AS205) on the menu.

The *Vier Jahreszeiten Restaurant* (Map 8; ☎ 711 22 140), in the Hotel Inter-Continental, is highly rated for gourmet food (closed at weekends), and also does standard Viennese fare. The sumptuous lunch buffet costs AS490 and à la carte dishes are AS195 to AS325. A pianist plays in the evening.

THE EAST

Wien Mitte station has several places for cheap and quick eating, like the *Interspar* supermarket, which has a self-service restaurant upstairs (meals AS50 to AS90; closes 7 pm weekdays and 5 pm Saturday).

Indian restaurants are not very numerous, but one good one in the city is *Zum Inder* (Map 5), 02, Praterstrasse 57, which serves dishes from about AS90 (open daily). Weekday lunches with soup start at just AS50.

Schweizerhaus (Map 7), in the Prater at 02, Strasse des Ersten Mai 116, is famous for its roasted pork hocks (Hintere Schweinsstelze). A meal consists of a massive chunk of meat on the bone (about 750g minimum at AS182 per kilogram – eat alone and end up the size of two people), best served with mustard (AS5) and freshly grated horseradish (AS10). Chomping your way through vast slabs of pig smacks of medieval banqueting, but it's very tasty when washed down with draught Budweiser (the Czech stuff). It gets incredibly busy, and there are many outside tables. It's open daily from 10 am to 11 pm, mid-March to 31 October only. *Café-Restaurant Luftberg* (Map 7), nearby on Walsteingarten Strasse, offers a similar meat orgy.

Vegetarians will have better luck in the Prater at *Estancia Cruz* (Map 7), 02, An der Prater Hauptallee 8, a large place with many outside tables in a shady garden. Latin American food costs from AS82 to AS196, including several non-meat choices (open 11 am to 1 am daily).

Gasthaus Hansy (Map 5), 02, Praterstern, serves Viennese food for AS75 to AS185. It's fairly bare inside but the food is reliably good, and there are outside tables (open 9 am to 10 pm daily).

Steirereck (Map 7; ☎ 713 31 68), 08, Rasumofskygasse 2, is gourmet territory; in fact, it's rated one of the best restaurants in Austria. Different parts of the restaurant have a different ambience, but it's pretty formal throughout. Even the toilets are stylish! Tempting main courses all top AS300 (choose from lobster, rabbit, pigeon, venison etc) yet you still have to book days in advance for the evening. The three course lunch menu is AS395; in the evening, the multi-course menu is AS880, or AS1430 including wine with each course. It's open Monday to Friday.

COFFEE HOUSES

The coffee house is an integral part of Viennese life. The story goes that the tradition started after retreating Turkish invaders left behind their supplies of coffee beans in the 17th century. Today Vienna has hundreds of coffee houses. They are a great place for observing the locals in repose and recovering after a hard day's sightseeing. Small/big coffees cost about AS24/38. Although that's expensive, the custom is to take your time. You can linger as long as you like and enjoy the atmosphere or read the café's newspapers – some places stock British and other foreign titles (saving you AS30 or so on purchase

price). Traditional places will serve a glass of water with your coffee.

Coffee houses basically fall into two types, though the distinction is rather blurred nowadays. A Kaffeehaus, traditionally preferred by men, offers games such as chess and billiards and serves wine, beer, spirits and light meals. Whereas a Café Konditorei attracts more women and typically has a salon look with rococo mouldings and painted glass. A wide variety of cakes and pastries is usually on offer.

Café Museum (Map 8), 01, Friedrichstrasse 6, is open daily from 8 am to midnight and has chess, many newspapers and outside tables. The building was created by Adolf Loos in 1899 but has since been renovated.

Café Bräunerhof (Map 8), 01, Stallburggasse 2, has classical music on weekends and holidays from 3 to 6 pm, and British newspapers. It's open weekdays to 7.30 pm (8.30 pm in winter) and weekends to 6 pm.

Café Central (Map 8), 01, Herrengasse 14, has a fine ceiling and pillars, and piano music from 4 to 7 pm. Trotsky came here to play chess. Say 'Hello' to the plaster patron near the door with the walrus moustache – a model of the poet Peter Altenberg. Opening hours are Monday to Saturday from 8 am to 10 pm; coffee costs from AS29.

Café Hawelka (Map 8), 01, Dorotheergasse 6, is another famous coffee house. At first glance it's hard to see what the attraction is: scruffy pictures and posters, brown-stained walls, smoky air, cramped tables. At second glance you see why – it's the people not the place; an ideal location for people-watching. The whole gamut of Viennese society comes here, from students to celebrities. It's also a traditional haunt for artists and writers (the Vienna Group came here in the 1950s and 60s). After 10 pm it gets busy. You're constantly being shunted up to accommodate new arrivals at the table, the organising elderly Frau seizing on any momentarily vacant chair (curtail those toilet visits!) to re-assign it elsewhere. Café Hawelka is open from 8 am (from 4 pm on Sunday and holidays) to 2 am, and it's closed on Tuesday.

PLACES TO EAT

PLACES TO EAT

Types of Coffee

Legend has it that coffee beans were left behind by the fleeing Turks in 1683, and it was this happy accident that resulted in today's plethora of coffee establishments. Vienna's first coffee house opened in 1685, but it could have been emulating successful establishments already opened in Venice (1647 – the first in Europe), Oxford (1650), London (1652), Paris (1660) and Hamburg (1677), rather than having anything to do with the Turks.

Austrian coffee consumption was modest in the ensuing centuries, and it was only after WWII that it really took hold among the population at large. Austrians now drink more coffee than any other beverage, gulping down 221L per person per year (next in line comes beer at 120L, followed by milk at 104L, soft drinks at 84L, mineral water at 76L, black tea at 39L and wine at 33L). Only Finland, Sweden and Denmark consume more coffee per person.

Different types of coffee you'll come across are:

Mocca (sometimes spelled *Mokka*) or *Schwarzer* – black coffee
Brauner – black but served with a tiny jug of milk
Kapuziner – with a little milk and perhaps a sprinkling of grated chocolate
Melange – served with milk, and maybe whipped cream too
Einspänner – with whipped cream, served in a glass
Masagran (or *Mazagran*) – cold coffee with ice and Maraschino liqueur
Wiener Eiskaffee – cold coffee with vanilla ice cream and whipped cream

Waiters normally speak English and can tell you about any specialities available. In particular, various combinations of alcohol may be added (eg *Mozart* coffee with Mozart liqueur, *Fiaker* with rum, *Mocca gespritzt* with cognac, *Maria Theresa* with orange liqueur). Some people find the basic coffee too strong, so there's the option of asking for a *Verlängerter* ('lengthened'), a *Brauner* weakened with hot water. Traditional places will serve the coffee on a silver tray and with a glass of water. Some types of coffee are offered in small *(kleine)* or large *(grosse)* portions. According to an old Viennese tradition, if the waiter fails to give you the bill after three requests you can walk out without paying (three instantaneous requests don't count!). ■

Alt Wien (Map 8), 01, Bäckerstrasse 9, is a rather dark coffee house, attracting students and arty types. At night it becomes a lively drinking venue; beer is AS34 for a Krügerl. Also well known for its goulash (AS80 large, AS55 small), it is open daily from 10 am to 2 am. After a hard night drinking or dancing, greet the dawn at *Café Drechsler* (Map 8), 06, Linke Wienzeile 22, where you'll rub shoulders with traders at the Naschmarkt. Opening hours are 3 am to 8 pm (Saturday 6 pm; closed Sunday). There are billiard tables (the pocketless variety), and meals are AS55 to AS75.

Café Sperl (Map 8), 06, Gumpendorfer Strasse 11, has been well established since 1880 (it was Hitler's favourite coffee house). Features include the Times newspaper, Jugendstil fittings, pocketless billiard tables, and influxes of people from the nearby Theater an der Wien. It's open daily from 7 am (3 pm Sunday and holidays) to 11 pm.

Café Restaurant Landtmann (Map 8), 01, Dr Karl Lueger Ring 4, has outside tables overlooking the Burgtheater. This elegant, upmarket café has English newspapers, coffee from AS28, meals above AS115 and a selection of cakes (open daily from 8 am to midnight).

Café Schwarzenberg (Map 8), 01, Kärntner Ring 17, is another traditional coffee house with seating inside and out. It's popular with all ages and open daily from 7 am (9 am Saturday) to midnight. There's live piano music Tuesday to Friday from 8 to 10 pm, and weekends from 4 to 7 pm and 8 to 10 pm.

The *Hotel Sacher Café* (Map 8), 01, Philharmonikerstrasse 4, behind the Staatsoper, is a picture of opulence with chandeliers, battalions of waiters and rich, red walls and carpets (open 6.30 am to 11.30 pm daily). It's famous for its chocolate apricot cake, Sacher Torte (AS50 a slice; coffee from AS32). Its main rival in terms of Torte is the elegant, equally expensive, mirrored environment of *Demel* (Map 8), 01, Kohlmarkt 14. It's the archetypal Konditorei establishment, open daily from 10 am to 7 pm.

HEURIGEN

Heurigen (wine taverns) can be identified by a green wreath or branch (the Busch'n) hanging over the door. Many have outside tables in large gardens or courtyards. Inside they are fairly rustic but have an ambience all their own. Heurigen almost invariably have food, which you select yourself from hot and cold buffet counters; prices are generally reasonable. It's traditionally acceptable to bring your own food along instead, but this isn't commonly done nowadays.

Heurigen usually have a relaxed atmosphere that gets more and more lively as the customers and mugs of wine get drunk. Many feature traditional live music, perhaps ranging from a solo accordion player to a fully fledged oompah band; these can be a bit touristy but great fun nonetheless. The Viennese tend to prefer a music-free environment. Opening times are approximately 4 pm (or before lunch on weekends) to 11 pm or midnight, though in the less touristy regions some may close for several weeks at a time before reopening. Similarly, some are only open in the summer, or maybe only from Thursday to Sunday. The common measure for Heuriger wine is a Viertel (250mL) in a glass mug, costing around AS25 to AS30, though you can also drink by the Achterl (125mL). A Viertel Gespritzer costs AS16 to AS20.

Heurigen are concentrated in the wine-growing suburbs to the north, west, north-west, and south of the city. Once you pick a region to explore, the best approach is to simply go where the spirit moves you (or to whichever places happen to be open at the time); taverns are very close together and it is easy to visit several on the same evening.

North-West

This is the best known region. The area most favoured by tourists is Grinzing (Map 3; count the tour buses lined up outside at closing time), and this is probably the best

The Heuriger

The *Heuriger* (wine tavern) tradition in Vienna dates back to the Middle Ages, but it was Joseph II in 1784 who first officially granted producers the right to sell their wine directly from their own premises. It proved to be one of his more enduring reforms. These taverns are now one of Vienna's most popular institutions with visitors. The term Heuriger refers not only to the tavern itself but also to the year's new vintage, which officially comes of age on St Martin's Day (11 November). It continues to be Heuriger wine up to its first anniversary, at which time it is promoted (relegated?) to the status of Alte (old) wine. St Martin's day is a day of much drinking and consumption of goose.

A *Buschenschank* is a type of Heuriger that within the Vienna region may only open for 300 days a year. It can only sell its own wine, either new or old, and must close when supplies have dried up. The term is protected. Not so 'Heuriger': taverns can adopt the name even when they don't produce their own wine.

Austrian wine production is 80% white and 20% red. The most common variety (36%) is the dry white Grüner Veltliner; it also tends to be the cheapest on the wine list. Other common varieties are Riesling and Pinot Blanc. Sekt is a sparkling wine. Some of the young wines can be a little sharp, so it is common to mix them with 50% soda water, called a *Gespritzer* or *G'spritzer*. The correct salute when drinking a Heuriger is *Prost* (cheers). But the Viennese can't wait for 11 November to drink the new vintage, and are prepared to consume it early, as unfermented must (Most), partially fermented (Sturm), or fully fermented but still cloudy (Staubiger); they taste a little like cider. The correct salute when drinking these versions is *Gesundheit* (health), perhaps in recognition of the risk taken by the palate. ∎

area to head for if you want to catch some live music and enjoy a lively atmosphere. However, bear in mind that this area is mostly eschewed as a tourist ghetto by the Viennese themselves. There are several good Heurigen in a row along Cobenzlgasse and Sandgasse, near the terminus of tram 38 (which starts at Schottentor on the Ring). *Reinprecht* (Map 3), 19, Cobenzlgasse 22, is a very large place with a lively, sing-along environment.

From Grinzing, you can hop on the 38A bus to Heiligenstadt, where in 1817 Beethoven lived in the Beethovenhaus (Map 3), 19, Pfarrplatz 3. This is a big hall with live music and many annexes. From Heiligenstadt it's just a few stops on tram D north to Nussdorf (Map 3), where a couple of Heurigen await right by the tram terminus. But don't just settle for these without exploring first; there are several along Kahlenberger Strasse.

Farther west are the areas of Sievering (terminus of bus No 39A) and Neustift am Walde (bus 35A). Both these buses link up with the No 38 tram route. Ottakring (Map 4) is a small but authentic Heurigen area a short walk west of the tram J terminus.

North

The Heurigen areas here in the 21st district are less visited by tourists and are therefore more typically Viennese, catering to a regular clientele. They are also cheaper: a Viertel costs around AS22. Live music is not the norm. Stammersdorf (Map 2; terminus of tram No 31) is Vienna's largest wine-growing district, producing about 30% of Vienna's wine. From the tram stop, get on to Stammersdorfer Strasse, the next street north and running east-west. Many Heurigen are

on this street in the westward direction; two good ones to try are *Weinhof Wieninger* at No 78 and *Weingut Klager* at No 14.

Strebersdorf (Map 2) is at the terminus of tram No 32, or about a 30 minute walk west of Stammersdorf. The Heurigen are north of the tram terminus. *Weingut Schilling*, Langenzersdorferstrasse 54, has a good reputation for wine. It's closed on odd-numbered months (January, March etc), at which time the next-door *Strauch* at No 50A is open. Another place to try is *Noschiel-Eckert* (☎ 292 25 96), Strebersdorfer Strasse 158, open every odd month. Paintings by a different artist are featured every month and there's occasional live music (anything from jazz to rock & roll).

South

As in the north, tourists are less prevalent in these Heurigen. Mauer is in the south-west, on the edge of the Wiernerwald (Vienna Woods). Take the U4 to Hietzing and then tram No 60 to Mauer Hauptplatz. Oberlaa (Map 2) is farther east. To get there, take the U1 to Reumannplatz, bus 66A or 67A to Wienerfeld, and then transfer to bus 17A. This runs along Oberlaaer Strasse where there are several Heurigen.

City

Esterházykeller (Map 8), 01, Haarhof 1, off Naglergasse, is a busy wine cellar with cheap wine from AS23 for 250mL. Meals and snacks are available and it's open daily from 11 am (4 pm weekends) to 11 pm.

St Urbani-Keller (Map 8; ☎ 533 91 02), 01, Am Hof 12, is an expensive Heuriger (AS38 a Viertel), though it does have live accordion music (open daily from 6 pm to midnight).

Entertainment

The tourist office produces a monthly listing of events covering theatre, concerts, film festivals, spectator sports, exhibitions and more; see also its seasonal magazine, *Vienna Scene*. Weekly magazines with extensive listings include *City* (AS10) and *Falter* (AS28). The Thursday edition of the *Neue Kronen Zeitung* newspaper (AS8) has the 'Wiener Stadt Krone' pull-out section giving a rundown on the week's cultural, sporting and entertainment events. Blue Danube Radio has 'What's on in Vienna' daily at 1 pm. Check with the tourist office for free events around town. For information on a variety of different cultural events throughout Vienna, see the Public Holidays & Special Events section in the Facts for the Visitor chapter.

Outside the bars and clubs, classical music is still the sound that dominates the Viennese streets. The programme of musical events is unceasing, and as a visitor you'll continually be accosted by Mozart lookalikes in the city centre trying to sell you tickets for concerts or ballets (at some events the musicians wear historical costumes too). Even some of the buskers playing along Kärntner Strasse and Graben are classical musicians.

For entertainment on the move, DDSG Blue Danube (☎ 588 80) offers Evergreen Dance Evenings on the Danube Canal from mid-May to late September (AS200), departing at 7.30 pm on Friday and Saturday.

See the Places to Eat chapter for information on coffee houses and Heurigen; fine places to relax or be entertained in a typically Viennese environment.

On the seedy side of life, the central zone has the usual smattering of go-go bars. There's no red-light district as such, though prostitutes greet passers-by along the Gürtel ring road. They're usually associated with a bar, and the practice is quite legal. The Prater also has sex shows and is the site for an unpleasant trade in underage prostitution, which is *not* legal!

OPERA & THEATRE
Buying Tickets

Cheap standing-room *(Stehplatz)* tickets for the Staatsoper (AS20 and AS30) and Volksoper (AS15 and AS20) go on sale one hour before the performance, as they do at the Burgtheater (AS15 and AS20) and Akademietheater (AS15). Queue up at the venue concerned. For major productions you may have to allow two or three hours; for less important works, you can often get tickets with minimal queuing. Once you get inside, reserve your place by tying a scarf or sweater to the rail, then go for a wander around. People also queue for student tickets: at these four venues they are the same price as the cheapest tickets (ie AS50 to AS120 for the Staatsoper) for any seats left unsold, and they are available to students under age 27 who can show both a university ID and an ISIC card. They are available 30 minutes (operas) or one hour (theatres) before productions start.

The state ticket office, charging no commission, is the Bundestheaterkassen (Map 8; ☎ 514 44-2959), 01, Goethegasse 1, open weekdays from 8 am to 6 pm and weekends and holidays from 9 am to noon. It only sells tickets for these four federal venues mentioned before and closes from 1 July to the last week in August, as all these places are closed in July and August. Tickets are available here in the month prior to the performance and credit cards are accepted (for September performances, apply in June); credit card sales can also be made by telephone (☎ 513 15 13). For postal bookings at least three weeks in advance, apply to the Bundestheaterverband (☎ 514 44-2653; fax -2969) at the same address. You pay only after your reservations are confirmed. The four venues also have their own box offices.

Tickets to all sorts of performances and events are available from various agents around town, but beware of hefty commission rates (20 to 30%!). Wien Ticket (☎ 588

85), in the hut by the Oper, is linked to the city government and charges either no commission or up to 6% (open 10 am to 7 pm daily).

Many of the other theatre and music venues around town offer cheap standing room and/or student tickets (eg the Theater an der Wien has AS30 standing-room tickets, and AS150 last-minute tickets for students under 25 who show an ISIC card).

Theatre

There are performances in English at the *English Theatre* (☎ 402 82 84), 08, Josefsgasse 12, and the *International Theatre* (☎ 319 62 72), 09, Porzellangasse 8 (entrance Müllnergasse). The English Theatre is the larger venue. Plays are cast and rehearsed in London before the company is flown to Vienna. There's a range of ticket prices, starting at AS180; students (under 27) pay from AS150 for last-minute leftovers. The International Theatre has a small (mainly American) company living locally; tickets cost AS220 to AS280, or AS140 for students (under 26) and senior citizens. It closes for around five weeks at the beginning of August, and has a linked venue, Fundus, at 09, Müllnergasse 6A.

Mime performances (generally avant-garde) are at the *Serapionstheater im Odeon* (☎ 214 55 62), 02, Taborstrasse 10.

If you can follow German, the prime place to go is the *Burgtheater* (Map 8), Dr Karl Lueger Ring, though there are plenty of other theatres, like the nearby *Volkstheater* (☎ 523 27 76), 07, Neustiftgasse 1. The *Theater an der Wien* (Map 8; ☎ 588 30 265), 06, Linke Wienzeile 6, usually puts on musicals.

CLASSICAL MUSIC

Productions in the *Staatsoper* (Map 8) are lavish affairs, and shouldn't be missed. Seats cost anything from AS50 to AS2300. Stehparterre standing-room tickets (AS30) put you in a good position at the back of the stalls, whereas the AS20 tickets leave you high up at the rear of the gallery. The Viennese take their opera very seriously and dress up accordingly. Wander around the foyer and the refreshment rooms in the interval to fully appreciate the gold and crystal interior. Opera in not performed in July and August, but the venue may be used for other events.

The other main opera venue is the *Volksoper* (Map 4), 09, Währinger Strasse 78, close to the Gürtel and the U6 line. It includes operettas and musicals in its repertoire.

The Vienna Philharmonic Orchestra performs in the Grosser Saal (large hall) in the *Musikverein* (Map 8; ☎ 505 81 90), 01, Bösendorferstrasse 12, which is said to have the best acoustics of *any* concert hall in Austria. The interior is suitably lavish and can be visited by occasional guided tour. Standing-room tickets in the main hall cost AS50; no student tickets. Smaller scale performances are held in the Brahms Saal, for which the cheapest tickets (AS60) have no view. The ticket office is open from Monday to Friday from 9 am to 7.30 pm, and Saturday from 9 am to 5 pm (closed July and August).

Another major venue is the *Konzerthaus* (Map 8; ☎ 712 12 11), 03, Lothringerstrasse 20, which can put on up to three simultaneous performances, in the Grosser Saal, the Mozart Saal and the Schubert Saal. Most programmes are classical, but you can also hear anything from ethnic music to gospel, pop or jazz. Student tickets (for those under 27 with an ISIC) are half price. The Konzerthaus Tageskasse (ticket office) is open Monday to Friday from 9 am to 7.30 pm and Saturday from 9 am to 1 pm. The Konzerthaus is closed in July and August except when it hosts Summer of Music events.

There are sometimes free concerts around town, such as at the Rathaus or in one of the churches; check with the tourist office. Schönbrunn Palace (Map 6) is the site of outdoor classical concerts in the summer, and year-round Mozart concerts in the Orangerie (at 8.30 pm; from AS390). The Kursalon (Map 8; ☎ 713 21 81) in the Stadtpark offers a so-so Waltz Show in the evening from Easter to mid-October (AS195 including a couple of glasses of wine), and a full concert by the Spa orchestra at 4 pm from 1 June to 31 August, which may be outside (from AS390).

THE VIENNA BOYS' CHOIR

The Vienna Boys' Choir (Wiener Sängerknaben), another famous institution, is actually four separate choirs; duties are rotated between singing in Vienna, touring the world, resting, and perhaps even occasionally going to school. The choir dates back to 1498 when it was instigated by Maximilian I and at one time numbered Haydn and Schubert in its ranks. The choir sings every Sunday (except during July and August) at 9.15 am in the *Burgkapelle* (Royal Chapel) in the Hofburg. Tickets for seats are AS60 to AS310 and must be booked weeks in advance, but standing room is free. Queue by 8.30 am to find a place inside the open doors, but you can get a flavour of what's going on from the TV in the foyer. Also interesting is the scrum afterwards when everybody struggles to photograph and be photographed with the serenely patient choir members.

The choir also sings a mixed programme of music in the *Konzerthaus* (Map 8) at 3.30 pm on Friday in May, June, September and October. Tickets cost AS390 to AS430, and are available through Reisebüro Mondial (☎ 588 04 141), 04, Faulmanngasse 4, but not from the Konzerthaus booking office.

CINEMAS

Entry prices start at AS70; Monday is known as *Kinomontag*, when all cinema seats are AS70. Sometimes films are in English: look out for *OF (Original Fassung)* or *OV (Original Version)*, meaning the film is shown in the original language; *OmU (Original mit Untertiteln)* means it's shown in the original language with subtitles. Cinemas that show original-language films include:

Österreichische Filmmuseum
(Hofburg map; ☎ 533 70 56/4) 01, Augustinerstrasse 1 – closed 1 July to 30 September; annual membership required (AS180), then AS50 entry; several films shown daily
Burg Kino
(Map 8; ☎ 587 84 06) 01, Opernring 19 – *The Third Man* is shown regularly here
Kino De France
(Map 8; ☎ 317 52 36) 01, Schottenring 5

Filmcasino
(☎ 587 90 62)
Filmhaus
(☎ 546 66 30) 05,
Flotten Center
(Map 4; ☎ 586 51 . 85-87
Audimax HTU
(Map 8; ☎ 588 01-5897, actually a lecture theatre i. university; prices lower than con\ . cinemas
IMAX Filmtheater
(☎ 894 01 01) 14, Mariahilfer Strasse 212 – giant screen, prices from AS110, or AS95 for students
Top Kino
(Map 8; ☎ 587 55 57) 06, Rahlgasse 1
Votivkino
(Map 4; ☎ 317 35 71) 09, Währinger Strasse 12

DISCOS & BARS

Despite its rather old-fashioned image, Vienna is a place where you can party all night. And unlike some other capital cities, you don't have to spend a lot of money in nightclubs to drink until late. Venues are by no means limited to the Innere Stadt – dozens of interesting small bars and cafés in the 6th, 7th, 8th and 9th districts stay busy until well after midnight. See the Getting Around chapter for information on getting home afterwards.

Keeping cool in the summer heat is a major consideration. In the Innere Stadt, owing to noise and nuisance regulations, most places with outside tables have to bring the punters inside after 11 pm. Exceptions are the cafés at the Kunsthalle, the Secession and the Volksgarten.

Innere Stadt

The best-known area for a night out is around Ruprechtsplatz, Seitenstettengasse, Rabensteig and Salzgries in the central zone near the Danube Canal. This area has been dubbed the 'Bermuda Triangle' (Bermuda-Dreieck) as drinkers can disappear into the numerous bars and clubs and apparently be lost to the outside world. This area is very compact so it's easy just to walk around and dive into whatever place takes your fancy. *Krah Krah* (Map 8), Rabensteig 8, has 50 different brands of beer (from AS37 for a

ENTERTAINMENT

), attracts a range of ages, and
ly until 1 or 2 am. Thursday there's
live music (from 8 to 9 pm; free entry)
r a karaoke evening.

A good jazz club is *Porgy & Bess* (☎ 512
84 38), Spiegelgasse 2. It's open weekdays
from 8 pm to 2 am and weekends from 8 pm
to 4 am (closed in summer). Entry costs
AS120 or more, except on Wednesday
(AS30), which is usually 'Session' night
when up-and-coming bands are featured.
Another place to try is *Jazzland* (Map 8;
☎ 533 25 75), Franz Josefs Kai 29; entry
costs from AS150.

P1, Rotgasse 9, is a disco, with dry ice and
a dance cage, which attracts a 20s crowd;
admission costs AS50 or AS80, though
Tuesday (hip-hop) is free. It's open till 4 or
6 am, and closed Sunday and Monday. *Tenne*
(Map 8; ☎ 512 57 08), Annagasse 3, aims for
a slightly older audience, offering live music
such as 'evergreen' classics, swing-time and
big band. Entry usually costs only AS20 (or
AS50 for the occasional variety acts), though
drinks are around AS50 or more. It's open
from 8.30 pm to 2.30 am or later.

The Volksgarten (Map 8) has three adjoining venues appealing to all tastes. The
Volksgarten Nightclub has different music
on successive nights, anything from garage,
hip-hop, house, rhythm and blues, or soul.
Check the weekly listings in newspapers.
Entry costs about AS100 (AS150 on Saturday) and it starts at 10 pm (11 pm on
Sunday). There's a garden bar with beer from
AS55 and the dance-floor roof can be
retracted to reveal the night sky.

In contrast, right next door is the *Tanz
Volksgarten* venue where serene and somewhat restrained couples waltz across the
dance floor to 'evergreen' classics. Dancing
is nightly in summer (it's closed in winter, as
the venue is largely open-air); entry costs
about AS55 unless there's a live concert,
when it costs about AS140.

The third Volksgarten venue is the
Pavillon Café, open daily from 11 am to 2
am. It has garden tables, a DJ and food. Beer
costs AS39 for 500mL. Entry is free, except
for occasional 'unplugged' concerts or gar-

den barbecues; it's closed from 1 October to
30 April. For information on these Volksgarten venues, call ☎ 533 05 18.

Bierhof (Map 8), which is on Haarhof just
off Naglergasse, has courtyard seating and
four varieties of draught Ottakringer to try
(AS38 per Krügerl). It's open from 10.30 am
(4 pm in winter) to 1 am, but is closed on
Sunday.

Irish bars are currently trendy in Vienna.
One of the best is *Molly Darcy's Irish Pub*
(Map 8), Teinfaltstrasse 6, open daily from
11 am to 2 am (1 am Sunday). It's staffed by
non-German-speaking Irish folk and serves
Irish stew (AS105), Guinness and Kilkenny
(AS65 per pint), and local beers (AS38 for
500mL).

Other Districts

Tunnel (Map 4; ☎ 405 34 65), 08,
Florianigasse 39, is a student-type bar/café
with low prices. There's a cellar bar with live
music nightly from 9 pm; entry costs from
AS30, though on Monday there's generally
a free 'Jazzsession'. *Engel* (Map 4; ☎ 523 14
74), 07, Neustiftgasse 82, is a bar and restaurant, often with free jazz on Friday night.

Chelsea (Map 4), 08, Lechenfelder Gürtel
29-31, is open daily from 4 or 6 pm to 4 am.
There's a DJ spinning loud sounds (usually
indie, sometimes techno) and live bands
weekly. There's also live TV coverage of
English premier league football at 5 pm
Sunday and one other time during the week.

Andino (Map 6; ☎ 587 61 25), 06,
Münzwardeingasse 2, is a Latin American
bar and restaurant with lively murals and
meals for under AS100. It's open daily from
6 pm to 2 am. Upstairs it has a venue for live
music or 'theme' parties, usually on Friday
and Saturday; entry costs AS60 to AS140
(cheaper in advance).

Camera Club (Map 4), 07, on Neubaugasse by Mariahilfer Strasse, is a relaxed
bar and disco featuring music (reggae to
rock; no techno) and rock videos. People
smoke dope here and the police seem to turn
a blind eye (at least at the time this research
was done). It's open nightly from 9 pm to 4
am and entry costs AS50, including AS20

towards a drink; ladies get in f[ree?]
Tuesday, Thursday and Sunday. From [ ]
to 9 pm the *Café Tralala* operates [on the]
same premises.

Club Köö (Map 4), 07, Kirchengasse [ ]
is a good place to play pool. Tables cost A[S]
per hour, or AS50 on weekdays before 5 [pm]
(open 10 am to 2 am daily). Although [it]
doesn't look it, this is different to the adjoining *Café Berg*, which also has pool tables
(AS78 per hour).

BACH (Map 4; ☎ 480 19 70), 16, Bach-
gasse 21, has different events depending
upon the night, with live music (usually
'alternative' bands; AS70 to AS150) and
discos (anything from rave to 1960s). Drink
prices are reasonable and it's open from 8 pm
to 2 or 4 am. *Szene* (☎ 749 33 41), 11,
Hauffgasse 26, also features alternative-style
bands (AS80 to AS200).

WUK (Map 4; ☎ 401 21), 09, Währinger
Strasse 59, is an interesting venue offering a
variety of events, including alternative
bands, classical music, dance, theatre,
children's events, political discussions and
practical-skills workshops. It is government
subsidised but has freedom to pursue an
independent course. Prices are not high;
some events are even free. There's also a
Beisl in a cobbled courtyard, open daily to 2
am.

Arena (Map 7; ☎ 798 85 95), 03, Baum-
gasse 80, is another good venue, centred in
a former slaughterhouse. From May to September, headline rock, soul and reggae bands
play on the outdoor stage (entry AS250 to
AS350), but in August this space becomes an
outdoor cinema. All year, smaller bands play
in one of two indoor halls (entry from
AS100), and there's sometimes theatre,
dance and discussions. Keep an ear open for
the once-a-month all-night parties (about
AS80), eg 'Iceberg' (German/British 1970s
new wave music) and various techno parties.

One of the best discos in Vienna is *U4*
(Map 6; ☎ 815 83 07), 12, Schönbrunner
Strasse 222. It's open nightly from (usually)
10 pm to 4 or 5 am. Drink prices aren't too
bad, and there are two dancing rooms and a
slide show. Each night has a different style

day, but if you try at around 11 am m[ost]
people have gone and you can get [ ]
quickly – indicative of the fact th[at]
is relatively dull except for [ ]
high points. If you only w[ant]
photos, you can try wai[ting]
between the sch[ ]
(stables), which [ ]
hour.

[ ]t[ ] ...programme of
c[ ] ...the audience cranes to
se[ ] ...pillared balconies, and chandeliers
shimmer above. The mature stallions are all
snow-white (though they are born dark) and
the riders wear traditional garb, from their
leather boots up to their bicorn hats. It's a
long established Viennese institution, truly
reminiscent of the old Habsburg era.

Reservations to see them perform are
booked up months in advance: write to the
Spanische Reitschule, Michaelerplatz 1, A-
1010 Wien; fax 535 01 86. (Buy direct –
travel agents charge 20 to 30% commission.)
Otherwise, ask in the office about cancella-
tions; cancelled tickets are sold around two
hours before performances. You need to be
pretty keen on horses to be happy about
paying AS250 to AS900 for seats or AS200
for standing room, although a few of the
tricks, such as seeing a stallion bounding
along on only its hind legs like a demented
kangaroo, do tend to stick in the mind.

Tickets to watch them train can be bought
the same day (AS100) at gate No 2, Josefsplatz in the Hofburg. Training is from 10 am
to noon, Tuesday to Friday and some Saturdays. The stallions go on their summer
holidays (seriously!) to Lainzer Tiergarten,
west of the city, during July and August.
They can be seen training for much of the
rest of the year (except Christmas to mid-
February), though they are sometimes away
on tour. Queues are very long early in the

ost
fairly
at training
few isolated
ant to grab a few
ing to see them cross
ool and the Stallburg
usually happens on the half

CASINO

Vienna's casino (Map 8) is opposite the tourist office in Kärntner Strasse. Ascend the stairs to play blackjack, roulette and other games; stakes are from AS50 (AS100 after 9 pm) up to much more than you can probably afford. There's no entry fee as such. Show identification to get in, whereupon you'll be given a voucher for AS300 worth of chips; to use the voucher you'll have to pay AS260. Smart dress is required, ie no trainers or jeans, a collared shirt, a tie (in winter) and jacket (a jacket and tie can be hired for a refundable deposit if required). Opening hours are 3 pm to 3 am. Downstairs, slot machines are open from 11 am to midnight (no dress code).

SPECTATOR SPORT

As in any large city, there are plenty of sports to choose from. International and domestic football (soccer) is played at the Ernst Happel Stadion (Map 7), 02, Meiereistrasse 7, in the Prater. The Stadthalle (Map 4; ☎ 98 100), 15, Vogelweidplatz 15, hosts a national football tournament at the end of December, and other events as diverse as a tennis tournament (mid-October) and a horse show (early November). The swimming pool here is one of the main venues for aquatic events including races, water polo and synchronised swimming. Another important pool is the Stadionbad, which also has swimming and diving competitions from time to time (check with the venue for dates).

Other popular sports that can be played and watched include golf, handball and baseball. Horse racing is at Freudenau (Map 2), 02, Rennbahnnstrasse 65. Call ☎ 728 95 31 for information. Also in the Prater, there are trotting races at Krieau (Map 7).

Vienna's Spring Marathon is run (jogged, walked, abandoned – depending upon the fitness of the participants) in April or May. The route takes in Schönbrunn, the Ringstrasse and the Prater.

Shopping

Vienna is not a place for cheap shopping but does offer numerous elegant shops and quality products. Local specialities include porcelain, ceramics, handmade dolls, wrought-iron work and leather goods. You'll also see many philately shops as you wander around. Many of the more expensive hotels have a free guide called *Shopping in Vienna*, listing products and outlets, mostly in the Innere Stadt. Another useful leaflet you can pick up at some hotels is *Wiener Kunst-Antiquitäten Führer*, detailing art and antique dealers in Vienna. Falter's *Best of Vienna* has a large and typically idiosyncratic section on shopping (in German).

Shops are generally open from 8 or 9 am to about 6 pm on weekdays and 8 am to noon or 1 pm on Saturday. Shops have recently been allowed to open till 7.30 pm on weekdays and 5 pm on Saturdays, but only some supermarkets and larger stores exercise this option. Some shops cling to the old habit of opening till 5 pm only on the first Saturday of the month (called *Langersamstag*). Major credit cards are usually accepted. For special reductions, look out for signs saying 'Aktion'. Bargaining is not the norm in shops, though you can certainly haggle when buying second-hand. There are various second-hand shops where you can sometimes pick up unusual items. The Viennese advertise their second-hand goods in *Bazar* or *Findegrube*; both magazines are available from pavement newsstands.

See Taxes & Refunds in the Facts for the Visitor chapter for information on reclaiming the VAT on large purchases (for non-EU residents only).

WHERE TO SHOP

The main shopping streets in the Innere Stadt are the pedestrian-only thoroughfares of Kärntner Strasse, Graben and Kohlmarkt. Mainly upmarket and specialist shops are to be found along here. Haas Haus on Stephansplatz also houses plush shops. Generally speaking, outside the Ring is where you'll find shops catering for those with shallower pockets. Mariahilfer Strasse is regarded as the best shopping street, particularly the stretch between the Ring and Westbahnhof, and has large department stores like Gerngross, which are missing from the central zone (though Kärntner Strasse does have the Steffl department store at No 19). Other prime shopping streets are Landstrasser Hauptstrasse, Favoritenstrasse and Alser Strasse.

Mexikoplatz in the vicinity of the church is an interesting place to have a wander. It has many shops selling cheap electrical goods and watches, and is also known as a location for obtaining goods on the black market. Various shady types may approach you on the pavement and offer foreign currency and other deals.

Niedermeyer has stores all round the city, and they're good places to buy a hi-fi, radios, TVs, video and audio tapes, photography equipment, computer hardware and software and other goods.

For major shopping expeditions, the Viennese head south of the city to Shopping City Süd, marketed simply as SCS. It's said to be the biggest shopping centre in Europe. Parking places are difficult to find here after about 10 am on Saturday, so a good alternative is to take the shuttle bus departing from opposite the Staatsoper (near the tram No 2 stop) to the IKEA furniture shop. The bus there is free. It's free coming back as well, provided you get a stamp in IKEA (which is close to the main SCS complex). The bus runs from the city every 90 minutes, weekdays from 10 am to 5.30 pm and Saturday from 8.30 am to 4 pm; the bus returns 45 minutes later. The Lokalbahn service to Baden, departing opposite the Hotel Bristol every 15 minutes, stops at SCS; the fare is AS34, or AS17 supplement if you already have a city travel card. Rail passes should be valid for half-price travel, but check first.

SHOPPING

🐜 🐜 🐜 🐜 🐜 🐜 🐜 🐜

Shopping Spree
When Hungary's borders opened in 1989 the Viennese flocked to the town of Sopron to do their shopping. Prices were a fraction of what they were in Vienna's plush boulevards. Just 8km from the Austrian border, Sopron was eastern Europe's first free trade shopping zone. It was a picturesque medieval town, but quickly changed its face to meet the new demand. It soon spawned 36 supermarkets (foie gras was highly prized, as was the cheap wine, spirits and cigarettes) and 24 fashion boutiques. There were also an incredible 127 dentists – dental work was described as half the price of Vienna and twice as good by happy punters.

Sopron is about an hour's drive south-east of Vienna. It's still a popular excursion for the Viennese, and accessible by Austrian trains (Austrian rail passes valid). The Hungarians, meanwhile, tend to come to Vienna for electrical goods, though no longer quite in the numbers that prompted local wits to dub Mariahilfer Strasse 'Magyarhilfer Strasse'. ∎

🐜 🐜 🐜 🐜 🐜 🐜 🐜 🐜

SCS is just south of the city precincts at Vösendorf, near the junction of the A21 and A2.

The Ringstrassen Galerien is a new shopping centre beside the Hotel Bristol (Map 8) on Kärntner Ring, in two adjoining buildings split by Akademiestrasse. Another good shopping centre is Lugner City (Map 4), in the 15th district on Gablenzgasse not far from the Gürtel ring road. This large shopping mall is cool in summer, with an atrium and a glass roof. Branches of all the main chain stores are here, plus there are restaurants, cafés and supermarkets. Opening hours are Monday to Friday from 8 am to 7 pm and Saturday to 5 pm; it has its own parking garage (first hour free, thereafter AS14 per hour). The even larger Donauzentrum shopping centre (Map 5) is farther afield, but conveniently next to the Kagran U1 station.

Markets
The biggest and best known market is the Naschmarkt (Map 4 & 8), extending for over 500m along Linke Wienzeile. It's a 'farmer's

market', mainly consisting of stalls selling meats, fruit and vegetables, but there are some stalls selling clothes and curios. Prices are said to get lower the farther from the Ring end you go. Opening times are Monday to Friday from 6 am to 6 pm, and Saturday from 6 am to 5 pm. The Naschmarkt is also a good place to eat cheaply in snack bars.

On Saturday a flea market (Flohmarkt; Map 6) is tacked on to the south-western end, extending for several blocks. It's very atmospheric and shouldn't be missed, with goods piled up in apparent chaos on the walkway. You can find anything you want (and everything you don't want): books, clothes, records, ancient electrical goods, old postcards, ornaments, carpets ... you name it. We even saw a blow-up doll (second-hand, of course). Bargain for prices here.

Food markets are also at 16, Brunnengasse, between Thaliastrasse and Gaullachergasse, and around the intersection of Landstrasser Hauptstrasse and Salmgasse.

Other markets are:

Antiques
01, Am Hof (Map 8); March to mid-December on Friday and Saturday, 10 am to 8 pm
Art & antiques
Along the Danube promenade between Schwedenplatz and Schottenring (Maps 4 & 8); weekends from May to September
Arts & crafts
01, Schönlaterngasse (Map 8); first weekend of the month from April to November and each weekend in December
Arts & crafts
07, Spittelberg (Map 8); weekends from April to November and daily in December

WHAT TO BUY
Souvenirs & Crafts
There are various souvenir shops in the arcade connecting the old and new Hofburgs (Map 8), selling typical artefacts like mugs, steins, dolls, petit-point embroidery, porcelain Lipizzaner stallions and so on. Kärntner Strasse (Map 8) has numerous souvenir shops; Pawalata, at No 14, seems to have lower prices than most, and also stocks lots of distinctive tableware from Gmunden.

The Augarten Porcelain Factory (☎ 512

14 94), 01, Stock im Eisen Platz 3 and 06, Mariahilfer Strasse 99, produces a variety of gifts and ornaments, including Lipizzaners. A specialist outlet for porcelain and crystal is Albin Denk, 01, Graben 13. Next door, Kober, 01, Graben 14-15, sells toys, souvenirs and tin soldiers. Spielzeug OASE, on the corner of Seilerstätte and Weihburggasse in the Innere Stadt, has many dolls and toys.

Österreichische Werkstätten (☎ 512 24 18), 01, Kärntner Strasse 6, is a co-operative with jewellery, handicrafts and ornaments, in eye-catching and colourful designs. Neues Design (☎ 402 87 32), 08, Piaristengasse 9, is a small gallery and workshop, constructing jewellery and ornaments in modern or traditional styles. Silver jewellery in Wiener Werkstätte style starts at about AS250.

J & L Lobmeyer, 01, Kärntner Strasse 26, is well known for glassware, and has a small museum upstairs (free; open weekdays 9 am to 6.30 pm and Saturday from 9 am to 5 pm).

For anything to do with Lower Austria, including traditional clothing, embroidery, music and pottery, go to NÖ Heimatwerk (Map 8), 01, Herrengasse 6-8.

Jewellery & Watches

Haben, at 01, Graben 12 and 01, Kärntner Strasse 2, has the largest range of clocks in Vienna, and a king's ransom of quality jewellery. CF Rothe & Neffe, 01, Kohlmarkt 7, sells traditional garnet jewellery. Other top outlets are: AE Köchert, 01, Neuer Markt 15; Hübner, 01, Graben 28; and Wagner, 01, Kärntner Strasse 32.

Art & Antiques

Selling works of art is big business; check the auctions at the state-owned Dorotheum (Map 8; ☎ 515 60), 01, Dorotheergasse 17. It was founded in 1707 by Joseph I and it's interesting to watch the proceedings even if you don't intend to buy anything. Lots can be inspected in advance with the opening prices marked. If you don't have the confidence to bid yourself you can commission an agent to do it for you. A range of objects wind up for sale, not only expensive antiques but also relatively undistinguished household knick-knacks. Prices sometimes include VAT, which you may be able to claim back (see Tax & Refunds in the Facts for the Visitor chapter). There are many antiques and art galleries along Dorotheergasse and the surrounding streets.

Dreimäderlhaus (Map 7; ☎ 505 85 28), 04, Wiedner Hauptstrasse 69, is a second-hand shop that buys and sells art and antiques. Most of it is good-quality stuff, though there are some junk-shop odds and ends like books, records and old postcards.

Furniture & Fittings

Orth-Blau (☎ 512 89 13), 01, Krugerstrasse 17, has Art Nouveau and Art Deco furniture, lamps, ornaments and jewellery.

Szaal (☎ 406 63 30), 08, Josefstädter Strasse 74, is a specialist in new Biedermeier furniture. The store can arrange shipment back to your home country.

Wiener Messing Manufaktur, 08, Lerchenfelder Strasse 27, sells modern lights and lampshades in interesting designs, including Art Nouveau styles, plus some ornaments. Opposite, is Beranek, with a similar selection. Design Rampf (☎ 402 17 01), 09, Kinderspitalgasse 3, covers the same ground, but even more creatively.

Fashion

High fashion commands high prices; renowned stores in the centre include: Eduard Kettner, 01, Seilergasse 12; Fürnkranz-Couture, 01, Kärntner Strasse 39; Jonak, 01, Trattnerhof 1; Silhouette, 01, Kärntner Strasse 35; and Boutique Vienne in the Hilton Hotel. Aigner, in the Ringstrassen Galerien, offers clothes and all sorts of leather accessories, such as handbags and belts.

Upmarket stores for men's fashion are: Adonis, 01, Kohlmarkt 11; Linnerth, 01, Am Lugeck 1-2; and E Braun & Co, 01, Graben 8. Loden-Plankl, 01, Michaelerplatz 6, is a specialist in traditional Austrian wear (eg the green collarless loden jackets, made of pressed felt).

For expensive and fashionable shoes go to Wunderl, 01, Bauernmarkt 8, or Dominici,

01, Singerstrasse 2. For those looking for something more affordable, look to the Humanic chain, with branches on all the main shopping streets (eg 01, Kärntner Strasse 51; 06, Mariahilfer Strasse 94; or 08, Alserstrasse 35).

Music

The biggest outlet is the Virgin Megastore (Map 8; ☎ 581 05 00) at 06, Mariahilfer Strasse 37-39; there are three floors crammed with CDs, records, tapes, videos and pop books and magazines. Another place with a wide selection is EMI Austria (☎ 512 36 73) at 01, Kärntner Strasse 30. To pursue operatic interests, try Arcadia, 01, Kärntner Strasse 40.

Teuchtler (Map 8; ☎ 586 21 33), 08, Windmühlgasse 10, is a second-hand shop that buys, sells and exchanges records and CDs, particularly rare and deleted titles. It specialises in classical and jazz but still has a large rock section, and is open weekdays from 1 to 6 pm and Saturday from 10 am to 1 pm. Prices start at AS70.

Other specialist record shops include Red Octopus (Map 4; ☎ 408 14 22), 08, Josefstädter Strasse 99, for jazz, and Black Market (☎ 533 76 170), 01, Gonzagagasse 9, for soul, funk, hip-hop and other genres.

Books & CD ROMs

Look for branches of the Libro chain for cheap books, stationery and CD ROMs (eg in the Ringstrassen Galerien). Wollzeile, near Stephansdom, is a street with many different bookshops; Morawa (Map 8; ☎ 515 62) at No 11 is the biggest. There are also

bookshops on Graben. The British Bookshop (Map 8; ☎ 512 19 45), 01, Weihburggasse 24-6, has the largest selection of English-language books. Shakespeare & Co Booksellers (Map 8; ☎ 535 50 53), 01, Sterngasse 2, is a smaller place and has some second-hand books. Big Ben, (Map 5; ☎ 319 64 12) 09, Servitengasse 4A, is another English bookshop.

Freytag & Berndt (Map 8; ☎ 533 20 94), 01, Kohlmarkt 9, stocks a vast selection of maps, and has travel guides in English. Reiseladen (Map 8; ☎ 513 75 77), 01, Dominikanerbastei 4, is a travel agency and travel bookshop with many Lonely Planet guides. Reisebuchladen (Map 8; ☎ 317 33 84), 09, Kolingasse 6, has an equally comprehensive selection of Lonely Planet and other travel books.

Alpha Buchhandlung (☎ 522 63 22), 07, Neustiftgasse 112, has a large selection of CD ROMs and sells computer accessories. Gerold (☎ /fax 535 54 05), 01, Kramergasse 7, specialises in CD ROMs.

Food & Drink

The best place to buy wine is Wein & Co: prices are low and the selection is wide. There are branches at 01, Habsburgergasse 3 (☎ 535 09 16) and 07, Mariahilfer Strasse 32-34 (☎ 522 39 13).

The Hotel Sacher has a shop on Kärntner Strasse, by the tourist office, selling its famous Sacher Torte. Close by on Kohlmarkt, Demel has a section selling its cakes to take away. Or look into Anzinger, 01, Tegetthoffstrasse 7, for a wide range of chocolatey concoctions.

Excursions

There are some excellent day trips near Vienna. Perhaps the best excursion is to the small towns and villages along the Danube, particularly the wine-growing stretch known as the Wachau. Other attractions are nearby Burgenland and the Wienerwald (Vienna Woods). If you stay overnight in one of these places, inquire at the tourist office or your hotel if there's a 'guest card', as these bring useful discounts. Cards are funded by a resort tax of about AS10.50 per adult per night, which is usually included in quoted accommodation prices.

If you're interested in taking a two or three day trip farther afield the possibilities are many. Graz, Salzburg, Prague and Budapest are all within easy reach and well worth a visit. For reasons of space these destinations aren't covered here, though the nearby Slovak capital of Bratislava is described briefly.

THE DANUBE VALLEY

The historical importance of the Danube (Donau) Valley as a corridor between east and west ensured that control of this area was hotly contested. As a result there are some 550 castles and fortresses in Lower Austria alone, including many monasteries and abbeys that have defences to match conventional castles. The Wachau section of the Danube, between Krems and Melk, is the most scenic, with wine-growing villages, forested slopes, vineyards and imposing fortresses at nearly every bend.

St Pölten is the state capital of Lower Austria, and its tourist office (☎ 02749-353 354) has some regional information. See also the Niederösterreich Touristik-Information (Map 8; ☎ 513 80 22; fax -30) in Vienna. Attractions are considered below in order from west to east.

Getting There & Away

It's very easy to take a day trip from Vienna to the Wachau, and include a boat trip along the river.

To Melk, direct trains depart from Westbahnhof and take an hour (AS142). Some trains involve changing at St Pölten, but that only adds about 10 minutes to the trip.

Trains to Krems go from Franz Josefs Bahnhof (AS119); they leave hourly and also take about an hour. From Krems a slowish train runs along the northern bank to St Valentin, stopping at all Wachau villages on that side. Another line links Krems to St Pölten.

Four weekday Bundesbuses (two or three on weekends) go between Melk and Krems. The fare is AS70 and it takes 65 minutes.

Getting Around

A popular way of exploring the Wachau is by boat. The stretch of Danube from Krems to Vienna is less interesting and scheduled boats no longer service this part of the river. DDSG Blue Danube (☎ 588 80; fax -440) operates steamers between Melk and Krems from early April to late October, with three departures daily (one only in April and October). The full trip takes 100 minutes going downstream and an hour longer going upstream (ie Krems to Melk). The cost is AS190, or AS260 return. From either town to Spitz costs AS100, or AS140 return. Boats also stop at Dürnstein. Commentary en route (in English) highlights points of interest. National and European rail passes earn the holder a discount of 20% on DDSG's Wachau fares. Bikes can be taken on board free of charge.

Brandner (☎ 07433-25 90-0) sends one daily boat between Krems and Melk, starting from 1 May; it stops at Dürnstein, Weissenkirchen and Spitz. Fares are slightly lower than with DDSG, but it costs AS20 extra to take a bicycle. Ardagger (☎ 07479-64 64-0) travels from Linz to Krems on Sunday, Tuesday and Thursday (7¾ hours), returning on Monday, Wednesday and Friday

(10¼ hours). The boat operates from late April to late October; the full fare is AS440 each way, and bicycles are transported for AS30.

The route by road is also scenic. Highway 3 links Vienna and Linz and stays close to the northern bank of the Danube for much of the way. Along the Wachau stretch another road hugs the southern bank. Cycling is extremely popular in summer. There is a bicycle track along the southern bank from Vienna to Krems, and along both sides of the river from Krems to Linz. Heading east, a bicycle track also runs north of the river to Hainburg.

Melk
• *pop 5000*   ☎ *0275*
Lying in the lee of its imposing monastery-fortress, Melk is an essential stop on the Danube trail.

Orientation & Information The train station is 300m from the town centre. Walk straight ahead for 50m down Bahnhofstrasse to get to the post office (Postamt 3390), where a money exchange is available to 5 pm on weekdays and 10 am on Saturday. Turn right for the youth hostel or continue straight on, taking the Bahngasse path for the central Rathausplatz. Turn right at Rathausplatz to get to the tourist office (☎ 02752-523 07 -32) on Babenbergerstrasse 1. It's closed from November to March; otherwise it's open weekdays to at least 6 pm, Saturday to 2 pm, and Sundays in summer. If you stay anywhere in the Wachau, your guest card entitles you to free entry to Melk's open-air swimming pool in the summer.

Things to See & Do The **Stift Melk** dominates the town from the hill and provides an excellent view. Guided tours (often in English, but phone ahead to be sure) of this Benedictine abbey explain its historical importance and are well worth the extra money.

The huge monastery church is Baroque gone mad, with endless prancing angels and gold twirls, but it's very impressive nonethe-less. The fine library and the mirror room both have an extra tier painted on the ceiling to give the illusion of greater height. The ceilings are slightly curved to aid the effect.

The monastery is open from the Saturday before Palm Sunday to All Saints' Day (1 November) from 9 am to 5 pm, except between May and September when it closes at 6 pm. Entry costs AS55, or AS30 for students up to 27 years, the guided tour is AS15 extra. During winter the monastery can only be visited on a guided tour (☎ 523 12 for information).

There are other interesting buildings around town. Try following the **walking tour** outlined in the tourist office map.

Schloss Schallaburg, 5km south of Melk, is a 16th century Renaissance palace with magnificent terracotta arches and various exhibitions. It's open from late April to late October and entry costs AS80, or AS30 for students. A reduced combination ticket (AS115) with Melk's monastery is available.

Places to Stay & Eat *Camping Melk* is on the west of the canal where it joins the Danube, and is open from April to October. Charges, excluding resort tax (AS10.50), are AS35 per person, AS35 per tent and AS25 for a car. The reception is in the *Melker Fähr-haus* restaurant (☎ 532 91), Kolomaniau 3, open every day in summer from 8 am to midnight; Wednesday to Sunday in winter. When it's closed, just camp and pay later. The restaurant has good lunch-time menus including soup from about AS75.

The HI *Jugendherberge* (☎ 526 81; fax 542 57), Abt Karl Strasse 42, has good showers and four-bed dorms, as well as sports and games facilities and parking spaces. Beds are AS150 (AS126 for those under 19), plus a AS25 surcharge for the first night only. The reception is closed from 10 am to 5 pm, but during the day you can reserve a bed and leave your bags in the bicycle room, to the left of the entrance. The hostel is closed from 1 November to mid-March.

Gasthof Weisses Lamm (☎ 540 85), Linzer Strasse 7, has a few singles/doubles for

AS350/550. On the premises is *Pizzeria Venezia* (open daily), with many tasty pizzas starting at AS60. *Gasthof Goldener Stern* (☎ 522 14), Sterngasse 17, provides slightly cheaper accommodation.

Gasthof zum Goldenen Hirschen (☎ 522 57), at Rathausplatz 13 in the centre of town, offers pleasant singles/doubles with private shower for AS381/622. Its *Rathauskeller* restaurant has daily menus with soup for about AS90, and other dishes from AS75.

There's a *supermarket* at Rathausplatz 9.

Getting There & Around For information on getting to Melk from Vienna see Getting There & Away under The Danube Valley earlier in this chapter. Boats leave from the canal by Pionierstrasse, 400m to the rear of the monastery. Bicycle rental is available in Melk at the train station.

Melk to Dürnstein

In addition to the grape vines, peaches and apricots are grown along this 30km stretch of the river. Shortly after departing Melk you pass **Schloss Schönbühel** on the southern bank, which marks the beginning of the Wachau. On the opposite bank **Willendorf** soon appears, where a 25,000-year-old sandstone statuette of Venus was discovered; another made from a mammoth tusk was also found.

A farther 5km brings **Spitz** into view, a village with attractive houses and a peaceful aura. The parish church at Kirchenplatz is unusual for its chancel, which is out of line with the main body of the church. Another noteworthy feature is the 15th century statues of the 12 apostles lining the organ loft. Most wear an enigmatic expression, as if being tempted by an unseen spirit to overindulge in the communion wine. The fountain in front of the church and the vine-covered hills rising behind make a pretty picture.

Six kilometres farther along the northern bank is **Weissenkirchen**. Its centrepiece is a fortified parish church rising from a hill. This Gothic church was built in the 15th century and has a Baroque altar. The garden

terrace, if open, provides good views of the river. Below the church is the charming Teisenhoferhof arcaded courtyard, with a covered gallery and lashings of flowers and dried corn. The **Wachau Museum** is here and has work by artists of the Danube School. It's open from April to October (closed Monday) and entry costs AS20 (students AS10).

After Weissenkirchen the river sweeps around to the right, and soon yields a fine perspective of Dürnstein.

Dürnstein
☎ 0271

One of the prime destinations in the Wachau, Dürnstein achieved 12th century notoriety by its imprisonment of King Richard the Lion-Heart of England.

Orientation & Information From the train station, walk ahead and then right for the village walls (five minutes). En route you pass the tourist office (☎ 02711-200), in a little hut in the corner of the east carpark. It's only open in the afternoon from April to October. All year during office hours you can get information from the Rathaus (☎ 02711-219) in Hauptstrasse, the main street. The boat landing stage is below the dominating feature of the village centre, the blue and white parish church.

Things to See & Do High on the hill, commanding a marvellous view of the curve of the Danube, stand the ruins of **Kuenringerburg**, where Richard was incarcerated from 1192 to 1193. His crime was to have insulted Leopold; his misfortune was to be recognised despite his disguise when journeying through Austria on his way home; his liberty was achieved only upon the payment of a huge ransom. The hike up from the village takes 15 to 20 minutes.

In the village, Hauptstrasse is a cobbled street with some picturesque 16th century houses and wrought-iron signs. The **parish church**, often called the abbey church (Chorherrenstift), has been meticulously restored. The Baroque interior effectively combines white stucco and dark wood balconies. Entry costs AS25, which includes access to the porch overlooking the Danube and a photo exhibition detailing the renovation process (open daily from 9 am to 6 pm between March and October).

Places to Stay & Eat *Pension Alte Rathaus* (☎ /fax 02711-252), Hauptstrasse 26, is reached through an attractive courtyard. Singles with hall shower are AS280 and doubles with private shower and WC are AS630. *Pension Böhmer* (☎ 02711-239), Hauptstrasse 22, has slightly smaller singles/ doubles with shower and WC for AS350/ 550. Private rooms are cheaper: *Maria Wagner* (☎ 02711-232), Hauptstrasse 41, has four doubles from AS360.

For food, try *Gasthof Sänger Blondel*, Klosterplatz, with a shady courtyard and food costing over AS90 (closed Sunday evening and Monday), or the cheaper and plainer *Goldener Strauss*, Hauptstrasse 18 (closed Tuesday). *Alter Klosterkeller* is a Buschenschank tavern on Anzuggasse, just outside the village walls and overlooking the vineyards. Wine is AS20 a Viertel and a selection of cold snacks and meals are served (AS25 to AS80). It opens at 3 pm (2 pm on weekends) and is closed on Tuesday.

Restaurant Loibnerhof (☎ 02732-828 90), Unterloiben 7, about 1.5km east of Dürnstein, is highly regarded and reasonably priced (closed Monday and Tuesday).

Getting There & Away By train, the fare is AS17 to either Krems or Weissenkirchen.

Krems
• *pop 23,000 ☎ 0273*
The historic town of Krems reclines on the northern bank of the Danube, surrounded by terraced vineyards.

Orientation & Information The town centre is 300m in front of the train station, stretching along Obere and Untere Landstrasser. The main post office is to the left of the station on Brandströmstrasse 4-6 (Postamt 3500). Two kilometres west of the station is

the suburb of **Stein**; the tourist office (☎ 826 76; fax 700 11) is halfway between, at Undstrasse 6, in the Kloster Und. It's open daily from 1 May to 31 October and weekdays only the rest of the year. Upstairs is the Tourismusregion Wachau office (☎ 856 20).

Things to See & Do The best thing to do in Krems is to relax and enjoy the peaceful ambience. Take your time and wander around the cobbled streets, quiet courtyards and ancient city walls. The most interesting streets are Landstrasser in Krems and Steiner Landstrasser in Stein. Krems is a wine-growing centre and there's wine-tasting in the Kloster Und (AS140). The street plan from the tourist office (AS10) details various points of interest.

Krems has several churches worth peeking inside: the **Pfarrkirche St Veit** on the hill, with frescoes by Martin Johann Schmidt, an 18th century local artist; the **Piaristenkirche**, up behind St Veit's, huge windows and Baroque altars; and the **Dominikanerkirche**, Dominikanerplatz, containing a collection of religious and modern art and wine-making artefacts.

By the Kremser Tor (gate) is a new arts centre, the **Kunsthalle**.

Places to Stay & Eat *Camping Donau* (☎ 844 55), near the boat station at Wiedengasse 7, is open Easter to mid-October and costs AS50 per person, from AS30 for a tent and AS40 for a car.

The HI *Jugendherberge* (☎ 834 52) is at Ringstrasse 77, and has excellent facilities for cyclists, such as a garage and an on-site repair service. Beds in four/six-bed dorms are AS150/160, plus a AS20 surcharge for stays of only one or two nights.

Many hotels also have a surcharge for short stays. The cheapest choice is the private rooms (summer only) at *Haus Hietzgern* (☎ 761 84), Untere Landstrasse 53. AS380/580 gets you a single/double with private shower, WC and TV at *Aigner* (☎ 845 58), Weinzierl 53. Weinzierl passes under the S33 dual carriageway east of the station.

Towering over the town of Melk is Stift Melk, a Baroque Benedictine abbey that houses a great library (with over 2000 old tomes) and a treasure trove of sculptures, paintings and other arts. The abbey was used in the opening and closing scenes of Umberto Eco's novel *The Name of the Rose*.

JON DAVISON

MARK HONAN

MARK HONAN

MARK HONAN

Top Left: Inside the dome of Stift Melk
Right: Steiner Landstrasser, Stein
Middle Left: A typical house in Durnstein
Bottom Left: Vineyards near Durnstein

In Stein, *Frühstückspension Einzinger* (☎ 823 16), Steiner Landstrasser 82, offers attractive rooms around a courtyard: singles/ doubles are AS330/570, also with shower, WC and TV.

Hotel Restaurant Alte Poste (☎ 822 76), Obere Landstrasse 32, is a historic 500-year-old house. It has good singles/doubles for AS300/580, or AS470/740 with private shower, and an enchanting courtyard. It's a good place to eat too, with daily menus from AS90 and local wine from AS30 per Viertel (closed Tuesday evening and Wednesday).

Supermarkets include a *Spar* at Obere Landstrasse and a *Löwa* in the shopping centre by the Steiner Tor. *Café Roma* on Untere Landstrasse, is an ice cream and drinks place, but often has one lunch dish (eg spaghetti bolognaise) for a giveaway price of AS20 or less. It's open daily. Nearby at No 8 is *Schwarze Kuchl* with cheap food till 7 pm on weekdays and 1 pm on Saturday. The restaurant *Zur Wiener Brücke*, also called Gasthof Klinglhuber (☎ 821 43), Wienerstrasse 2, has meals from AS120 to AS220 and is open daily from 7 am to at least 10 pm.

Getting There & Away The boat station is a 20 minute walk from the train station towards Stein on Donaulände. Bikes can be rented at the train station and campsite.

Tulln
• *pop 11,300*   ☎ *02272*

Formerly a Roman camp called Comagena, and named as a town settlement in 791, Tulln trumpets itself as the 'Birthplace of Austria', and was in effect the nation's first capital.

Orientation & Information Tulln is 29km west of Vienna. The centre of town is Hauptplatz; the tourist office (☎ 02272-65836) is one block north at Albrechtgasse 32. It's open daily (after 1 pm on weekends) from 1 May to 30 September, and only weekday mornings the rest of the year.

Things to See & Do Next to the tourist office is **Tullner Museen**, a complex of museums dealing with the city's history,

ancient and modern (AS30; closed Monday). On the riverside is the **Egon Schiele Museum**, open Tuesday to Sunday from 9 am to noon and 2 to 6 pm (5 pm in winter), which tells the story of the artist who was born in Tulln in 1890. The premises are a former jail – appropriate as Schiele was imprisoned in 1912 following the furore over some of his more erotic works. Admission costs AS40.

Churches of interest include the newly restored **Minoritenkirche** and the Romanesque **Pfarrkirche St Stephan**. Behind the latter is a polygonal funerary chapel dating from the 13th century, with frescoes depicting some not very evil-looking devils.

Places to Stay & Eat The *Donaupark Camping Ground* (☎ 02272-65200; fax 65201), open from May to September, is east of the centre near the river. Beside the river and 500m west of the Schiele Museum is *Alpenvereins Herberge* (☎ 02272-62692), with dorm beds for AS163 and a mattress on the floor for AS133 (open 1 May to 31 October). The three-star Hotel-Restaurant *Zur Rossmühle* (☎ 02272-62411-0), Hauptplatz 13, has singles/doubles with shower, WC and TV from AS590/880. There are cheaper pensions and private rooms.

China Restaurant Asia, Brudergasse 5, off Hauptplatz, has good weekday lunch menus from AS58, with plenty of food. For Austrian cooking, go to *Albrechtsstuben*, Albrechtsgasse 24, it has a garden and three-course lunch menus from about AS60 (closed Monday).

Getting There & Away Tulln is reached by train or S-Bahn (S40) from Franz Josefs Bahnhof (AS51). The train is quicker (25 minutes), but only stops at the main Tulln station. Save yourself a 10 minute walk by getting the S40 to Tulln Stadt.

Klosterneuburg
☎ *02243*

Overlooking the river, only a little northwest of Vienna's provincial territory and within hiking distance of Kahlenberg (at the

EXCURSIONS

end of bus No 38A from Vienna), Klostern-euburg is known for its large Augustinian abbey (Stift Klosterneuburg), founded in 1114. The Baroque interior is outshone by St Leopold's Chapel, which has the Verdun Altar, covered in 51 enamelled panels showing biblical scenes. The abbey can be visited daily by guided tour.

Petronell
• *pop 1250*   ☎ *02163*

The village of Petronell lies near the Danube, 38km east of Vienna. In Roman times it was the site of Carnuntum, a regional capital believed to have 50,000 inhabitants. Relics of former glories are not particularly stunning, but added together they make a reasonably diverting day. They include a museum in nearby Bad Deutsch-Altenburg (which is also a spa town), a grass-covered amphitheatre that formerly seated 15,000, and an archaeological park (open April to October) that contains ruins and a reconstructed temple. The Heidentor (Heathen Gate) was once the south-west entrance to the city and now stands as an isolated anachronism amid fields of corn. Get further information from the archaeological park office (☎ 02163-337 70), or Bad Deutsch-Altenburg's tourist office (☎ 02163-624 59).

Places to Stay & Eat *Gasthof Zum Heidentor* (☎ 02163-2201), Hauptstrasse 129, has singles/doubles for AS300/500 with shower, WC and TV. The restaurant offers a lunch menu for AS60 with soup (not Sunday; closed Monday), and has a beer garden and children's play area. Bad Deutsch Altenburg has a wider range of places to stay and eat.

Getting There & Away Take the hourly S7 from Wien Nord or Wien Mitte (direction: Wolfsthal); the one hour journey costs AS68, or AS51 if you have a city travel pass. To Bad Deutsch Altenburg costs an extra AS17.

BRATISLAVA
The capital of Slovakia is 65km east of Vienna and a popular day trip. People come here to shop and eat, not because the quality

and range is particularly good but because prices are about half those in Vienna. Slovak *koruna* (crowns) are easily changed at the boat station or banks.

Orientation & Information
The boat station is on the northern bank of the Danube. Get information, maps and help with accommodation from the Bratislava Information Service (BIS; ☎ 533 37 15), Klobuànícká 2, open weekdays from 8 am to 4.30 pm (to 7 pm in summer) and Saturday from 8.30 am to 1 pm.

Things to See & Do
Bratislava hasn't the charm of Prague or Budapest; the old centre has been scarred by soulless Soviet-style edifices, and the sea of standardised apartment blocks to the south is a depressing sight. **Bratislava Castle** stands on the hill but it has little to excite the visitor except a historical museum (closed Monday) and the view from the top. There are many other museums, the best being the **Municipal Museum** in the old town hall, featuring historical artefacts, decorated rooms and torture chambers.

The **Nový Bridge** is an absurd lopsided structure with a restaurant at the top. A lift will whisk you up there, after which you can enjoy a beer, the view, and the unnerving quivering of the floor as the traffic rumbles below and the wind buffets the windows. Historical resonances are best experienced in the **cathedral**, where 11 Habsburg kings were crowned, and the **Primatial Palace**, where Napoleon signed a peace treaty with Austria's Franz I in 1805.

The main shopping district (and hub for trams) is Kamenné námestie (square).

Places to Eat
You'll have no problem finding somewhere suitable – the centre of town offers plenty of cheap cafeteria-style buffets, as well as some reasonably-priced restaurants.

Vegetarian buffets are at *Jedáleñ*, Obchodná 68, and *Divesta*, Laurinská 8; they're open on weekdays till 3 pm. A *food market* on the corner of Hviezdoslavovo námestie and Rybárska brána (open daily from 10.30 am to 10 pm) has various stand-up counters, or go next door for pizza and pasta at *Spaghetti & Co*, open daily to 1 am.

Getting There & Away

See the Getting There & Away chapter for information on boats, buses and trains to Bratislava. Bratislava's main train station is 1.5km north of the centre (take tram No 1); the bus station is to the east, but walkable.

WIENERWALD

The Wienerwald (Vienna Woods), west of Vienna, is a place to get off the beaten track and enjoy nature. Attractive settlements speckle the area, such as the wine-growing centres of Perchtoldsdorf, Mödling and Gumpoldskirchen. **Mayerling** has little to

see now, but the bloody event that occurred there still brings people to the site; the Carmelite convent can be visited (see the Mystery at Mayerling boxed text).

About 6km to the north-east is **Heiligenkreuz**, where Marie's grave can be seen. The 12th century Cistercian abbey here is the final resting place of most of the Babenburg dynasty that ruled Austria until 1246. The church and the cloister combine Romanesque and Gothic styles. The abbey museum contains models by Giovanni Giuliani, who also created the trinity column in the courtyard. Tours are conducted daily and cost AS40 (students AS25).

Between Mödling and Heiligenkreuz, boat tours can be taken of **Seegrotte Hinterbrühl** (☎ 02236-263 64), Europe's largest underground lake.

EXCURSIONS

Mystery at Mayerling

It's the stuff of lurid pulp fiction: the heir to the throne found dead in a hunting lodge with his teenage mistress. It became fact in Mayerling on 30 January 1889, yet for years the details of the case were shrouded in secrecy and denial. Even now a definitive picture has yet to be established – the 100th anniversary of the tragedy saw a flurry of books on the subject, and Empress Zita claimed publicly that the heir had actually been murdered.

The heir was Archduke Rudolf, 30-year-old son of Emperor Franz Josef, husband of Stephanie of Coburg, and something of a liberal who was fond of drinking and womanising. Rudolf's marriage was little more than a public façade by the time he met 17-year-old Baroness Marie Vetsera in the autumn of 1888. The attraction was immediate, but it wasn't until 13 January of the following year that the affair was consummated, an event commemorated by an inscribed cigarette case, a gift from Marie to Rudolf.

On 28 January Rudolf secretly took Marie with him on a shooting trip to his hunting lodge in Mayerling. His other guests arrived a day later; Marie's presence, however, remained unknown to them. On the night of the 29th, the valet, Loschek, heard the couple talking until the early hours, and at about 5.30 am a fully dressed Rudolf appeared and instructed him to get a horse and carriage ready. As he was doing his master's bidding two gun shots resounded through the still air. He raced back to discover Rudolf lifeless on his bed, with a revolver by his side. Marie was on her bed, also fully clothed, also dead. Just two days earlier Rudolf had discussed a suicide pact with a former mistress. Apparently he hadn't been joking.

Almost immediately the cover-up began. Count Hoyos, a guest at the lodge, told Marie's mother that it was Marie who killed both herself and the archduke with the aid of poison. The official line was proffered by Empress Elisabeth, who claimed Rudolf died of heart failure. There was no hint of suicide or a mistress. The newspapers swallowed the heart-failure story, though a few speculated about a hunting accident. It was only much later that Rudolf's suicide letter to his wife was published in her memoirs, in which he talked of going calmly to his death.

Throughout the lies and misinformation, the real victim remains Marie. How much of a willing party she was to the suicide will never be known. What has become clear is that Marie, after her death, represented not a tragically curtailed young life but an embarrassing scandal that had to be discreetly disposed of. Her body was left untouched for 38 hours, after which it was loaded into a carriage in such a manner as to imply that it was a living person being aided rather than a corpse beyond help. Her subsequent burial was a rude, secretive affair, during which she was consigned to the ground in an unmarked grave (her body was later moved to Heiligenkreuz). Today the hunting lodge is no more – a Carmelite nunnery stands in its place. ■

Getting There & Away

To explore this region, it's best if you have your own transport. Trains skirt either side of the woods and the bus service is patchy. Bundesbus Nos 1140 and 1142 go regularly between Baden and St Pölten, usually stopping at Heiligenkreuz and sometimes also at Mayerling.

Baden

• *pop 24,000*   ☎ *02252*

On the eastern edge of the Wienerwald, the spa town of Baden has a long history. The Romans were prone to wallow in its medicinal springs. Beethoven heard about its healing properties and came here many times in hope of a cure for his deafness. The town flourished in the early 19th century after being adopted by the Habsburgs as their favourite summer retreat.

Orientation & Information The centre is a 10 minute walk north-west of the train station: cut across the small park, continue along Bahngasse and then bear right on Wassergasse. This will bring you to Hauptplatz and the centre of town. Follow the signs to the left for the tourist office (☎ 02252-44531-59) at Brusattiplatz 3.

Things to See & Do Baden exudes health and 19th century affluence. Nowhere is this more evident than in the **Kurpark**, a wonderful place for a stroll. Rows of white benches are neatly positioned under manicured trees in front of the bandstand, and fountains and statues of famous composers are embellished by elaborately laid-out flower beds. Added to this are the spa features such as the Trinkenhalle for imbibing the salubrious springs. Baden also has a casino and a couple of museums. The **Dreifaltigkeitssäule** (trinity column) on Hauptplatz dates from 1714.

Places to Stay & Eat The private rooms at *Lakics* (☎ 02252-22938), Vöslauer Strasse 11, south of the river, is the only budget choice at AS180 per person. *Pension Garni Margit* (☎ 02252-89718), Mühlgasse 15-17, is an eight minute walk east of Hauptplatz

and has singles/doubles with shower from AS400/650. There are lots of restaurants in the centre. *Wassergasse* has some cheapish choices, or get Chinese lunches at *Goldener Löwe*, Badner Braitner Strasse 1, for AS59 (not Sunday).

Getting There & Away Regional and S-Bahn trains run to and from Baden up to four times an hour from Südbahnhof (AS51, or AS34 if you have a Vienna city pass), with services till around 11 pm. The trip takes 20 to 30 minutes. For the same price, you could instead take the small 'Lokalbahn' from opposite the Hotel Bristol on Kärntner Ring, which terminates at Josefsplatz in Baden and goes every 15 minutes (64 minutes). Austrian and European rail passes are apparently valid for half-price travel on this service, though none of the staff seems sure of the rules.

BURGENLAND

When Austria lost control of Hungary after WWI, it was at least ceded the German-speaking part of that country in 1921 following a favourable plebiscite. Renamed Burgenland, this agricultural province is known for its wines, and wine-tasting tours are popular with visitors. One-fifth of present-day Burgenland is owned by the Esterházys, erstwhile employers of Josef Haydn and one of the richest families in Austria.

Eisenstadt

• *pop 11,000*   ☎ *02682*

Orientation & Information The provincial capital of Burgenland lies 50km south of Vienna. From the train station, walk straight ahead down Bahnstrasse until you get to the pedestrian-only Hauptstrasse, a street with cafés, shops and restaurants (10 minutes). Turn left for Schloss Esterházy, which houses the two tourist offices, Eisenstadt Tourismus (☎ 02682-673 90) and the provincial office (☎ 02682-633 84-16; fax -20; email info@burgenland-tourism.co.at). Both are open daily from 9 am to 5 pm (closed weekends from 1 November to 31

March). Free maps are available, and a bro-chure listing hotels, private rooms and museum openings and prices.

A post office and Bundesbus ticket office are by the cathedral at Domplatz.

Things to See & Do Joseph Haydn lived and worked in Eisenstadt for 31 years, and although he died in Vienna his remains were transferred here to the **Bergkirche**, where they lie in a white marble tomb. His skull was actually stolen from a temporary grave shortly after he died in 1809, and it wasn't reunited with the body until 1954. The church itself is remarkable for the Kalva-rienberg, a unique calvary display round the other side. Life-sized figures depict the sta-tions of the Cross in a series of suitably austere, dungeon-like rooms. It's open daily from 9 am to noon and 2 to 5 pm, but only between 1 April and 31 October. Entry is AS25 (students AS10) and includes the mau-soleum.

The Baroque **Schloss Esterházy** features the frescoed Haydn Hall, open the same hours as the tourist offices. The last tour is at 4 pm. Entry costs AS50, or AS30 for students and seniors, and a 40 minute guided tour (phone ahead and you might be able to get one of the occasional English tours, or ask for the English notes). A festival of Joseph Hayn's music is staged here in September. Behind the palace is a large, relaxing park, the **Schlosspark**, the setting for the Fest der 1000 Weine in late August. There are several museums in the town, most of which are shut on Monday.

Places to Stay & Eat Ask the tourist office about the few private rooms; otherwise, *Gasthof Kutsenits Ludwig* (☎ 02682-63511), Mattersburger Strasse 30, has the cheapest singles/doubles (from AS250/400), though it's not convenient for the centre.

For lunch, think Chinese: *Asia*, Haupt-strasse 32, entrance on Matthias Markhl Gasse, and *Mandarin*, Wiener Strasse 2, by the Bergkirche, both have three-course weekday menus for about AS60 (both open daily). Or there's a branch of the fast-food *Schnitzelhaus* chain at Esterházystrasse 16. *Gasthof Zum Haydnhaus*, Josef Haydn Gasse 24, has regional and Austrian dishes for AS65 to AS150 (open daily). Near the cathedral is a *Billa* supermarket.

Getting There & Away Regular trains depart from Vienna's Südbahnhof. There's a direct train leaving at 10.03 am (AS68; 66 min-utes), which also stops at Wien Meidling. At other times you have a choice of two routes but each involves a change, at Neusiedl am See (AS68; 80 minutes) or Wulkaproders-dorf (AS85; 68 minutes). Buses take 70 minutes and depart from Wien Mitte (AS85). Wiener Neustadt is on the Vienna-Graz train route; buses from there take 30 minutes.

Lake Neusiedl

Bird-watchers flock to Neusiedler See, the only steppe lake in central Europe. It's ringed by a wetland area of reed beds, providing an ideal breeding ground for nearly 300 bird species. The lake only averages 1m in depth and there is no natural outlet, giving the water a slightly saline quality. Naturalists are particularly attracted to **Seewinkel** on the east shore, a national park of grassland inter-spersed with a myriad of smaller lakes. A cycle track winds all the way around the reed beds, making it possible to complete a circuit of the lake, but remember to take your pass-port as the southern section is in Hungary.

Water sports are also emphasised here, with boats and windsurfers for hire at various resorts around the lake. The main town on the shores is **Neusiedl am See**, 50 minutes by train from Vienna's Südbahnhof. It has a tourist office (☎ 02167-2229) in the Rathaus on Hauptplatz, and a HI *Jugendherberge* (☎ /fax 02167-2252) at Herbergsgasse 1 (open March to November). Hostel beds are AS166 (AS144 for those under 19); sheets are AS17.

A bus ride south-east of Neusiedl is **Pod-ersdorf**, a holiday resort on the shore of the lake. Get more details from its tourist office (☎ 02177-2227; fax 2170).

Rust

• *pop 1700*   ☎ *02752*

Rust, 14km east of Eisenstadt, is famous for storks and wine, though its name derives from the word for elm tree. The town's prosperity has been based on wine for centuries. In 1524 the emperor granted local vintners the exclusive right to display the letter 'R' on their wine barrels; corks today bear the same insignia.

Storks descend on Rust from the end of March, rear their young, then fly off in late August. Many homes in the centre have a metal platform on the roof to try to entice storks to build a nest there. A good vantage point is attained from the tower of the **Katholische Kirche** (AS10, students AS5). The **Fischerkirche** is the oldest church in Rust (12th to 16th century).

Access to the **lake** is 1.5km down the reed-fringed Seepromenade. Here you'll find a swimming pool (AS30 per day) as well as motor boats, pedal boats and sailing boats for hire, and schools for windsurfing and sailing.

Places to Stay & Eat Rust's *campsite* (☎ 02685-595) is near the lake. The tourist office (☎ 02685-502; fax -10) is in the Rathaus and has lists of hotels and private rooms, or there's an accommodation board outside. *Pension Halwax* (☎ 02685-520), Oggauer Strasse 21, has seven doubles from AS480, each with their own shower and WC. Ruster Jugendästehaus (☎ 20685-591; fax -4) opened in the summer of 1998; there's a kitchen and beds cost up to AS150. It's open year-round but reservations are required.

To eat, look no further than the many *Buschenschenken* (wine taverns) around town. A place with good food and wine is *Schandl* at Hauptstrasse 20, open daily from 4 pm (11 am on weekends and holidays) to midnight. Another option is to compile a picnic at the *ADEG* supermarket, Oggauer Strasse 3, to eat by the lake.

Getting There & Away Buses run approximately hourly to and from Eisenstadt (AS34; 30 minutes). Services stop in the early evening. Several places rent bikes in the centre.

Mörbisch

• *pop 2400*   ☎ *02685*

Six kilometres around the lake from Rust, Mörbisch is just a couple of kilometres short of the Hungarian border. It's worth spending an hour or so here, enjoying the relaxed atmosphere and the quaint whitewashed houses with hanging corn and flower-strewn balconies. There's a tourist office (☎ 02685-8430) on the main street, which can fill you in on the Seefestspiele, a summer operetta festival.

Getting There & Away By bus, the fare to Rust is AS17, though to/from Eisenstadt costs the same (AS34) as only going from Rust to Eisenstadt. South of Mörbisch, cyclists may cross into Hungary but there's no road for cars.

Glossary

Abfahrt – departure (trains)
Achterl – 125mL glass (drinks)
Ankunft – arrival (trains)
ANTO – Austrian National Tourist Office
Apotheke – pharmacy
Ausgang – exit
Autobahn – motorway
Autoreisezug – motorail train

Bad – bath (spa resort)
Bahnhof – train station
Bahnsteig – train station platform
Bankomat – automated teller machine
Bauernhof – farmhouse
Besetzt – occupied, full (ie no vacancy) in a hotel/pension
Bezirk – (town or city) district
Biedermeier period – 19th century art movement in Germany and Austria; applies particularly to a decorative style of furniture from this period
Bierkeller – beer cellar
Brauerei – brewery
Bundesbus – state bus
Bundesländer – federal province (government)
Bundesrat – Federal Council (upper house – government)
Buschenschank – wine tavern

Dirndl – traditional skirt

EEA – European Economic Area, comprising European Union states plus Iceland, Liechtenstein and Norway
Einbahnstrasse – one-way street
Eingang, Eintritt – entry
Einkaufsamstag – 'long' Saturday, when shops have extended opening hours (usually on the first Saturday of the month)
EU – European Union

Fahrplan – timetable
Feiertag – public holiday
Ferienwohnungen – self-catering holiday apartments

Flohmarkt – flea market
Flugpost – air mail
Föhn – hot, dry wind that sweeps down from the mountains, mainly in early spring and autumn
FPÖ – Freedom Party (political party)

Glockenturm – clock tower
Glockenspiel – carillon
Gästekarte – guest card
Gästehaus/Gasthaus – guesthouse
Gasthof – inn
Gemütlichkeit – 'cosiness'; a quality much revered by Austrians
Gendarmerie – police

Haltstelle – bus or tram stop
Hauptbahnhof – main train station
Hauptpost – main post office
Heurigen – wine tavern

Imbiss – snack bar

Jugendherberge/Jugendgästehaus – a youth hostel

Kaffeehaus/Café Konditorei – coffee house
Konsulat – consulate
Kurzparkzone – short-term parking zone

Landesmuseum – provincial museum
Landtag – provincial assembly (government)
Langersamstag – another name for Einkaufsamstag
LIF – Liberal Forum (political party)

Maut – toll (or indicating a toll booth); also Viennese dialect for a tip (gratuity)
Mehrwertsteuer (MWST) – value-added tax
Mensa – university restaurant
Mitfahrzentrale – hitching organisation

Nationalrat – National Council (lower house – government)
Not(ruf) – Emergency (call)

ÖAMTC – national motoring organisation
ÖAV – Austrian Alpine Club
ÖBB – Austrian federal railway
ÖKISTA – student travel agency
ÖVP – Austrian People's Party (political party)

Parkschein – parking voucher
Pedalos – paddle boats
Pfarrkirche – parish church
Polizei – police
Postamt – post office
Postlagernde Briefe – poste restante

Rathaus – town hall
Red Vienna – describes the period of socialist reforms instigated by the city government from 1919 to 1934
Ruhetag – 'rest day', on which a restaurant is closed

Schlossberg – castle hill
Schrammelmusik – popular Viennese music for violins, guitar and accordion
Secession movement – early 20th century movement in Vienna seeking to establish a more functional style in architecture; led by Otto Wagner (1841-1918)
Selbstbedienung (SB) – self-service (restaurants, laundries etc)
SPÖ – Social Democrats (political party)

Stadtmuseum – city museum
Studentenheime – student residences

Tabak – tobacconist
Tagestellar/Tagesmenu – the set meal or menu of the day in a restaurant
Telefon-Wertkarte – phonecard
Tierpark – zoo
Tor – gate

Urlaub – holiday

Vienna Circle – group of philosophers centred on Vienna University in the 1920s and 30s
Vienna Group (Wienergruppe) – literary/art movement formed in the 1950s, whose members incorporated surrealism and Dadaism in sound compositions, textual montages and actionist happenings
Viertel – 250mL glass (drinks); also a geographical district

Wien – Vienna
Wiener Werkstätte – workshop established in 1903 by Secession artists
Wäscherei – laundry
Würstel Stand – sausage stand

Zimmer frei/Privat Zimmer – private rooms (accommodation)

Index

Map references are in **bold** type.
Map numbers refer to the colour
maps at the back of the book.

LONELY PLANET PHRASEBOOKS

Building bridges,
Breaking barriers,
Beyond babble-on

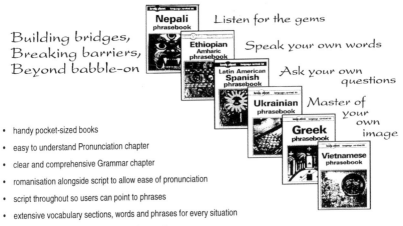

Listen for the gems

Speak your own words

Ask your own
questions

Master of
your
own
image

- handy pocket-sized books
- easy to understand Pronunciation chapter
- clear and comprehensive Grammar chapter
- romanisation alongside script to allow ease of pronunciation
- script throughout so users can point to phrases
- extensive vocabulary sections, words and phrases for every situation
- full of cultural information and tips for the traveller

'...vital for a real DIY spirit and attitude in language learning' – Backpacker

'the phrasebooks have good cultural backgrounders and offer solid advice for challenging situations in remote locations' – San Francisco Examiner

'...they are unbeatable for their coverage of the world's more obscure languages' – The Geographical Magazine

---

Arabic (Egyptian)
Arabic (Moroccan)
Australia
  Australian English, Aboriginal and Torres Strait languages
Baltic States
  Estonian, Latvian, Lithuanian
Bengali
Brazilian
Burmese
Cantonese
Central Asia
Central Europe
  Czech, French, German, Hungarian, Italian and Slovak
Eastern Europe
  Bulgarian, Czech, Hungarian, Polish, Romanian and Slovak
Ethiopian (Amharic)
Fijian
French
German
Greek

Hindi/Urdu
Indonesian
Italian
Japanese
Korean
Lao
Latin American Spanish
Malay
Mandarin
Mediterranean Europe
  Albanian, Croatian, Greek, Italian, Macedonian, Maltese, Serbian and Slovene
Mongolian
Nepali
Papua New Guinea
Pilipino (Tagalog)
Quechua
Russian
Scandinavian Europe
  Danish, Finnish, Icelandic, Norwegian and Swedish

South-East Asia
  Burmese, Indonesian, Khmer, Lao, Malay, Tagalog (Pilipino), Thai and Vietnamese
Spanish (Castilian)
  Basque, Catalan and Galician
Sri Lanka
Swahili
Thai
Thai Hill Tribes
Tibetan
Turkish
Ukrainian
USA
  US English, Vernacular, Native American languages and Hawaiian
Vietnamese
Western Europe
  Basque, Catalan, Dutch, French, German, Irish, Italian, Portuguese, Scottish Gaelic, Spanish (Castilian) and Welsh

---

LONELY PLANET JOURNEYS

JOURNEYS is a unique collection of travel writing – published by the company that understands travel better than anyone else. It is a series for anyone who has ever experienced – or dreamed of – the magical moment when they encountered a strange culture or saw a place for the first time. They are tales to read while you're planning a trip, while you're on the road or while you're in an armchair, in front of a fire.

JOURNEYS books catch the spirit of a place, illuminate a culture, recount a crazy adventure, or introduce a fascinating way of life. They always entertain, and always enrich the experience of travel.

THE GATES OF DAMASCUS
Lieve Joris
Translated by Sam Garrett

This best-selling book is a beautifully drawn portrait of day-to-day life in modern Syria. Through her intimate contact with local people, Lieve Joris draws us into the fascinating world that lies behind the gates of Damascus. Hala's husband is a political prisoner, jailed for his opposition to the Assad regime; through the author's friendship with Hala we see how Syrian politics impacts on the lives of ordinary people.

Lieve Joris, who was born in Belgium, is one of Europe's leading travel writers. In addition to an award-winning book on Hungary, she has published widely acclaimed accounts of her journeys to the Middle East and Africa. *The Gates of Damascus* is her fifth book.

'Expands the boundaries of travel writing' – Times Literary Supplement

---

KINGDOM OF THE FILM STARS
Journey into Jordan
Annie Caulfield

Kingdom of the Film Stars is a travel book and a love story. With honesty and humour, Annie Caulfield writes of travelling in Jordan and falling in love with a Bedouin. Her book offers fascinating insights into the country – from the traditional tent life of nomadic tribes to the first woman MP's battle with fundamentalist colleagues. *Kingdom of the Film Stars* unpicks some of the tight-woven Western myths about the Arab world, presenting cultural and political issues within the intimate framework of a compelling love story.

Annie Caulfield, who was born in Ireland and currently lives in London, is an award-winning playwright and journalist. She has travelled widely in the Middle East.

'Annie Caulfield is a remarkable traveller. Her story is fresh, courageous, moving, witty and sexy!' – Dawn French

PLANET TALK

Lonely Planet's FREE quarterly newsletter

We love hearing from you and think you'd like to hear from us.

When...is the right time to see reindeer in Finland?
Where...can you hear the best palm-wine music in Ghana?
How...do you get from Asunción to Areguá by steam train?
What...is the best way to see India?

For the answer to these and many other questions read PLANET TALK.

Every issue is packed with up-to-date travel news and advice including:

*   a letter from Lonely Planet co-founders Tony and Maureen Wheeler
*   go behind the scenes on the road with a Lonely Planet author
*   feature article on an important and topical travel issue
*   a selection of recent letters from travellers
*   details on forthcoming Lonely Planet promotions
*   complete list of Lonely Planet products

To join our mailing list contact any Lonely Planet office.

Also available: Lonely Planet T-shirts. 100% heavyweight cotton.

LONELY PLANET ONLINE

Get the latest travel information before you leave or while you're on the road

Whether you've just begun planning your next trip, or you're chasing down specific info on currency regulations or visa requirements, check out Lonely Planet Online for up-to-the minute travel information.

As well as travel profiles of your favourite destinations (including maps and photos), you'll find current reports from our researchers and other travellers, updates on health and visas, travel advisories, and discussion of the ecological and political issues you need to be aware of as you travel.

There's also an online travellers' forum where you can share your experience of life on the road, meet travel companions and ask other travellers for their recommendations and advice. We also have plenty of links to other online sites useful to independent travellers.

And of course we have a complete and up-to-date list of all Lonely Planet travel products including guides, phrasebooks, atlases, Journeys and videos and a simple online ordering facility if you can't find the book you want elsewhere.

www.lonelyplanet.com
or
AOL keyword: lp

LONELY PLANET PRODUCTS

Lonely Planet is known worldwide for publishing practical, reliable and no-nonsense travel information in our guides and on our web site. The Lonely Planet list covers just about every accessible part of the world. Currently there are nine series: *travel guides, shoestring guides, walking guides, city guides, phrasebooks, audio packs, travel atlases, Journeys – a unique collection of travel writing and Pisces Books - diving and snorkeling guides.*

EUROPE

Amsterdam • Austria • Baltic States phrasebook • Britain • Central Europe on a shoestring • Central Europe phrasebook • Czech & Slovak Republics • Denmark • Dublin • Eastern Europe on a shoestring • Eastern Europe phrasebook • Estonia, Latvia & Lithuania • Finland • France • French phrasebook • Germany • German phrasebook • Greece • Greek phrasebook • Hungary • Iceland, Greenland & the Faroe Islands • Ireland • Italian phrasebook • Italy • Lisbon • London • Mediterranean Europe on a shoestring • Mediterranean Europe phrasebook • Paris • Poland • Portugal • Portugal travel atlas • Prague • Romania & Moldova • Russia, Ukraine & Belarus • Russian phrasebook • Scandinavian & Baltic Europe on a shoestring • Scandinavian Europe phrasebook • Slovenia • Spain • Spanish phrasebook • St Petersburg • Switzerland • Trekking in Spain • Ukrainian phrasebook • Vienna • Walking in Britain • Walking in Switzerland • Western Europe on a shoestring • Western Europe phrasebook

Travel Literature: The Olive Grove: Travels in Greece

NORTH AMERICA

Alaska • Backpacking in Alaska • Baja California • California & Nevada • Canada • Chicago • Deep South• Florida • Hawaii • Honolulu • Los Angeles • Mexico • Mexico City • Miami • New England • New Orleans • New York City • New York, New Jersey & Pennsylvania • Pacific Northwest USA • Rocky Mountain States • San Francisco • Southwest USA • USA phrasebook • Washington, DC & the Capital Region

Travel Literature: Drive thru America

CENTRAL AMERICA & THE CARIBBEAN

• Bahamas and Turks & Caicos • Bermuda • Central America on a shoestring • Costa Rica • Cuba •Eastern Caribbean •Guatemala, Belize & Yucatán: La Ruta Maya • Jamaica

SOUTH AMERICA

Argentina, Uruguay & Paraguay • Bolivia • Brazil • Brazilian phrasebook • Buenos Aires • Chile & Easter Island • Chile & Easter Island travel atlas • Colombia Ecuador & the Galápagos Islands • Latin American Spanish phrasebook • Peru • Quechua phrasebook • Rio de Janeiro • South America on a shoestring • Trekking in the Patagonian Andes • Venezuela

Travel Literature: Full Circle: A South American Journey

ISLANDS OF THE INDIAN OCEAN

Madagascar & Comoros • Maldives• Mauritius, Réunion & Seychelles

AFRICA

Africa - the South • Africa on a shoestring • Arabic (Moroccan) phrasebook • Cairo • Cape Town • Central Africa • East Africa • Egypt • Egypt travel atlas• Ethiopian (Amharic) phrasebook • Kenya • Kenya travel atlas • Malawi, Mozambique & Zambia • Morocco • North Africa • South Africa, Lesotho & Swaziland • South Africa, Lesotho & Swaziland travel atlas • Swahili phrasebook • Tunisia Trekking in East Africa • West Africa • Zimbabwe, Botswana & Namibia • Zimbabwe, Botswana & Namibia travel atlas

Travel Literature: The Rainbird: A Central African Journey • Songs to an African Sunset: A Zimbabwean Story

MAIL ORDER

Lonely Planet products are distributed worldwide. They are also available by mail order from Lonely Planet, so if you have difficulty finding a title please write to us. North American and South American residents should write to Embarcadero West, 155 Filbert St, Suite 251, Oakland CA 94607, USA; European and African residents should write to 10a Spring Place, London NW5 3BH; and residents of other countries to PO Box 617, Hawthorn, Victoria 3122, Australia.

NORTH-EAST ASIA

Beijing • Cantonese phrasebook • China • Hong Kong • Hong Kong, Macau & Guangzhou • Japan • Japanese phrasebook • Japanese audio pack • Korea • Korean phrasebook • Mandarin phrasebook • Mongolia • Mongolian phrasebook • North-East Asia on a shoestring • Seoul • Taiwan • Tibet • Tibet phrasebook • Tokyo

Travel Literature: Lost Japan

MIDDLE EAST & CENTRAL ASIA

Arab Gulf States • Arabic (Egyptian) phrasebook • Central Asia • Central Asia phrasebook • Iran • Israel & the Palestinian Territories • Israel & the Palestinian Territories travel atlas • Istanbul • Jerusalem • Jordan & Syria • Jordan, Syria & Lebanon travel atlas • Lebanon • Middle East • Turkey • Turkish phrasebook • Turkey travel atlas • Yemen

Travel Literature: The Gates of Damascus • Kingdom of the Film Stars: Journey into Jordan

ALSO AVAILABLE:

Brief Encounters • Travel with Children • Traveller's Tales

INDIAN SUBCONTINENT

Bangladesh • Bengali phrasebook • Delhi • Goa • Hindi/Urdu phrasebook • India • India & Bangladesh travel atlas • Indian Himalaya • Karakoram Highway • Nepal • Nepali phrasebook • Pakistan • Rajasthan • Sri Lanka • Sri Lanka phrasebook • Trekking in the Indian Himalaya • Trekking in the Karakoram & Hindukush • Trekking in the Nepal Himalaya

Travel Literature: In Rajasthan • Shopping for Buddhas

SOUTH-EAST ASIA

Bali & Lombok • Bangkok • Burmese phrasebook • Cambodia • Ho Chi Minh City • Indonesia • Indonesian phrasebook • Indonesian audio pack • Jakarta • Java • Laos • Lao phrasebook • Laos travel atlas • Malay phrasebook • Malaysia, Singapore & Brunei • Myanmar (Burma) • Philippines • Pilipino phrasebook • Singapore • South-East Asia on a shoestring • South-East Asia phrasebook • Thailand • Thailand's Islands & Beaches • Thailand travel atlas • Thai phrasebook • Thai audio pack • Thai Hill Tribes phrasebook • Vietnam • Vietnamese phrasebook • Vietnam travel atlas

AUSTRALIA & THE PACIFIC

Australia • Australian phrasebook • Bushwalking in Australia • Bushwalking in Papua New Guinea • Fiji • Fijian phrasebook • Islands of Australia's Great Barrier Reef • Melbourne • Micronesia • New Caledonia • New South Wales • New Zealand • Northern Territory • Outback Australia • Papua New Guinea • Papua New Guinea phrasebook • Queensland • Rarotonga & the Cook Islands • Samoa • Solomon Islands • South Australia • Sydney • Tahiti & French Polynesia • Tasmania • Tonga • Tramping in New Zealand • Vanuatu • Victoria • Western Australia

Travel Literature: Islands in the Clouds • Sean & David's Long Drive

ANTARCTICA

Antarctica

THE LONELY PLANET STORY

Lonely Planet published its first book in 1973 in response to the numerous 'How did you do it?' questions Maureen and Tony Wheeler were asked after driving, bussing, hitching, sailing and railing their way from England to Australia.

Written at a kitchen table and hand collated, trimmed and stapled, *Across Asia on the Cheap* became an instant local bestseller, inspiring thoughts of another book.

Eighteen months in South-East Asia resulted in their second guide, *South-East Asia on a shoestring*, which they put together in a backstreet Chinese hotel in Singapore in 1975. The 'yellow bible', as it quickly became known to backpackers around the world, soon became *the* guide to the region. It has sold well over half a million copies and is now in its 9th edition, still retaining its familiar yellow cover.

Today there are over 240 titles, including travel guides, walking guides, language kits & phrasebooks, travel atlases and travel literature. The company is the largest independent travel publisher in the world. Although Lonely Planet initially specialised in guides to Asia, today there are few corners of the globe that have not been covered.

The emphasis continues to be on travel for independent travellers. Tony and Maureen still travel for several months of each year and play an active part in the writing, updating and quality control of Lonely Planet's guides.

They have been joined by over 70 authors and 170 staff at our offices in Melbourne (Australia), Oakland (USA), London (UK) and Paris (France). Travellers themselves also make a valuable contribution to the guides through the feedback we receive in thousands of letters each year and on our web site.

The people at Lonely Planet strongly believe that travellers can make a positive contribution to the countries they visit, both through their appreciation of the countries' culture, wildlife and natural features, and through the money they spend. In addition, the company makes a direct contribution to the countries and regions it covers. Since 1986 a percentage of the income from each book has been donated to ventures such as famine relief in Africa; aid projects in India; agricultural projects in Central America; Greenpeace's efforts to halt French nuclear testing in the Pacific; and Amnesty International.

'I hope we send people out with the right attitude about travel. You realise when you travel that there are so many different perspectives about the world, so we hope these books will make people more interested in what they see. Guidebooks can't really guide people. All you can do is point them in the right direction.'

– Tony Wheeler

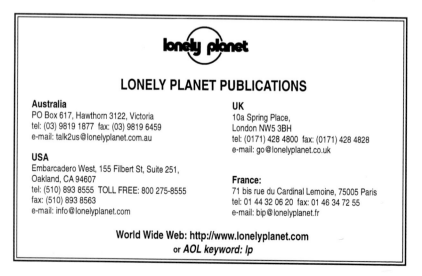

LONELY PLANET PUBLICATIONS

Australia
PO Box 617, Hawthorn 3122, Victoria
tel: (03) 9819 1877 fax: (03) 9819 6459
e-mail: talk2us@lonelyplanet.com.au

USA
Embarcadero West, 155 Filbert St, Suite 251,
Oakland, CA 94607
tel: (510) 893 8555 TOLL FREE: 800 275-8555
fax: (510) 893 8563
e-mail: info@lonelyplanet.com

UK
10a Spring Place,
London NW5 3BH
tel: (0171) 428 4800 fax: (0171) 428 4828
e-mail: go@lonelyplanet.co.uk

France:
71 bis rue du Cardinal Lemoine, 75005 Paris
tel: 01 44 32 06 20 fax: 01 46 34 72 55
e-mail: bip@lonelyplanet.fr

World Wide Web: http://www.lonelyplanet.com
or *AOL keyword: lp*

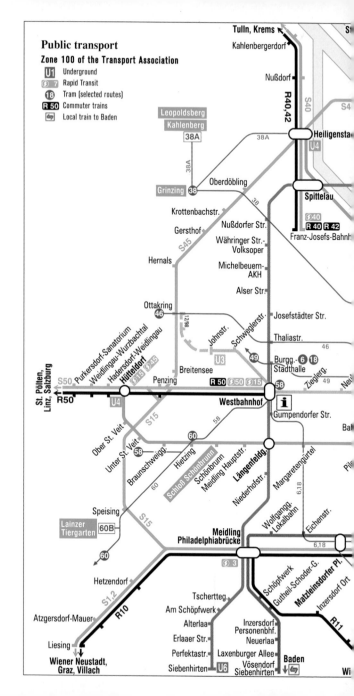

MAP 1

Public transport
Zone 100 of the Transport Association

- **U1** Underground
- **S 7** Rapid Transit
- **18** Tram (selected routes)
- **R 50** Commuter trains
- Local train to Baden

Tulln, Krems

Kahlenbergerdorf

Nußdorf

R40, 42

S40

S4

Leopoldsberg
Kahlenberg
38A

38A

Heiligensta...
U4

Oberdöbling

Grinzing 38

38

Spittelau

S40
R 40 R 42
Franz-Josefs-Bahn...

Krottenbachstr.

Nußdorfer Str.

Gersthof

Währinger Str.-
Volksoper

S45

Hernals

Michelbeuern-
AKH

Alser Str.

Ottakring
46

12/98

Josefstädter Str.

Johnstr.

Schweglerstr.

Thaliastr.

46

U3

49

Burgg.- 6 18
Stadthalle

Ziegler...

49

Purkersdorf-Sanatorium

Weidlingau-Wurzbachtal

Hadersdorf-Weidlingau

St. Pölten, Linz, Salzburg

Hütteldorf

S15 S45

Breitensee

R 50 S50 S15

58

Ne...

Penzing

S50

R50

U4

Westbahnhof

i

Gumpendorfer Str.

S15

58

Ober St. Veit

60

58

Ba...

Unter St. Veit
58

Braunschweig...

Hietzing

Schloß Schönbrunn

Längenfeldg.

60

Schönbrunn

Schönbrunn
Meidling Hauptstr.

Margaretengürtel

Niederhofstr.

6,18

Pi...

Speising

S15

Wolfgangg.
Lokalbahn

Eichenstr.

Lainzer
Tiergarten
60B

Meidling
Philadelphiabrücke

6,18

60

S1,2

Hetzendorf

S 3

Schöpfwerk

Gutheil-Schoder-G.

Matzleinsdorfer Pl.

Inzersdorf Ort

Tschertteg.

Am Schöpfwerk

R10

R11

Atzgersdorf-Mauer

Alterlaa

Inzersdorf
Personenbhf.

Erlaaer Str.

Neuerlaa

Liesing

Perfektastr.

Laxenburger Allee

Baden

Wiener Neustadt,
Graz, Villach

Siebenhirten

U6

Siebenhirten

Vösendorf

Wi...

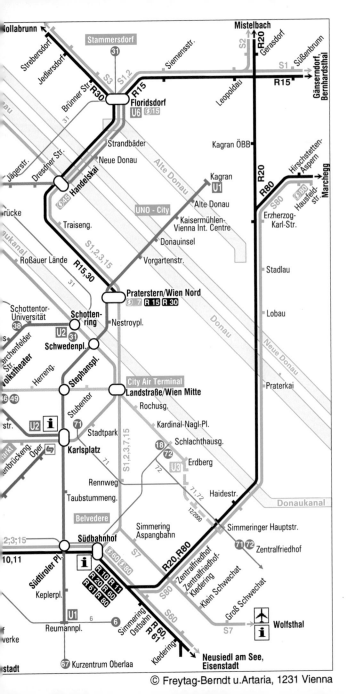

MAP 1

© Freytag-Berndt u.Artaria, 1231 Vienna

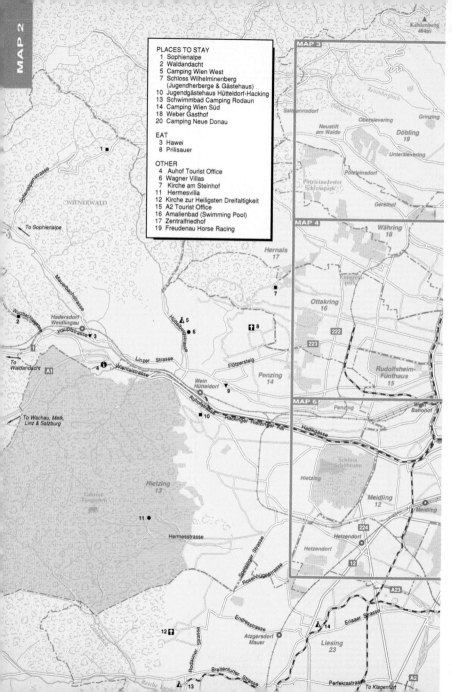

PLACES TO STAY
1 Sophienalpe
2 Waldandacht
5 Camping Wien West
7 Schloss Wilhelminenberg
  (Jugendherberge & Gästehaus)
10 Jugendgästehaus Hütteldorf-Hacking
13 Schwimmbad Camping Rodaun
14 Camping Wien Süd
18 Weber Gasthof
20 Camping Neue Donau

EAT
3 Hawei
8 Prilisauer

OTHER
4 Auhof Tourist Office
6 Wagner Villas
7 Kirche am Steinhof
11 Hermesvilla
12 Kirche zur Heiligsten Dreifaltigkeit
15 A2 Tourist Office
16 Amalienbad (Swimming Pool)
17 Zentralfriedhof
19 Freudenau Horse Racing

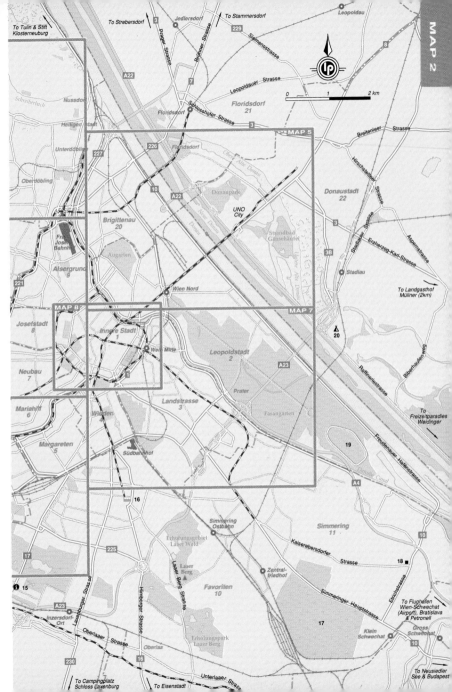

MAP 3

Höhenstrasse

Höhenstrasse

Cobenzl

Ob. Reisenbergweg

Himmelstrasse

Bellevuestrasse

Rosenbergbach

Sieveringer Strasse

Alsbach

Reinischgasse

Zierleitengasse

Obersievering

Salmannsdorfer Strasse

Celtesgasse

Agnesgasse

Mittewurzergasse

Nottebohmstrasse

1

Hameaustrasse

Neustift am Walde

Rathstrasse

Hackenberweg

Ahrengrubenweg

Breebargasse

Karthäuserstrasse

Windhabergasse

Hackenbergweg

Untersievering

Strehlgasse

Krottenbachstrasse

Dr.-Heinrich-Maier-Strasse

Khevenhüllergasse

Glanzinggasse

Raimund-Zoder-Gasse

Pötzleinsdorfer Strasse

Pötzleinsdorf

Starkfriedgasse

Glanzinggasse

Gustav-Pick-Gasse

Felix-Dahn-Strasse

Pötzleinsdorfer Schlosspark

Schafberggasse

Pötzleinsdorfer Strasse

Währing

Hockegasse

Buchleitengasse

Gersthof

Josef-Redl-Gasse

Gersthofer Strasse

Gerergasse

Scheibenberggasse

MAP 3

1 Celtes
2 Krapfenwaldbad
3 Reinprecht
4 Clima Villenhotel
5 Beethovenhaus
6 Casa Culinaria
7 Eroica House
8 Katholisches Studentenhaus
9 Haus Döbling
10 Schnitzelhaus
11 Spittelau Incinerator

MAP 4

PLACES TO STAY
2 Auge Gottes
3 Hotel Arkadenhof
6 Albatros
15 Porzellaneum
16 Hotel Alpha
17 Hotel Atlanta
19 Pension Falstaff
22 Hotel Am Schottenpoint
28 Auer
30 Thüringer Hof
32 Hotel Maté
33 Hotel Donauwalzer
34 Pension Ani
39 Hostel Zöhrer
43 Theater-Hotel
49 Hotel Avis (& Reception
   for Haus Pfeilgasse)
50 Auersperg
51 Pension Wild
54 Believe it or Not
55 Jugendherberge Myrthengasse
56 Jugendherberge Neustiftgasse
59 Hostel Panda and Lauria
60 Pension Atrium
65 Alla Lenz
70 Pension Carantania
75 Matauschek
81 Pension Continental
82 Pension Esterházy
84 Pension Hargita

PLACES TO EAT
1 Restaurant Sailer
9 Vegi Rant
10 Feuervogel
23 Café Berg
24 Afro-Asiatisches Institut Mensa
31 Thai Haus
36 Kräuterdrogerie
38 Laudon Stüberl
42 Tunnel Bar & Café
44 Fromme Helene
62 Burg-Keller
63 Gaunkerl
66 Ungar-Grill
68 Schnitzelwirt Schmidt
69 Amerlingbeisl
74 Schutzhaus am Ameisbach

76 Pulkautaler Weinhaus
77 Il Mare
78 Beim Novak
86 Schnitzelhaus

OTHER
4 Schnell & Sauber Waschcenter
   (Laundrette)
5 Schubert's Birth House
7 Volksoper
8 WUK
11 Hofer Supermarket
12 Niedermeyer (Store)
13 US Embassy
14 Museum Moderner Kunst
   (Liechtenstein Palace)
18 Josephinium (Museum of Medical
   History)
20 Sigmund Freud Museum
21 Polizeifundamt (Lost Property
   Office)
25 Votivkino (Cinema)
26 ÖKISTA (Travel Agency)
27 Café Stein
29 Allgemeines Krankenhaus (Hospital)
35 Niedermeyer (Store)
37 Odyssee Mitwohnzentrale
   (Accommodation Agency) &
   Beislbar Geralala
40 Mitfahrzentrale Josefstadt
41 Städtische Hauptbücherei (Library)
45 Miele (Laundrette)
46 Red Octopus
47 Chelsea
48 BACH
52 Hofer Supermarket
53 Club Köö
57 Engel
58 Alpha Buchhandlung
61 Lugner City (Shopping Centre)
64 Mondo Supermarket
71 Schnell & Sauber Waschcenter
   (Laundrette)
72 Stadthalle
73 Ottakringer Bad (Swimming Pool)
79 Gerngross Department Store
80 Niedermeyer (Store)
83 Camera Club & Café Tralala
85 Flotten Center (Cinema)
87 Majolikahaus

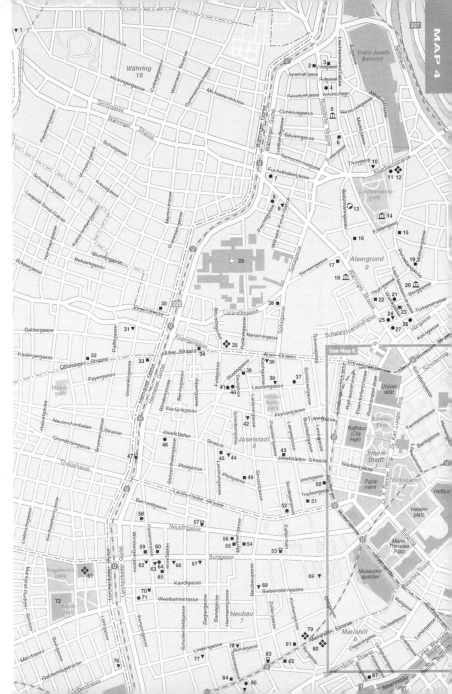

MAP 4

227

Franz Josefs
Bahnhof

Auhainse

Spittelau

Sternwartestrasse

Währing
18

Haslingergasse

Gentzgasse

Währinger   Strasse

Schulgasse

Kreuzgasse

Martinstrasse

Theresiengasse

Blumengasse

Beheimgasse

Rötzergasse

Geblergasse

Liechtensteinstrasse

Viriotgasse 3
2
Ayrenhoffgasse   4
Pulverturmgasse   Vereinsstiege
Canisiusgasse   5
Säulengasse   6
Sechschimmelgasse   Thurygasse 10
Fuchsthallergasse   11 12
7
8
9
Liechtenstein-
park
13
14

16
17   Alsergrund
9
18
Warhinger Strasse
15

Liechtensteinstrasse

29
Lazarettgasse
Lazarettgasse
28
Marianngasse

Schlagigasse

Sensengasse

Schwarzspanierstrasse

19
20
21 22
23
24
25
26 27

30   220

31

Körnergasse

Kindspitalgasse 35
Alser Strasse   34

Pelikangasse

Alser   Strasse

See Map 8

Universitätsstrasse

Universität

Haslingergasse
Ottakringer Strasse 32
33
Payergasse

Huber-
park

Veronikagasse

Hernalser Gürtel

Hernalser Gürtel

Bennogasse

Strozzigasse
39
36
Kochgasse
38
37
Schlösselgasse
41
40   Laudongasse
Floriangasse
42   Schönborn-
park
Parisergasse
43

Rathaus
(City
Hall)

Rathaus-
Park

Innere
Stadt

Neulerchenfelder

Grundsteingasse

Thaliastrasse

Brunnengasse

Florianigasse

Josefstädter
Strasse
46
47
45   44
49
Pfeilgasse

Joselstadt
8

Langegasse

Buchfeldgasse

Lenaugasse

Josefstädter Strasse

Stadiongasse

Parlament

Volksgarten

Hofburg

Lerchenfelder Strasse

Bernardgasse

58

57

Neustiftgasse

56
55 54
53

59   60
62
63 64
61
65 66 67

Burggasse

Kandlgasse

70
71

Westbahnstrasse

72
Mär-
park

Siebensterngasse
68
69

Neubau
7

Schottenfeldgasse

Zieglergasse

Bandgasse

Neubaugasse

Kirchengasse

Mariahilfer Strasse 79

78
77
76

83
84   85

81   80

82

87

Mariahilf
6

Museums-
quartier

Maria
Theresia
Platz

Helden-
platz

Burgring

Naschmarkt

MAP 5

Wasserpark

2 ℹ

3 ➤

Floridsdorfer
Brücke

Strandbäder

Nordbahnbrücke

Nordbahnbrücke

Josef-Melicher-Gasse

Bruckhaufnerstr.

Forsthausgasse

1 ■

Adalbert Stifter Strasse

Brigittenau
20

Donau

Brigittenauer
Brücke

Stromstrasse

Universumstrasse

Donaueschingenstrasse

Traisengasse ⊙

Leystrasse

Traisengasse

Vorgartenstrasse

Leipziger

Pöchlarnstrasse

Pappenheim

Nordwestbahnstrasse

Pöchlarnstrasse

Engerthstrasse

Rebhanngasse

Juxgasse

Bäuerlegasse

Wallenstein

Wasnergasse

Augarten

Leopoldstadt
2

Obere Augartenstrasse

ℹ 23

Am

Taborstrasse

Lessinggasse

Taborstrasse

Am Taborstrasse

Darwingasse

Heinestrasse

Rueppgasse

Castellezgasse

Leopoldsgasse

Obermüllerstrasse

Grosse Stadtgutgasse

Mühlfeldgasse

Stuwerstrasse

Untere Augartenstrasse

🏛 22

Schiffamtsgasse

Novaragasse

Blumauergasse

12 ●

Ausstellungsstrasse

18 ▼

ℹ Wien Nord
Train Station

19

Praterstern

20 ▼ 17 ▼

🏛 21

14 ●

15 ●

Calatatti-
platz

MAP 8

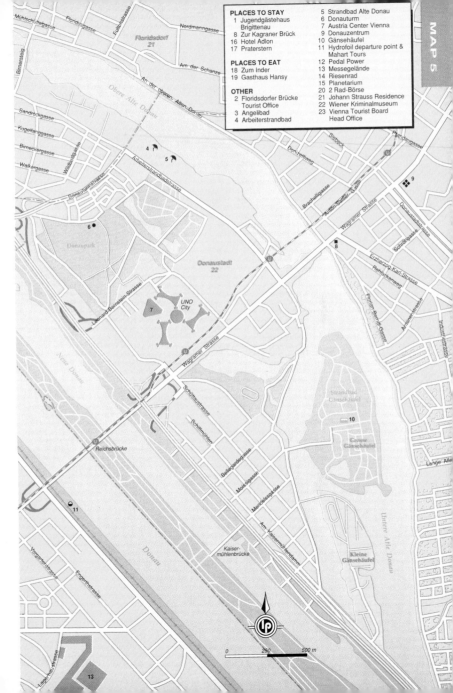

MAP 6

PLACES TO STAY
1 Rustler
2 Fünfhaus
3 Hostel Ruthensteiner
4 Hotel Fürstenhof
5 Hotel Westend
7 Pension Kraml
13 Goldenes Einhorn
14 Hotel Cryston
15 Altwienerhof
16 Reither
17 Renaissance
19 Kolpingsfamilie Meidling
31 Parkhotel Schönbrunn &
   Hotel Victoria
48 Zum Goldenen Stern Gasthof

PLACES TO EAT
11 Schnitzelhaus
24 Snack Bar
25 DO & CO Restaurant

SCHLOSS SCHÖNBRUNN
21 Meidling Gate
22 Orangerie
23 Entrance to Tours
26 Palace Entrance
27 Toilet
28 Schönbrunn Palace

29 Wagenburg (Imperial Coach
   Collection)
30 Hietzing U-Bahn
32 Post Office
33 Hietzing Gate
34 Schmetterlinghaus
   (Butterfly House)
35 Toilet
36 Palmenhaus (Palm House)
37 Maxing Gate
38 Toilet
39 Neptune Fountain
40 Toilet
41 Schöner Brunnen (Fountain)
42 Roman Ruins
43 Swimming Pool
44 Maria Theresia Gate
45 Gloriette Monument
46 Toilet
47 Meierei Gate

OTHER
6 Haydn Museum
8 Andino
9 Rosa Lila Villa
10 Flohmarkt
12 Schubert Commemorative
   Rooms
18 U4 (Nightclub)
20 Schönbrunn U-Bahn

MAP 7

Innere Stadt

Michaeler-
platz

Josefs-
platz

Opernring

Karlsplatz

Wieden

Südbahnhof

Südtiroler
Platz

Wien Mitte

Stadtpark

Botanic
Gardens

Alpine
Garden

Landstrasse

Rotunden-
brücke

1
3
5
7
8
10
11
12
13
14
15
16
17
18
19
20
21
22
25
26
27
28
29
30
31
32
33
34
35
36
37

0   250   500 m

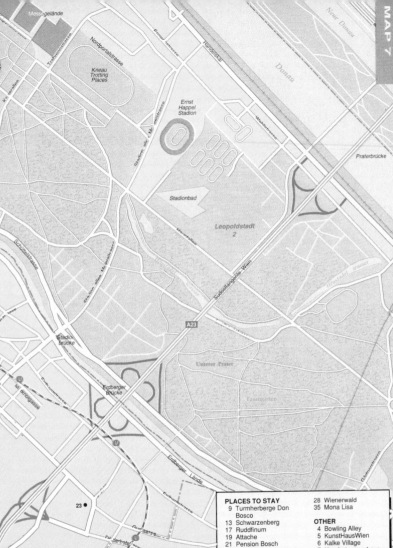

MAP 7

Messegelände

Nordportalstrasse

Krieau Trotting Places

Ernst Happel Stadion

Stadionbad

Leopoldstadt 2

Donau

Neue Donau

Praterbrücke

Handelskai

A23

Stadion brücke

Erdberger Brücke

Unterer Prater

Fasangarten

Erdberger Lände

Simmeringer Hauptstrasse

Simmering Aspangbahn

PLACES TO STAY
9 Turmherberge Don Bosco
13 Schwarzenberg
17 Ruddfinum
19 Attache
21 Pension Bosch
22 Artis
29 Hotel Congress
32 Hotel Kolbeck
33 Favorita
34 Cyrus
36 Pension Caroline

PLACES TO EAT
1 Schweizerhaus
2 Café-Restaurant Luftberg
3 Estancia Cruz
8 Steirereck
14 Oxen Steak
26 Kristall
27 China Restaurant Phoenix

28 Wienerwald
35 Mona Lisa

OTHER
4 Bowling Alley
5 KunstHausWien
6 Kalke Village
7 Hundertwasserhaus
10 UK Embassy
11 Unteres Belvedere
12 Orangery
15 Argus
16 Österreich Werbung
18 Dreimöderlhaus
20 Oberes Belvedere
23 Arena
24 St Marxer Friedhof
25 Museum Moderner Kunst (20er Haus)
30 Post Office & Airport Bus
31 Sixt Car Rental & Parking Garage
37 Billa Supermarket

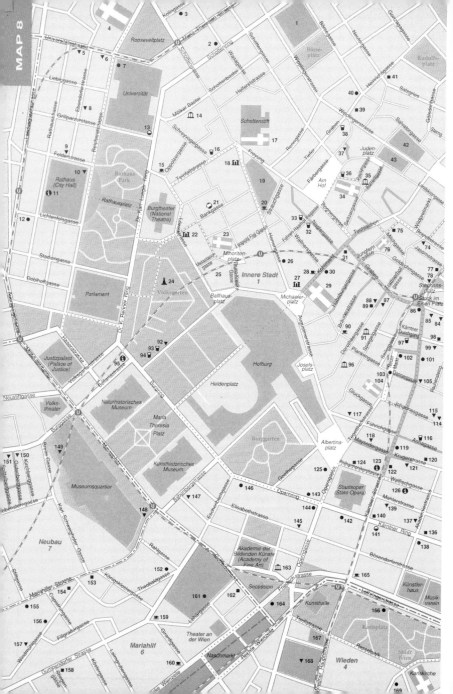

MAP 8

Kolingasse 3

4

Rooseveltplatz

Universitätsstrasse 5

6 7

Liebiggasse

Grillparzerstrasse 8

Universität

13

Felderstrasse 9

10

Rathaus Park

Rathaus (City Hall) 11

Lichtenfelsgasse

12

Stadiongasse

Doblhoffgasse

Parlament

Dr. Karl Renner Ring

Rathausplatz

Burgtheater (National Theatre)

Volksgarten 24

Schmerlingplatz

Justizpalast (Palace of Justice)

95

Neustiftgasse

Volkstheater

Burggasse

Naturhistorisches Museum

Maria Theresia Platz

Kunsthistorisches Museum

Museumsquartier

Neubau 7

149 150

151

154 153

155

156

157 158

Mariahilf 6

152

159

160

161 162

164

Theater an der Wien

Naschmarkt

1

Börseplatz

Rudolfsplatz

41

40 39

Schottenstift

17

Freyung

14

Schreyvogelgasse

16

15

18

19

Bankgasse 21

22 23

25

Minoritenplatz

26 27 28 29 30 31 32 33

Innere Stadt 1

Michaelerplatz

Ballhausplatz

Heldenplatz

Hofburg

Josefsplatz 96

Burggarten

Albertinaplatz

92 93 94

147

148

146

143

144

145

Akademie der Bildenden Künste (Academy of Fine Art) 163

Secession

168

Wieden 4

38 37 36 35 34

Judenplatz 42 43

75 76 74 77 78

Stock im Eisen Platz

Stephansplatz

85 84 86 87 88 89 90 91

98 99 97 101 102 100

103 104 105

115 114

117 116

118 119

120 121 122 123 124 125

Krugerstrasse

Wallnerstrasse

Staatsoper (State Opera)

126 139 140 137 141 142 136 138

Kärntner Ring

Bösendorferstrasse

165

166

167

Kunsthalle

Künstlerhaus

Musikverein

Karlsplatz

Stadt Wien

Karlskirche

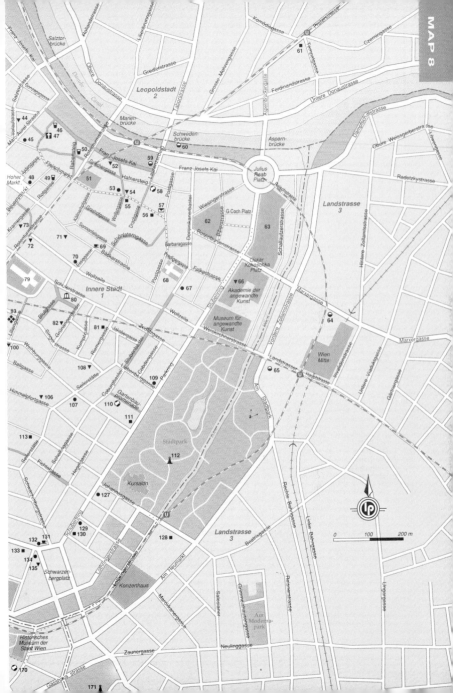

MAP 8

Leopoldstadt 2

Salztor-brücke

Obere Donaustrasse

Donau Canal

Hollandstrasse

Komödiagasse

Tempelgasse

61

Ferdinandstrasse

Grosse Mohrengasse

Gredlerstrasse

Czerningasse

Marc Aurel Strasse

44

46
47

45

Marien-brücke

Schweden-brücke

60

Aspern-brücke

Obere Weissgerberstrasse

Radetzkystrasse

Dampfschiffstrasse

50

Rabensteig

Franz Josefs Kai

59

Franz Josefs Kai

Julius Raab Platz

Landstrasse 3

Gonzagagasse

52

Griechengasse

Hafnersteig

58

Seitenstettengasse

Fleischmarkt

Judengasse

48

49

Hoher Markt

53

54

55

56

57

Drahtgasse

Rotgasse

Blumenstockgasse

Kramergasse

73

Rotenturmstrasse

51

Griechengasse

Sonnenfelsgasse

Schönlaterngasse

62

63

Wiesingerstrasse

G.Coch Platz

Rosenburgenstrasse

Ebendorferstrasse

Dominikanerbastei

Schaulautzerstrasse

Nestroyasse

Hintere Zollamtsstrasse

71

72

69

70

Bäckerstrasse

Wollzeile

Barbaragasse

68

Postgasse

Predigergasse

Falkestrasse

Stubenring

Oskar Kokoschka Platz

66

Akademie der angewandte Kunst

Marxergasse

Marxergasse

79

Schulerstrasse

80

Innere Stadt 1

67

Wollzeile

Museum für angewandte Kunst

Weiskirchnerstrasse

Vordere Zollamtsstrasse

64

83

82

81

Jakobergasse

Riemergasse

Zedlitzgasse

Stubenbastei

Landstrasser Hauptstrasse

65

U

Wien Mitte

Untere Viaduktgasse

Invalidenstrasse

Gärtnergasse

100

Ballgasse

Weihburggasse

Singerstrasse

Grünangergasse

Kumpfgasse

Seilerstätte

Coburgbastei

108

Liebenberggasse

Parkring

109

Am Stadtpark

Himmelpfortgasse

106

107

110

Gartenbau-promenade

111

113

Seilerstätte

Schwarzenbergstrasse

Fichtegasse

Hegelgasse

Sonnenfelsgasse

Stadtpark

112

Untere Viaduktgasse

Reichsratsstrasse

Linke Bahngasse

Reisnerstrasse

127

Kursalon

Johannesgasse

Schubring

129

130

131

128

Landstrasse 3

Am Heumarkt

Beatrixgasse

Am Modena-park

132

133

134

135

Schwarzen-bergplatz

Lothringerstrasse

Konzerthaus

Marokkanergasse

Grimmelshausengasse

Salesianergasse

Neulinggasse

Ungargasse

Historisches Museum der Stadt Wien

170

Gusshausstrasse

Zaunergasse

171

0   100   200 m

LP

MARK HONAN

Fiacres complement the backdrop of Viennese architecture

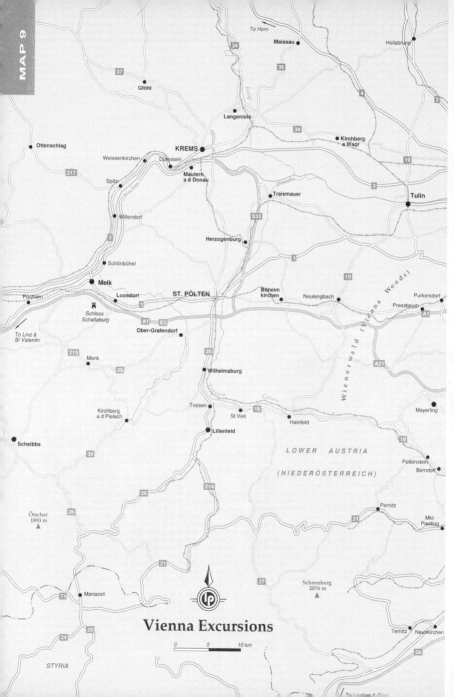

MAP 9

To Horn

Maissau

Hollabrunn

35

37

Gföhl

4

2

Langenlois

34

Kirchberg
a Wagr

19

Ottenschlag

KREMS

217

Weissenkirchen

Dürnstein

Spitz

Mautern
a d Donau

3

Tulln

Willendorf

Traismauer

S33

Herzogenburg

Schönbühel

1

19

Melk

Böheim
kirchen

Neulengbach

Purkersdorf

Pöchlarn

Loosdorf

ST. PÖLTEN

Pressbaum

A1

Schloss
Schallaburg

A1

E5

To Linz &
St Valentin

Ober-Grafendorf

20

W i e n e r w a l d   (V i e n n a   W o o d s)

A21

215

Mank

Wilhelmsburg

29

Kirchberg
a d Pielach

Traisen

St Veit

18

Mayerling

Hainfeld

18

Scheibbs

Lilienfeld

39

L O W E R   A U S T R I A

Pottenstein

Berndorf

20

214

(N I E D E R Ö S T E R R E I C H)

Ötscher
1893 m

28

Pernitz

Mkt-
Piesting

21

21

Schneeberg
2076 m

27

Ternitz

Neunkirchen

71

Mariazell

S6

24

20

STYRIA

Vienna Excursions

0   5   10 km

MAP 9

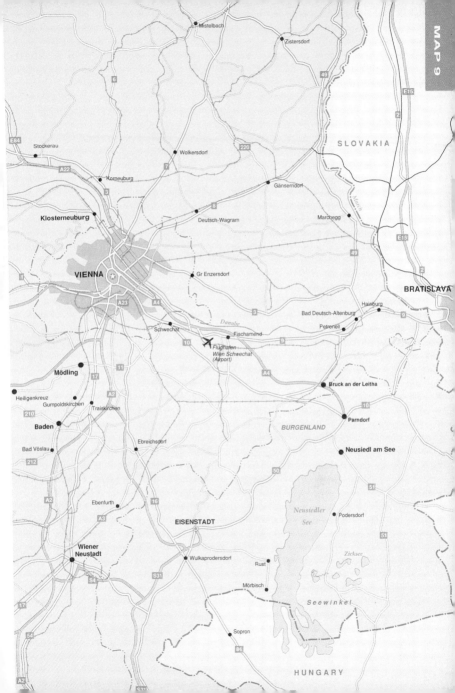

Map Legend

Note: not all symbols displayed above appear in this book